Contemporary Migration to South Africa

Contemporary Migration to South Africa

A Regional Development Issue

Aurelia Segatti and Loren B. Landau

Editors

A copublication of the Agence Française de Développement and the World Bank

ISBN: 978-0-8213-8767-2
eISBN: 978-0-8213-8768-9
DOI: 10.1596/978-0-8213-8767-2

Library of Congress Cataloging-in-Publication data has been requested.

Cover photograph: Township of Alexandra, north of Johannesburg, 2011, by Becca Hartmann for the African Centre for Migration and Society, University of the Witwatersrand, South Africa
Cover design: Naylor Design

Africa Development Forum Series

The **Africa Development Forum** series was created in 2009 to focus on issues of significant relevance to Sub-Saharan Africa's social and economic development. Its aim is both to record the state of the art on a specific topic and to contribute to ongoing local, regional, and global policy debates. It is designed specifically to provide practitioners, scholars, and students with the most up-to-date research results while highlighting the promise, challenges, and opportunities that exist on the continent.

The series is sponsored by the Agence Française de Développement and the World Bank. The manuscripts chosen for publication represent the highest quality in each institution's research and activity output and have been selected for their relevance to the development agenda. Working together with a shared sense of mission and interdisciplinary purpose, the two institutions are committed to a common search for new insights and new ways of analyzing the development realities of the Sub-Saharan Africa Region.

Advisory Committee Members

Agence Française de Développement
Pierre Jacquet, Chef Économiste
Robert Peccoud, Directeur de la Recherche

World Bank
Shantayanan Devarajan, Chief Economist, Africa Region
Jorge Arbache, Senior Economist

Titles in the Africa Development Forum Series

Africa's Infrastructure: A Time for Transformation (2010) by the World Bank
Challenges for African Agriculture (2011) by Jean-Claude Devéze, editor
Gender Disparities in Africa's Labor Market (2010) by Jorge Saba Arbache, Alexandre Kolev, and Ewa Filipiak, editors

Southern African Development Community (SADC) Countries

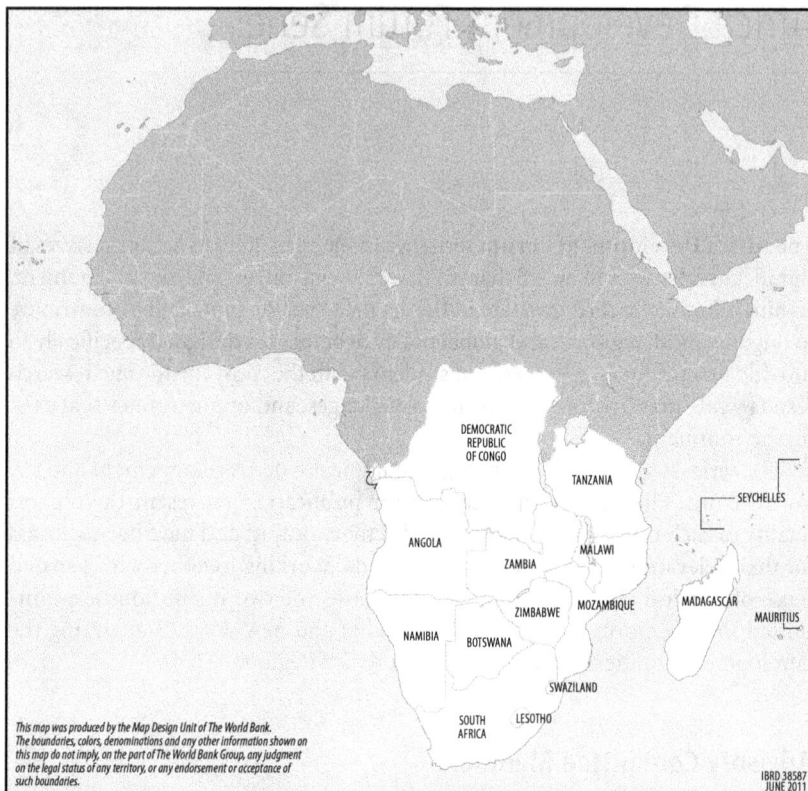

DEMOCRATIC
REPUBLIC
OF CONGO

TANZANIA

SEYCHELLES

ANGOLA

MALAWI

ZAMBIA

MOZAMBIQUE

MADAGASCAR

ZIMBABWE

MAURITIUS

NAMIBIA

BOTSWANA

SWAZILAND

SOUTH
AFRICA

LESOTHO

IBRD 38587
JUNE 2011

Source: World Bank.

Contents

Boxes

Figures

Maps

Tables

Preface

Southern Africa's economy and society have been shaped by human mobility and elaborate efforts to control it. The results include spatialized patterns of poverty and politically volatile inequality. The end of apartheid in South Africa and conflicts elsewhere, coupled with shifting modes of production and political reforms, mean that more people are moving for ever more diverse reasons. For some, these new forms of mobility offer the promise of moving out of poverty. They also generate new governance challenges.

Although migration is now a central component of people's livelihoods across the region, policies to manage and capitalize on these movements have lagged, creating two disjunctures. The first is the gap between what migrants are already doing—or trying to do—and the understanding of the long-term impact of mobility on livelihoods and poverty. The second is the chasm between governments' commitments to promoting regional integration, protecting human rights, and countering poverty on the one hand and their migration policies, administrative practices, and policing strategies on the other.

Building on more than a decade of research by the African Centre for Migration and Society (formerly the Forced Migration Studies Programme) at the University of the Witwatersrand, in Johannesburg, this volume documents what is known about migration into and within South Africa, explores its impacts on livelihoods, and outlines policies that help shape movements and their consequences. It takes stock of what is known about migration, identifies key sectors for policy intervention, and clarifies the reasons behind conspicuous bottlenecks.

This book is a call to rethink migration regimes in Southern Africa in ways that are more explicitly developmental and focused on poverty. Current policy debates are devoted almost exclusively to border control and policing; they pay only lip service to local and regional developmental strategies. This volume takes a different approach. Its contributors are scholars who are convinced that empirically based policy making stands a better chance of succeeding than untested preconceptions that risk reproducing recipes that have failed elsewhere.

The book is therefore strong on empirics, providing a wealth of original data. It also reframes existing approaches and reexamines secondary data from fresh perspectives. Although the focus remains South Africa, the book reflects South Africa's regional role and draws on data from across the Southern African Development Community (SADC).

Countries and regions around the world are recognizing that although migration is inevitable and potentially beneficial, it raises the specters of social unrest and political backlash. Despite declining demographics and stalled growth and innovation, European leaders are reasserting the need to seal their borders. North America maintains a more open immigration regime, but there, too, political pressures have drawn attention away from the potential benefits of human movement. Developing countries reveal a diversity of policy situations and options. In some, such as Bangladesh, Mexico, and the Philippines, emigration has become central to national development strategies. In others, such as China and India, internal migration is so massive that it has been the main source of urbanization and economic development. Elsewhere, as in Argentina, Brazil, the Republic of Korea, Singapore, and Thailand, immigration from within the subregion shapes sections of the labor markets and allows the sustained specialization of growth strategies. These experiences offer a range of policy models. If South Africa is to fulfill its aspirations for economic growth and regional power, it will need to consider the viability of these options and weigh the costs and benefits of action and inaction. Doing so means clearly identifying priorities and taking a pragmatic look at the government's potential role in managing mobility and its consequences.

This book broadens the "migration" agenda beyond the boundaries of migration studies and migration policy silos. Understanding its effects and maximizing its benefits requires identifying how mobility intersects with a range of policy sectors at different scales (multilaterally and bilaterally; nationally, regionally, and locally). Although migration policy is often considered a national issue, we devote a chapter to the local governance of mobility and lessons to be drawn from it. The consideration of health, local policing, and labor policy highlights the inseparability of mobility from other pressing policy concerns.

A version of this book focusing exclusively on South Africa was published by the Agence Française de Développement (AFD, the French Development Agency) in 2008. Based on a report commissioned by the Fonds d'Analyse des Sociétés Politiques (FASOPO) directed by Jean-François Bayart, it has been widely disseminated among scholars and policy makers in South Africa. It is also available on the AFD website. Although it remains a valuable reference, recent developments (including the Zimbabwean crisis, changes in legislation in South Africa, adoption of the regional protocol on the Facilitation of Movement of Persons by the SADC Assembly) and additional research warranted updating its analysis and recommendations.

This book is intended to become a resource for a range of audiences in Southern Africa and the continent. If successful, it will find a place among national and local government departments, university scholars and students interested in migration, regional integration organizations, and the NGO community. We hope it will also interest people outside the region, including migration and social science scholars, students and consultants, and staffs of international organization and donor agencies. The annexes are useful guides for readers attempting to rapidly capture key information on policy developments and statistical data or debates. We hope that this volume will serve as a starting point for people interested in participating actively in the field of migration policy making or its critique in order to take further the questions raised here.

Contributors

Stephen Ellis is a researcher at the African Studies Centre in Leiden, the Netherlands, and a professor at the VU University of Amsterdam, where he occupies the Desmond Tutu chair in the Faculty of Social Science. He is the author of *Season of Rains: Africa in the World* (2011) and *The Mask of Anarchy: The Destruction of Liberia and the Religious Dimension of an African Civil War* (1999) and the co-author (with Gerrie ter Haar) of *Worlds of Power: Religious Thought and Political Practice in Africa* (2004). He sits on several editorial boards, including the board of *African Affairs*, of which he is a former editor. He holds a Ph.D. in history from Oxford University.

Loren B. Landau is director of the African Centre for Migration and Society at the University of the Witwatersrand in Johannesburg.* His research explores sovereignty, urban transformation, and state-society relations. He is the author of *The Humanitarian Hangover: Displacement, Aid and Transformation in Western Tanzania* (2008). He sits on the editorial board of *The Journal of Refugee Studies*, the executive committee of the Consortium for Refugees and Migrants in South Africa (CoRMSA), and the South African Immigration Advisory Board. He holds a Ph.D. in political science and development studies from the University of California at Berkeley.

Jean Pierre Misago is a researcher at the African Centre for Migration and Society, University of the Witwatersrand. His research explores the effects of displacement on identity and belonging. He is working toward a Ph.D. in migration studies on the local politics of xenophobic violence in South Africa.

---

* The African Centre for Migration and Society (http://www.migration.org.za) is an independent, interdisciplinary, and internationally engaged research and teaching center that shapes global discourse on human mobility, development, and social transformation. Until 2010, it was known as the Forced Migration Studies Programme.

Aurelia Segatti is the former research director of the French Institute of South Africa in Johannesburg, and a Senior Research Fellow with the African Centre for Migration and Society at the University of the Witwatersrand. Her research interests include public policy, immigration policy analysis, regional policy coherence, xenophobic mobilizations, and local governance. She holds a Ph.D. in political science from the Centre of African Studies, in Bordeaux, France, and the University of Réunion.

Joanna Vearey is a postdoctoral research fellow with the African Centre for Migration and Society at the University of the Witwatersrand. For her doctoral dissertation, she investigated the urban health challenges of migration and informal settlements in the context of HIV/AIDS and developed a revised approach to guide local developmental responses. She is coordinating a regional research project on HIV/AIDS and youth funded by the Health Economics and AIDS Research Division (HEARD) of the University of KwaZulu-Natal in Durban, South Africa. She holds a Ph.D. in public health from the University of the Witwatersrand.

Darshan Vigneswaran is an associate researcher with the African Centre for Migration and Society and a research fellow with the Max Planck Institute for the Study of Religious and Ethnic Diversity in Göttingen, Germany. He holds a Ph.D. in politics from Monash University (Australia).

Acknowledgments

The editors wish to thank the team at the African Centre for Migration and Society for their contributions to the empirical material on which this volume draws. Véronique Gindrey deserves special recognition for her statistical analysis and mapping, as does Markus Sperl, from the International Centre for Migration Policy Development (ICMPD), for providing us with Eurostat data.

The research on which this work is based would not have been possible without the support of the African Centre for Migration and Society's funders and research programs. In this regard, we wish to acknowledge the U.K. Department for International Development, the French National Research Agency, the French Institute of Research for Development, the Atlantic Philanthropies, the Programme to Support Pro-Poor Policy Development based in the Office of the President of South Africa, the South African Local Government Association, the International Organization for Migration, Oxfam–UK, the Centre for Population and Development, the European Commission, the Foundation for Human Rights, the Ford Foundation, the MacArthur Foundation, the German Academic Exchange Service (DAAD), the Consortium for Refugees and Migrants in South Africa, the University of the Witwatersrand, the Open Society Foundation for Southern Africa, the British Academy UK/Africa Partnership Scheme, and South Africa's National Research Foundation.

Initial support and encouragement by the Fonds d'Analyse des Sociétés Politiques; Agence Française de Développement (AFD, the French Development Agency); and the French Institute of South Africa to publish the 2006 report is gratefully acknowledged. Thanks also go to Germaine Moolman for her initial editing of the manuscript and to Marguerite Duponchel, Jessica Anderson, and Iriann Freemantle, for assistance in researching SADC migration policies and updating chronological data. We would not have been able to manage the fieldwork necessary for many of the chapters without logistical support from Lenore Longwe.

Abbreviations

AFD	Agence Française de Développement
ANC	African National Congress
ASGISA	Accelerated and Shared Growth Initiative for South Africa
CoRMSA	Consortium for Refugees and Migrants in South Africa
COSATU	Congress of South African Trade Unions
EU	European Union
IDASA	Institute for Democracy in South Africa
JIPSA	Joint Initiative on Priority Skills Acquisition
MP	Member of Parliament
NEPAD	New Partnership for Africa's Development
NGO	nongovernmental organization
OAU	Organization of African Unity
SADC	Southern African Development Community
SAMP	Southern African Migration Programme
SETA	Sector Education and Training Authority
StatsSA	Statistics South Africa
UNDESA	United Nations Department of Economic and Social Affairs
UNHCR	United Nations High Commissioner for Refugees

Overview

This volume examines the approach to international migration that has informed South Africa's migration policies since the end of apartheid and analyzes the implications of these choices for regional development. In doing so, it aims to provide policy makers and migration and development scholars with insight into the specific policy challenges faced by Africa's new migration hub.

Volume Overview

The book has five chapters and four appendixes. Chapter 1 describes South Africa's historical experience of migration and analyzes the changes in official attitudes in the 20th century that explain the roots of contemporary ideas and policy dilemmas. Chapters 2–5 complement this analysis by looking at three often neglected dimensions of migration in a development context. Chapter 2 explores skilled labor, a crucial issue given the structure of the South African labor market. Chapter 3 examines the impact of migration on local government in South African cities, with an emphasis on the importance of local government responses, the costs of failing to respond, and the implications for urban planning, service delivery, health, security, and political accountability. Chapter 4 examines undocumented migration and the challenges it raises for both state and nonstate actors. Chapter 5 describes the importance of providing health care for migrants. Using a public health framework, it examines the developmental implications of the relationship between access to health care and international migration in light of recent data.

Chapter 1. Reforming South African Immigration Policy in the Postapartheid Period (1990–2010)

Chapter 1 explores three issues: the position on international migration developed by the ruling party in the postapartheid period, the capacity (or lack thereof) of the ruling party to reform public policy, and the role played by

South African and foreign nonstate actors in engaging with the South African government on migration issues.

The new regime that came into office in 1994 had to face a rapidly changing migrant situation with a legal instrument focused on policing and coercion. It lacked the political distance required to assess pressing issues such as the increasing numbers of asylum seekers, brain drain and brain gain, skill needs, and the rights of undocumented migrants. Existing practices, administrations, and institutions in charge of migration management and the legal apparatus available ensured the continuity of a national immigration policy awaiting redefinition.

The 10-year period between 1994 and 2004 saw a wide consultative and legislative process and passage of the Immigration Act in 2002 and the Immigration Amendment Act in 2004. This period was crucial in shaping positions and structuring networks on migration issues perhaps as never before in South African history and certainly as in very few other African countries. Clusters of actors then followed three diverging routes:

- The Department of Home Affairs pursed a rather neoliberal-inspired agenda that supported state withdrawal, the subcontracting of administrative processing of control to employers, incentives to investors and high-skilled labor, and accelerated policy reform by simplifying administrative procedures.

- Nongovernmental organizations supported an interventionist approach that sought balanced migration control, taking into account democratic commitments and state capacity for a flexible, reactive, and transparent migration policy. This approach called for more profound policy transformation and a regional thrust.

- Sections of the African National Congress (ANC) and the lower- to mid-level bureaucratic strata of government departments pursued a security- and sovereignty-centered agenda based on a narrowly defined notion of national interest. This approach bore many resemblances to that pursued by the apartheid regime.

In recent years, immigration has been reintegrated within the broader ANC political line thanks to ideological inputs from the African Renaissance and a neo-Marxist analysis of the world economy. Meanwhile, however, the gap between elite and rank-and-file ANC members on immigration seems to be widening. The ANC is confronted with the tensions shared by most social-democratic governments caught between the acceptance of market rules that include the free circulation of labor and the sometimes painful consequences for the domestic economy. Unlike their counterparts in Western social-democratic regimes, South African political elites are caught between their strong commitment to human rights, inherited from years of struggle against the apartheid regime, and the xenophobic perceptions of the majority of the population.

Chapter 2. The Role of Skilled Labor

Chapter 2 examines the domestic and regional implications of the role of skilled labor in South Africa's international migration policy. The main questions raised relate to the nature of the "skills problem" in South Africa and of labor market imbalances resulting from the departure of the highly skilled, the availability of skilled professionals from the region and beyond, and the employability of black South African graduates. The challenges these issues present raise broader questions about the efficacy of the postapartheid education system and employment equity measures as well as initiatives by the Southern African Development Community (SADC) to counter brain drain from and within the region. The chapter also describes government policy and explains why certain constituencies (such as trade unions) resist efforts to build a regional labor market. It concludes by assessing the obstacles to improving the management of skilled labor migration, with emphasis on the Department of Home Affairs.

The government seems divided on the approach to take to migration. Its policies lack continuity with the previous government, an aspect revealing the ANC's difficulty in defining a long-term strategy on the skills issue. Under President Mbeki, there was a sense that South Africa's serious shortage of skilled labor could be rectified in the short to medium term only by attracting skills from abroad and that a globalized economy implies a global market in labor. The Zuma administration does not appear to share these views. In addition, the capacity of the Department of Home Affairs to manage the skills crisis through labor imports has not improved. Such pendulum effects and administrative inertia are not conducive to testing the benefits or shortcomings of any policy over the mid- to long term.

Chapter 3. Mobility and Municipalities: Local Authorities, Local Impacts, and the Challenges of Movement

Global debates on migration and development have tended to address national policy frameworks and aggregate economic and social effects. South Africa illustrates the importance of subnational dynamics. The consequences of migration, positive and negative, are most acute at the provincial and, especially, municipal level. In previous decades, international migration into South Africa concentrated in agricultural and mining areas. Since the early 1990s, both international and domestic migrants increasingly concentrate in the country's urban centers. Indeed, population movements, some predictable, some spontaneous, some voluntary, some forced, are now perennial features of South African cities and secondary towns. Chapter 3 explores local governments' responsibilities for addressing migration, examines the localized effects of migration, and identifies the challenges of developing effective local responses. It argues that South Africa's inability to develop effective, contextualized policies on migration is having significant negative impacts on development.

Citizenship and asylum laws must remain national, but there is a growing need for increased attention to subnational actors. Cities and provinces need to recognize that they can, and indeed should be encouraged to, actively advocate for an immigration regime that helps foster inclusion and service delivery for all residents—working in collaboration with national, provincial, and neighboring local government officials. These efforts must be accompanied by broader discussions about the meaning of inclusion.

Chapter 4. Migration Control, Documentation, and State Transformation

South Africa's government has been struggling to develop a coherent response to migration for more than a decade. Ever since the transition to democratic rule in the mid-1990s, "illegal migration" from neighboring countries has been viewed as a major challenge to the country's ambitious agendas of political transformation, economic development, and poverty alleviation. Lacking clear direction from above, government agencies, offices, and officials have developed immigration policies and practices "on the fly." These divisive tendencies have been mirrored by the lack of significant regional initiatives by the SADC. As evidenced by the tepid response by the SADC to the ongoing Zimbabwean crisis, the region has limited capacity for a coordinated response to migration and refugee flows.

Chapter 4 gauges the long-term impacts of this bureaucratic stasis on governance in South Africa. It explores how an ongoing state of crisis in this policy sphere is shaping the everyday practices of government bureaucracies, including both those charged with specific responsibility for immigration policy and those that have taken up this task. The main theme is the disjuncture between policy and practice. Although there is consensus across government that current law and policy are inadequate and require substantial reworking, there is de facto acceptance that government agencies and officials must continue to implement control-oriented policies and practices, including through arrests, detentions, and deportations. This disjuncture opens the way for opportunism and corruption at lower and local levels of state institutions. Reform of immigration policy can thus not be a mere matter of designing new legislation. Rather, reformers need to engage with the grassroots of departments and provide new incentive structures to ensure that new policies are taken up and mainstreamed in everyday bureaucratic practice.

Chapter 5. Migration and Health in South Africa: Implications for Development

Through a public health framework, chapter 5 examines the developmental implications of the relationship between migration and health. It shows that migrants are often unable to access positive determinants of health, creating negative health outcomes, which place an additional burden on the host area. Denying migrant populations timely access to appropriate healthcare (including both preventative and curative services) puts the health of the entire population at risk. In a region where communicable diseases—including tuberculosis and HIV/AIDS—are prevalent, it is essential that access to healthcare for all be ensured.

Research on migration and health in South Africa highlights the "othering" of international migrants, which is amplified in a context of HIV/AIDS. There is an urgent need to return to a public health approach to address the health of regional migrant populations. Such an approach calls on regional bodies, governments, civil society, public health professionals, and researchers to advocate for and ensure that the right to access healthcare for all migrant groups is upheld.

Appendixes

The main text is supplemented by four appendixes. Appendix A presents a chronology of immigration legislation and policy in South Africa and other SADC countries from 1986 to 2010. Appendix B discusses methodological issues in understanding migration in South Africa. Appendix C presents migration statistics for Southern Africa. Appendix D provides statistics on urbanization in Africa.

Recommendations for Research and Policy Development

This book provides the historical, institutional, economic, and social contexts for understanding migration to South Africa from a regional perspective. Although the focus is on documenting these issues, the chapters point to a series of recommendations for research and policy development:

1. *Develop policy frameworks recognizing that migration is critical to Southern Africa's prosperity.* Given South Africa's economic ambitions, ongoing efforts to foster regional integration, and acute skills shortages, immigration is critical to achieving international competitiveness in the corporate, small business, and tourism sectors. Continued formal and informal restrictions on and mismanagement of immigration—including laws, administrative practice, human rights abuses, and widespread xenophobia—can only have a negative impact on the country's economic development.

2. *Develop efficient interdepartmental tools for gathering data, ensuring policy cohesion, and building capacity.* Inconsistencies in policy making across government departments stem partly from the lack of centralized, reliable

data and consistent data gathering methods across departments. Divergence of policy views, inherent to different departments' mandates, would benefit from the creation of interdepartmental avenues to express differences and explore better coordination. Lack of capacity, especially within the Department of Home Affairs, is one of the most critical problems plaguing the management of migration. Addressing this issue is important within the Department of Home Affairs itself, but only the development of interdepartmental skills that make staff responsible for migration aware of immigration control regulations as well as social, economic, and human rights dimensions will foster a general improvement in the management of migration.

3. *Improve subregional convergence and coordination.* Many elements point to the lack of subregional policy consultation, the reinforcement of bilateral rather than multilateral agreements, and the ineffectiveness of existing nonspecific (SADC) and specific (Migration Dialogue for Southern Africa) platforms. The very limited scope of the Protocol on the Facilitation of the Movement of People in Southern Africa is emblematic of the difficulty SADC has counterbalancing South Africa's political and economic weight in the region. Regular and effective consultation with labor organizations (trade unions, labor recruitment agencies) and the private sector at the regional level is lacking, despite recommendations to that effect formulated in the 1997 South African Green Paper on International Migration.

4. *Increase subnational engagement in migration management.* Although citizenship and asylum laws must remain national, there is a heightened need for increased attention to subnational actors as they continue to assert their influence—through commission and omission—on South Africa's immigration and asylum regime.

5. *Adopt pragmatic approaches to health care and service delivery.* Facilitating access to primary care clinics, lifesaving medical care, and legal services without regard to nationality or immigration status can help build safer and more accountable communities The practice of excluding migrants from access to public health care, a behavior based on prejudice and misinformation, places entire communities at risk rather than contributing to the improvement and prevention of communicable diseases. Countering exclusion based on community of origin will not ensure secure and sustainable livelihoods, accountable institutions, and unified communities. It can, however, make achieving these objectives possible.

6. *Conduct ongoing contextualized research.* Although understanding aggregate trends is important, responses and attitudes are often shaped by the racial, economic, and political histories of smaller units, such as neighborhoods. Differences within cities may be as important as differences across

cities. Developing context-specific understandings will require increasing the capacity for statistical, institutional, and social analyses. All spheres of government should be encouraged to collaborate and develop the capacity for data collection and analysis. Mechanisms should also be created to ensure that these analyses are fed into decision-making processes. Only by mainstreaming migration can South Africa hope to avoid policy failures and help allay fears about the effects of human mobility on prosperity and security.

7. *Develop a realistic understanding of the scope for policy reform.* The debate on migration and development is often premised on the idea that reducing barriers to human mobility will reduce poverty. This report warns against naive recommendations about migration policy reform. Even where policy reforms may spur development, there is a need to recognize the lack of institutional capacity to overcome pockets of entrenched corruption and to ensure that policy priorities are uniformly translated into practice. This capacity issue should always be weighed against incentives for reform.

Migration to South Africa: Regional Challenges versus National Instruments and Interests

Aurelia Segatti

The domestic and international migrant labor on which mine-based capital accumulation in Southern Africa relied for decades has helped shape the region's economies, forms of urban settlement, primary livelihood strategies, and forms of political leadership and resistance. The profound economic and political upheaval of the 1990s transformed international migration to South Africa. Alongside organized regional migrant labor flows, negotiated between governments and business, varied patterns of mobility rapidly emerged or expanded, from cross-border trading to asylum to seasonal migration for commercial farming to temporary stays for study and training. In a single decade, between 1990 and 2000, South Africa became the new migration hub at the southern-most tip of the continent, drawing hundreds of thousands of new migrants from Central, East, and West Africa and as well as Bangladesh, China, Eastern Europe, and Pakistan. For some of these migrants, South Africa is a second-best choice, a temporary haven en route to Europe or North America. For others, and unintentionally for many, it has become a final destination.

Although the governance and development implications of this shift from collective mining labor agreements to largely informal and more individual migration are immense, the responses by governments in Southern Africa have generally been defensive and noncommittal. Although governments in other regions, South and Southeast Asia in particular, have (controversially) built their national development strategies around migration, Southern Africa's national policies and regional initiatives remain marooned in an approach rigidly based on border control and national sovereignty. The consequence has been a stalemate in developing progressive regional management instruments. Where progress has been made, as in South Africa's asylum regime, inadequate administrative capacity and coordination are undermining policies. Similarly, the lack of an adequate migration policy has undermined efforts to ensure refugee protection. Waves of public sector reforms in the region—in public health, education, trade, labor and employment, local government, anticorruption, industrialization, and social cohesion, both donor driven and endogenous— have consistently ignored migration, overlooking both its real societal dangers and its developmental potential.

In societies with ailing economies, poor education systems, and chronic unemployment that are now undergoing profound socioeconomic transformations as a result of integration into world systems of trade and services, the voiceless and marginalized often turn to violence. Deeply entrenched and widespread across class and racial divides, xenophobia is not just a South African phenomenon. It was therefore little surprise that a series of events in South Africa in May and June 2008 left 62 people dead and about 150,000 displaced, primarily foreign nationals and members of South Africa's ethnic minorities. Although some called for a reconsideration of South Africa's position within and toward the continent, many within the ruling party, the African National Congress (ANC), and society at large saw the attacks as a reminder that the government should prioritize its own citizens (box 1).[1]

BOX 1

The Xenophobic Riots of 2008

On May 11, 2008, violent attacks began in the symbolically significant township of Alexandra, north of Johannesburg. The violence rapidly spread to many separate settlements across the Johannesburg-Pretoria province of Gauteng before flaring up at sites across the country. After a slow initial reaction, the government responded strongly, calling in the armed forces to quell the violence. After a month, widespread violence subsided.

During the attacks, at least 62 people were killed and another 670 were wounded. More than 150,000 people were displaced or forced to flee South Africa. Most of the victims were nonnationals from Southern Africa and farther afield. Some were South African citizens. The initial security crisis rapidly transformed into a humanitarian emergency as thousands of people were left without shelter, protection, food, and clothing. The scope of damage to property is not clear, but damage was estimated at millions of rands in the course of a few weeks.

There has been widespread speculation about the nature and causes of the violence. Research suggests that while structural forces were at work, violence was triggered by patterns of local governance: gangsters, leadership competition, and poor policing. Although South Africa has not seen a recurrence of the kind of violence it witnessed in 2008, few of the underlying factors have been addressed, and threats against and killing of foreigners and other outsiders continue.

Source: Misago, Landau, and Monson 2008.

South Africans are not the only ones to have turned on migrants in their midst. Similar, if milder, episodes of xenophobic violence have been reported in Botswana, Mozambique, and elsewhere on the continent. These incidents point to the need for governments to start developing approaches to socio-economic and political transformation that recognize that migration is, and will remain, an indelible feature of the region. The violence calls for renewed political thinking about the kind of interdependency migration creates between states and peoples in terms of regional growth, labor market imbalances, skills circulation, portable social security benefits, protection from persecution, cultural exchanges, and democratic values.

Migration policy making is a broad and complex issue confronting any government, involving a wide range of national and international stakeholders. There has long been a sense within the South African government of being caught between a rock and a hard place. On the one hand, the economy is highly dependent on, and increasingly important for, the rest of the region in terms of labor and employment, skills circulation, trade and technology transfers, and financial markets. In this context, migration is a necessity and can be a developmental tool. On the other hand, South Africa, as well as Botswana and Namibia, have achieved levels of political stability and economic growth that the ruling parties (the ANC, the Botswana Democratic Party, and the South West African People's Organisation) wish to sustain. Social tensions related to migration and xenophobia clearly constitute a threat to social order that could jeopardize their majorities and political domination.

This book addresses a number of these concerns through an in-depth study of some key aspects of South Africa's past and current migration experience within the Southern African region. It addresses the broader issue of development interdependence between Southern African countries from the angle of migration dynamics, by definition a transnational sector of state intervention.

South Africa in Southern Africa: The Other Migration Hub

The global media and scholarship have devoted much attention to migration to the Euro-Mediterranean zone, migration to the United States from Latin America, and migration within and out of Asia. Far less has been reported about Southern Africa's emergence as a major migration hub in the past 15 years.

Although not a new phenomenon—the migrant labor system goes back to the early twentieth century—international migration in Southern Africa has been radically transformed in recent years. Migration within Southern Africa is now far more numerically significant than migration to Europe. The change reflects political changes, particularly the end of apartheid and stronger migration controls in Europe, as well as deep restructuring in the mineral extracting industries and commercial farming, the expansion of the construction and hospitality industries, and continuous political instability in the Democratic Republic of Congo, Zimbabwe, and the Horn.

Despite regular national censuses in some countries, migration data remain scarce and poorly maintained, even in South Africa, which has perhaps the best data collection systems in this subregion. National censuses usually address migration in passing. Moreover, because of the vast numbers of undocumented migrants, actual migration flows are not captured in migration statistics. When statistics are collected, they are often not collated or tracked, because of technology and training. In such conditions and in the absence of systematic data collection work, only rough projections and estimates are possible.[2] Some large-scale subregional surveys have been completed in the past decade, which complement national censuses. They include the Migration and Remittances Survey conducted by the Southern African Migration Programme, the Potential Skills Base Survey, and the Migration and Poverty Study. Countries surveyed include Botswana, Lesotho, Malawi, Mozambique, Namibia, Swaziland, and Zimbabwe. The National Immigration Policy Survey, conducted by the Southern African Migration Programme, documents anti-immigrant attitudes between 1998 and 2008.[3] The Forced Migration Studies Programme African Cities Survey, conducted in 2006, provides information on different communities of migrants and nationals in Johannesburg as well as Lubumbashi, Democratic Republic of Congo; Maputo, Mozambique; and Nairobi, Kenya. The vulnerability pilot survey conducted by the Forced Migration Studies Programme and the United Nations Office for the Coordination of Humanitarian Affairs provides microdata on two areas of Johannesburg.[4]

These initiatives are valuable sources of information about internal and cross-border migration across the region. Nonetheless, they contain significant gaps and inconsistencies. Bearing these limitations in mind, it is possible to identify a few longer-term changes in volume, direction, urban settlement, and distribution of migrants across the subregion and in comparison with other subregions in Africa.

The general overview provided in tables 1–6 reveals at least four important trends.[5] First, although other subregions in Africa still receive much larger numbers of international migrants (5 million in Eastern Africa and 8 million in Western Africa in 2010) the number of international migrants in Southern Africa has increased steadily, reaching 2.1 million migrants in 2010, 10.9 percent of Africa's 19.2 million migrants.[6] More significantly, the percentage of international migrants is higher in Southern Africa (3.7 percent) than in any other subregions of Africa (the average for the continent as a whole is 1.9 percent).

Second, the rate of increase is accelerating. After a decade of decrease (from 1990 to 2000), the migrant stock in Southern Africa increased by 3.8 percent a

(continued on page 16)

Table 1 Population and Migration Data on Africa, 1990–2010

Indicator	1990	1995	2000	2005	2010
Estimated number of international migrants at midyear	15,972,502	17,921,345	17,062,143	17,735,600	19,263,183
Estimated number of refugees at midyear	5,350,411	6,362,573	3,575,274	2,895,101	2,567,719
Population at midyear (thousands)	638,729	726,285	819,462	921,073	1,033,043
Estimated number of female migrants at midyear	7,377,764	8,440,578	7,967,059	8,290,605	9,009,835
Estimated number of male migrants at midyear	8,594,738	9,480,767	9,095,084	9,444,995	10,253,348
International migrants as percentage of population	2.5	2.5	2.1	1.9	1.9
Female migrants as percentage of all international migrants	46.2	47.1	46.7	46.7	46.8
Refugees as percentage of international migrants	33.5	35.5	21.0	16.3	13.3
	1990–95	**1995–2000**	**2000–05**	**2005–10**	
Annual rate of change of migrant stock (percent)	2.3	−1.0	0.8	1.7	

Source: UN 2009a.

Table 2 Population and Migration Data on Western Africa, 1990-2010

Indicator	1990	1995	2000	2005	2010
Estimated number of international migrants at midyear	4,845,025	6,440,729	7,279,178	7,703,228	8,440,269
Estimated number of refugees at midyear	476,047	1,466,746	772,210	366,248	231,096
Population at midyear (thousands)	183,210	208,805	237,781	269,990	306,058
Estimated number of female migrants at midyear	2,224,440	3,002,795	3,364,345	3,563,105	3,922,614
Estimated number of male migrants at midyear	2,620,585	3,437,934	3,914,833	4,140,123	4,517,655
International migrants as percentage of population	2.6	3.1	3.1	2.9	2.8
Female migrants as percentage of all international migrants	45.9	46.6	46.2	46.3	46.5
Refugees as percentage of international migrants	9.8	22.8	10.6	4.8	2.7
	1990–95	**1995–2000**	**2000–05**	**2005–10**	
Annual rate of change of migrant stock (percent)	5.7	2.4	1.1	1.8	

Source: UN 2009a.

Table 3 Population and Migration Data on Eastern Africa, 1990–2010

Indicator	1990	1995	2000	2005	2010
Estimated number of international migrants at midyear	5,949,525	5,347,098	5,220,236	5,124,070	5,034,099
Estimated number of refugees at midyear	3,314,900	2,186,818	1,638,596	1,465,167	1,281,399
Population at midyear (thousands)	192,959	219,874	252,710	287,413	327,186
Estimated number of female migrants at midyear	2,845,675	2,602,234	2,562,761	2,533,823	2,496,466
Estimated number of male migrants at midyear	3,103,850	2,744,864	2,657,475	2,590,247	2,537,633
International migrants as percentage of population	3.1	2.4	2.1	1.8	1.5
Female migrants as percentage of all international migrants	47.8	48.7	49.1	49.4	49.6
Refugees as percentage of international migrants	55.7	40.9	31.4	28.6	25.5
	1990–95		**1995–2000**	**2000–05**	**2005–10**
Annual rate of change of migrant stock (percent)	−2.1		−0.5	−0.4	−0.4

Source: UN 2009a.

Table 4 Population and Migration Data on Middle (Central) Africa, 1990–2010

Indicator	1990	1995	2000	2005	2010
Estimated number of international migrants at midyear	1,455,922	2,651,377	1,392,181	1,566,684	1,615,402
Estimated number of refugees at midyear	446,837	1,693,843	539,052	642,174	609,155
Population at midyear (thousands)	72,813	86,424	98,060	113,185	128,909
Estimated number of female migrants at midyear	713,700	1,335,388	677,209	760,730	783,129
Estimated number of male migrants at midyear	742,222	1,315,989	714,972	805,954	832,273
International migrants as percentage of population	2.0	3.1	1.4	1.4	1.3
Female migrants as percentage of all international migrants	49.0	50.4	48.6	48.6	48.5
Refugees as percentage of international migrants	30.7	63.9	38.7	41.0	37.7
	1990–95		**1995–2000**	**2000–05**	**2005–10**
Annual rate of change of migrant stock (percent)	12.0		−12.9	2.4	0.6

Source: UN 2009a.

Table 5 Population and Migration Data on Northern Africa, 1990–2010

Indicator	1990	1995	2000	2005	2010
Estimated number of international migrants at midyear	2,278,422	2,185,783	1,924,530	1,836,287	2,010,070
Estimated number of refugees at midyear	1,070,685	916,010	590,099	379,067	400,580
Population at midyear (thousands)	147,767	163,943	179,525	195,444	212,921
Estimated number of female migrants at midyear	1,036,749	982,891	849,699	797,280	871,657
Estimated number of male migrants at midyear	1,241,673	1,202,892	1,074,831	1,039,007	1,138,413
International migrants as percentage of population	1.5	1.3	1.1	0.9	0.9
Female migrants as percentage of all international migrants	45.5	45.0	44.2	43.4	43.4
Refugees as percentage of international migrants	47.0	41.9	30.7	20.6	19.9
	1990–95	**1995–2000**	**2000–05**	**2005–10**	
Annual rate of change of migrant stock (percent)	−0.8	−2.5	−0.9	1.8	

Source: UN 2009a.

Table 6 Population and Migration Data on Southern Africa, 1990–2010

Indicator	1990	1995	2000	2005	2010
Estimated number of international migrants at midyear	1,443,608	1,296,358	1,246,018	1,505,331	2,163,343
Estimated number of refugees at midyear	41,942	99,156	35,317	42,445	45,489
Population at midyear (thousands)	41,981	47,240	51,387	55,041	57,968
Estimated number of female migrants at midyear	557,200	517,270	513,045	635,667	935,969
Estimated number of male migrants at midyear	886,408	779,088	732,973	869,664	1,227,374
International migrants as percentage of population	3.4	2.7	2.4	2.7	3.7
Female migrants as percentage of all international migrants	38.6	39.9	41.2	42.2	43.3
Refugees as percentage of international migrants	2.9	7.6	2.8	2.8	2.1
	1990–95	**1995–2000**	**2000–05**	**2005–10**	
Annual rate of change of migrant stock (percent)	−2.2	−0.8	3.8	7.3	

Source: UN 2009a.

year over the following five years before increasing 7.3 percent a year in 2006–10. Over the 2006–10 period, the changes in migrant stocks were 1.8 percent in Western and Northern Africa, 0.6 percent in Middle Africa, and –0.4 percent in Eastern Africa. In Botswana the proportion of international migrants in the population rose from 2.0 percent in 1990 to 5.8 percent in 2010 (UN 2009a). Most other countries in the subregion have fairly stable or decreasing percentages of international migrants. The exception is South Africa, where the migrant stock increased steadily, from 3.3 percent to 3.7 percent of the population between 1990 and 2010 (UN 2009a).

Third, refugees account for a very small share of migrants in Southern Africa (2.1 percent). This figure is lower than in Western Africa (2.7 percent) and much lower than in all other subregions: Northern Africa (19.9 percent), Eastern Africa (25.5 percent), and Middle (Central) Africa (37.7 percent) (UN 2009a). South Africa leads the world in pending asylum seekers' applications, which numbered more than 300,000 in 2009 (UNHCR 2010).

Fourth, female migration in Southern Africa remains relatively low, at 43 percent in 2010, despite a steady progression from 39 percent in 1990. The percentage of female migrants in other regions has been stable or declining (as in Northern Africa, for instance) (UN 2009a).

Regional surveys reveal certain livelihood patterns across the region.[7] In terms of lifetime patterns, migration affected a substantial part of the regional population (about 40 percent of people have moved). Cross-border migration accounted for 6 percent of regional lifetime migration, with South Africa the leading regional destination. Cross-border migration from South Africa was primarily to developed countries, such as Australia, Canada, the United Kingdom and the United States.

Multiple factors influence the decision to migrate (economic and family concerns, living conditions and education). A substantial proportion of regional migration (22 percent) was seasonal over periods of one to two years, with total migration of five years on average. The data strongly show that remittances played a vital role in household economics. For the countries surveyed, cash remittances and wage income were the most or second-most important source of household income. This income was used mainly to buy food, rarely for investment. Households with cross-border migrants were consistently better off than average households.

Although it is difficult to assess the share of domestic and international migration in urbanization, trends indicate that Southern Africa is no longer urbanizing rapidly, with an annual rate of urban growth of 1.37 percent in 2010—far lower than the 3.36 percent average for Africa as a whole. The slowdown probably reflects the fact that Southern Africa is by far the most urbanized subregion of Africa, with 58.7 percent of its population urbanized (comparable figures are 51.2 percent in Northern Africa, 44.9 percent in Western Africa, 43.1

percent in Middle Africa, and 23.6 percent in Eastern Africa) (see appendix tables D.1–D.6). In South Africa these averages must be contrasted with the impact of both domestic and international migration on specific urban areas. Movements into and out of South Africa's municipalities are far more frequent than movements at the national or provincial levels and directly influence the work of local authorities.

Domestic migration is far more significant than international migration in terms of the local governance challenges it raises (maps 1 and 2 and table 7). International and domestic migrants tend to concentrate in the main urban areas, particularly in Johannesburg. At the national level, the percentage of foreigners is estimated at 2.5–3.7 percent for 2005–10; it is about 5.6 percent in the Gauteng Province (Tshwane-Johannesburg area) and about 50 percent in some areas of Johannesburg, according to the 2010 survey conducted by the Forced Migration Studies Programme and the United Nations Office for the Coordination of Humanitarian Affairs.[8] Although far less sensitive politically than international migration, domestic migration is a much more pressing issue demographically and, consequently, in terms of the planning challenges it poses for housing, education, and public health services. The importance of domestic migration is particularly evident in several peri-urban areas around Johannesburg, Tshwane, and Cape Town that experienced in-migration rates of 20–35 percent over a seven-year period (Gindrey for SALGA report 2011). By global standards, these are extraordinary figures. Areas affected by this hypermobility are often the same as those in which international migrants settle.

Migration and Recent Labor Market Transformation in South Africa

Most analysts concur that labor market conditions in South Africa deteriorated from the early 2000s as a result of at least two main factors (Barker 2003; Posel and Casale 2003; Altman and Valodia 2006). First, large numbers of people entered the market, particularly young low-skilled South Africans and migrants from across the region.[9] Second, there were drastic reductions in job opportunities in the formal economy, as a result of both a slowdown in job creation (particularly between 2007 and 2009) and losses in key sectors of the economy (especially mining). The effects of the global economic crisis were initially buffered by certain structural aspects of the South African economy—specifically, its low levels of external debt, fiscal and monetary policies, and flexible exchange rate (Baxter 2008). The economy nevertheless entered its first period of recession in 17 years. In 2008 the mining, automotive, and retail sectors began experiencing slowdowns in activities,

Map 1 Percentage of Recent Migrants in South Africa, by District, 2001

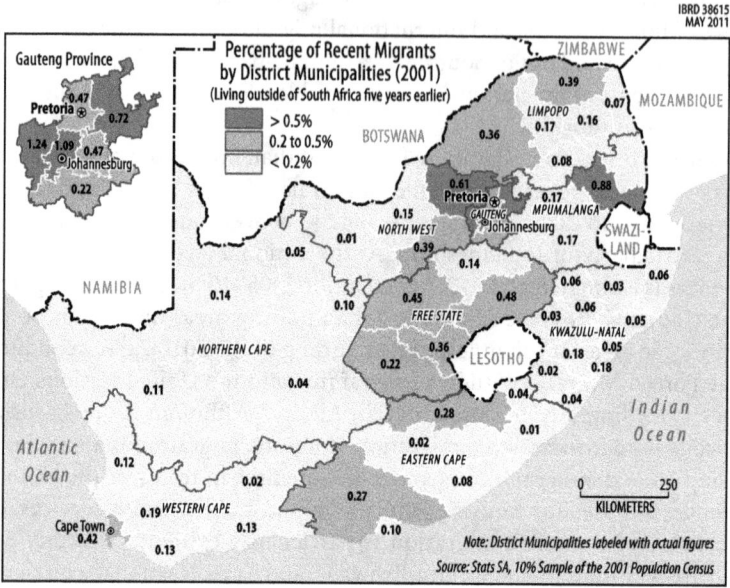

Source: Designed by V. Gindrey, in collaboration with the UN Office for the Coordination of Humanitarian Affairs (OCHA), for the Forced Migration Studies Programme from 2001 Census data.

Map 2 Percentage of Internal Migrants in South Africa, by District, 2001

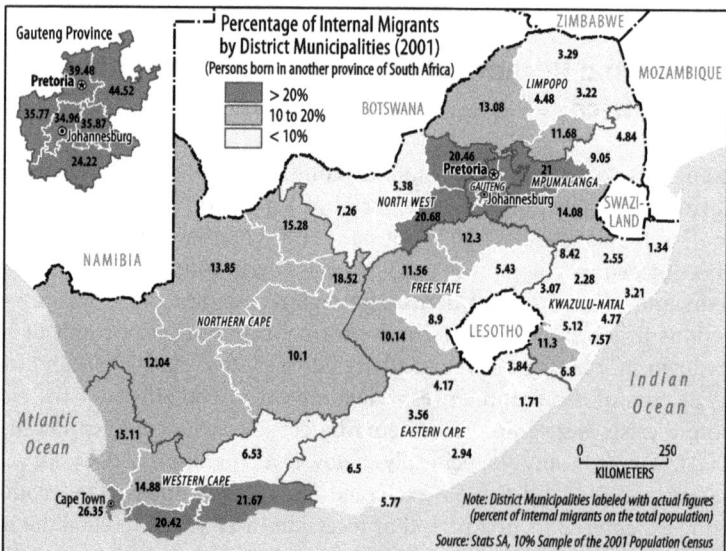

Source: Designed by V. Gindrey, in collaboration with the UN Office for the Coordination of Humanitarian Affairs (OCHA), for the Forced Migration Studies Programme from 2001 Census data.

Table 7 Origin of Migrants in South African Provinces, 2001–07
(percent)

Destination province	Province of origin									Number of migrants from all provinces
	Western Cape	Eastern Cape	Northern Cape	Free State	KwaZulu-Natal	Northwest	Gauteng	Mpumalanga	Limpopo	
Western Cape	0	54	5	3	7	1	25	2	3	197,212
Eastern Cape	29	0	5	8	19	2	31	3	3	85,392
Northern Cape	20	6	0	10	3	43	17	1	1	46,054
Free State	6	18	10	0	8	14	34	4	4	67,832
KwaZulu-Natal	6	45	2	4	0	3	29	8	3	124,276
Northwest	3	16	4	15	4	0	40	6	12	152,933
Gauteng	6	11	2	7	17	16	0	15	27	609,169
Mpumalanga	2	7	1	6	13	5	27	0	39	128,903
Limpopo	3	5	1	5	3	11	45	26	0	71,269

Source: V. Gindrey for the Forced Migration Studies Programme, based on data from the Statistics South Africa 2001 Census and 2007 Community Survey.

forcing large-scale retrenchments. More than 400,000 jobs may have been lost between 2008 and 2009 (Marais 2010). This figure only partly reflects losses of temporary and casual jobs and therefore renders estimates of unemployment rates more complicated and inaccurate.

In the mining sector, the proportion of foreign workers began to decline after 1994 (figure 1). During the 1960s, foreign workers represented more than 70 percent of miners in South Africa but would fluctuate substantially. Their numbers stabilized above 50 percent in the 1990s but from 2002, foreigners other than Mozambicans consistently represented less than 50 percent of the mining labor force (Crush and Williams 2010). By 2006 foreigners represented 38 percent of workers in South African gold mines (figure 2).

With increasing levels of subcontracting and little regulation or monitoring, it is difficult to know how many foreign miners currently work in South Africa. The older generation (particularly the Basotho) is gradually retiring and is not being replaced. Younger generations, especially of Mozambicans, tend to be employed in the most dangerous positions (Crush and others 1999; Anseeuw and Pons-Vignon 2007), suggesting that estimates of job losses in mining in South Africa, which have been placed at 14,000–40,000, understate the impact on the subsectors of the mining industry where foreigners are most represented.

Figure 1 Migrant Labor in South African Gold Mines, 1990–2006

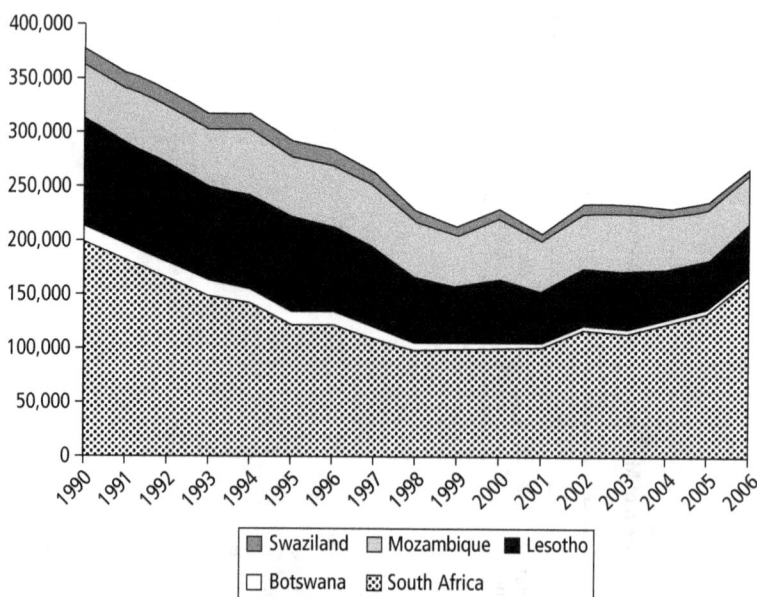

Source: Employment Bureau of South Africa.

Figure 2 Nationality of Workers in South African Gold Mines, 2006

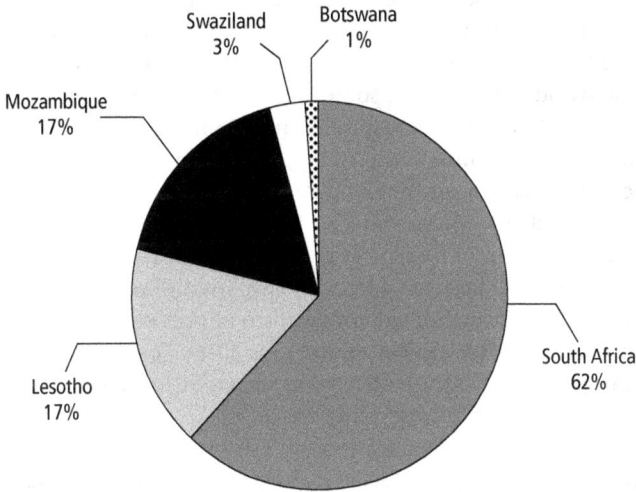

Source: Employment Bureau of South Africa.

The South African labor market remains highly dependent on foreign labor, and employment in South Africa remains crucial to the livelihoods of millions of people across the region. The slowdown of the economy as a result of the global crisis, as well as restructuring in the mining and manufacturing sectors, forced thousands of migrants to search for other means of survival. Extractive industries have been very seriously affected across Southern Africa. Therefore, although mining remains the backbone of the regional economy and new projects continue to be launched, the industry's employment capacity has contracted. According to the Southern Africa Resource Watch (2009), more than half a million mining workers in the region could lose their jobs between 2009 and 2011, from about 20 percent to 60 percent or more of mining workers in countries such as the Democratic Republic of Congo, Zambia, and Zimbabwe.

Unless new mining opportunities and export outlets emerge, the regional decline in mining will exacerbate unemployment and trigger new forms of mobility as part of workers' redeployment strategies. With decreased social spending by companies and governments, job losses will mean a return to poverty for many.

The situation in other sectors of the South African economy is more mixed. The 2010 *Statistics South Africa Labour Survey Quarterly* suggests that international migrants are most prevalent in the most labor-intensive sectors, which absorb large numbers of unskilled workers (construction, agriculture, mining, hospitality, domestic work, and to some extent the security sector). The food and beverages sector of the hospitality industry, a major employer of informal foreign labor, does not seem to have suffered significantly, perhaps because of the boost from the 2010 World Cup (Araia 2011). The construction sector has been affected. The government's large infrastructure programs and preparations for the World Cup mitigated some of the worst effects of the crisis but may have provided only short-term respite. As in the mining sector, there has been a steady increase in the number of foreign workers in construction, with the replacement of Mozambicans by Zimbabweans, particularly after 2005 (Araia, Polzer, and Kola 2010). Although lack of good data precludes proper assessment of the proportion of foreigners in construction, a recent study indicates that the key distinction between decent and exploitative conditions of employment depends on the nature of employment (more regular or more casual jobs) rather than on workers' (Araia, Polzer, and Kola 2010). Foreigners may therefore not necessarily be the ones most affected by the crisis. Impacts on workers may depend on workers' specific position in the sector.

Little is known about other sectors, such as domestic work, security, and agriculture. Domestic work and security may not have been subject to downscaling as a result of the global crisis. Although agriculture may have suffered from inflation and the general slowdown of the economy, it has benefitted from the growing availability of cheap labor, particularly from Zimbabwe. A 2007 report on Zimbabweans in Limpopo, the South African province that shares a border with Zimbabwe, recorded local testimonies about a general disrespect for minimum wages, concerns for workers' safety, the employment of under-age school leavers, and a policy of systematic deportation by the South African authorities (Forced Migration Studies Programme and Musina Legal Advice Office 2007).

The Institutional Framework: Regional Divergence and the Preference for Bilateralism

Regional integration in Southern Africa initially emerged as a reaction to protracted colonial domination. Southern African states first united as a coalition of independent "front-line" states under the Southern African Development Coordination Conference, which, after the end of apartheid, became the Southern African Development Community (SADC). The end of the Cold War and the advent of the European Union as a unified regional power counterbalancing the United States and Russia contributed to a new momentum for regional integration organizations (Bach 2008).

Adoption of the SADC Treaty in 1992, implied, among other things, a commitment to lifting obstacles not only to capital and goods circulation but also to the circulation of people. Following the signature of the treaty, however, the initial consensus about "free movement" as a goal of regional integration seemed to vanish. There was clear reluctance from SADC's "richest" member states (South Africa, Botswana, and Namibia) to institutionalize the principle of free movement (Oucho and Crush 2001). Oucho and Crush (2001), Oucho (2006), and Williams (2006, 2009) all retrace the origins of, and the developments behind, the adoption of the Protocol for the Facilitation of Movements of Persons in the SADC in August 2005. They show how South Africa stalled the original initiative, substituting a protocol that confirmed current legislation in the region.

The decade before 2005 witnessed the gradual but consistent move away from free movement. After the 1992 SADC Treaty, the position of member states moved toward mutual defiance and a lack of political will to develop a common understanding or practical implementation plans. Article 5 of the treaty explicitly called for the development of "policies aimed at the progressive elimination of obstacles to the free movement of capital and labor, goods and services, and of the peoples of the region generally, among member states." However, freer movement vanished from other protocols in which it would have applied (for instance, the 2003 Charter of Fundamental Social Rights in the SADC or the SADC Regional Indicative Strategic Development Plan [RISDP], adopted in 2003).

The provisions of the 2005 Protocol on the Facilitation of Movements of Persons are subject to the domestic legislation and policies of member states. The treaty also strongly encourages bilateral agreements between member states on crossing points, border passes, and immigration staff to the SADC secretariat (Williams 2009). The treaty does not include binding mechanisms or specific time frames.

Day-to-day management of migration in the region has given rise to a number of ad hoc pragmatic arrangements between states. In addition to the bilateral labor agreements that have been in place between South Africa and some of its neighbors (Lesotho, Mozambique, Swaziland) since the colonial period, with minor amendments, other agreements have been signed. A review of these agreements shows that they either attempt to regulate irregular moves at particular ports of entry (Malawi–Mozambique; South Africa–Mozambique; South Africa–Mozambique–Swaziland; South Africa–Lesotho) and therefore acknowledge some kind of back-door entry into labor markets or facilitate survival trade through cross-border passes.[10] The 2005 agreement between South Africa and Mozambique on a 30-day visa for Mozambican nationals entering South Africa has had a decisive impact on the lives of thousands of Mozambican migrants (Vidal 2008). Although not giving them access to the South African labor market, this measure allows them to enter legally and move about the country. The numbers of Mozambicans deported from South Africa as undocumented migrants decreased significantly after this agreement was signed (see appendix C).

Another area of bilateral cooperation has been the management of migration, which has consisted largely of exporting South Africa's expertise in the field of documentation through technical assistance and support of migration policy development, often in partnership (or in competition) with the European Union (comment made by an official from the European Commission in Kinshasa, Democratic Republic of Congo in 2008).

Given the regional focus on control and tightly framed bilateral agreements for the extractive industries (and to some extent commercial farming through specific permits), it is not surprising that market labor integration has not progressed in Southern Africa. The thorny issue of the "brain drain," which affects all states in the region, is complicated by the attractiveness of the labor markets in Botswana, Namibia, and South Africa, which recruit regional professionals and other highly skilled people (see chapter 2). Despite anti–brain drain positions within the SADC, the regional skills market is characterized by emigration toward countries in the Organisation for Economic Co-operation and Development and the replacement of skilled labor from Botswana, Namibia, and South Africa by skilled nationals from the rest of the continent. In 2002 the South African Institute of Statistics indicated that 322,499 South Africans had emigrated between 1970 and 2001 (Statistics South Africa 2003)—a gross underestimate, according to many analysts, as departures are unrecorded. In 2006 the Mbeki government acknowledged that South Africa would have to face a net skills (or job) deficit of 1.2 million positions until 2014 (ASGISA 2006). His statement led to an official change in attitude by the South African government toward the immigration of skilled labor to South Africa, but it has not changed policies drastically. Legal immigration from SADC countries to South Africa has remained very limited, with only about 15,000 permits delivered between 1994 and 2004.

In the field of humanitarian intervention and protection of vulnerable populations, ad hoc bilateral arrangements prevail in the absence of a SADC binding framework (Landau 2008). Southern Africa witnessed several protracted civil conflicts (Angola, Mozambique) until the mid-1990s and continues to include chronically unstable countries (the Democratic Republic of Congo, Zimbabwe) and natural catastrophes in the face of which states have little capacity to intervene. Various humanitarian crises have regularly marked interstate relations. They resulted in streams of refugees from Angola into the Democratic Republic of Congo in the 1980s and 1990s; from the Democratic Republic of Congo into Angola and Zambia in the late 1990s; from Mozambique into Malawi, South Africa, Zambia, and Zimbabwe in the 1980s and 1990s; and regularly as a result of floods, and more recently, political and economic uncertainty, which has brought thousands of Zimbabweans into Botswana, Namibia, South Africa, and other countries. In none of these cases did the SADC play a prominent role in the organization of relief. Agreements were generally signed between states and the UN High Commissioner for Refugees for the management of camps, documentation processes, and sometimes voluntary repatriation. The September 2010 agreement between South Africa and Zimbabwe (which legalized undocumented Zimbabwean migrants in South Africa before their pending deportation) illustrates the preference for flexible, nonbinding arrangements favored by SADC member states in crisis situations (see chapter 1).

Bilateral agreements and ad hoc arrangements between SADC member states have multiplied in the past decade alongside preexisting labor agreements between South Africa and its neighbors. The state of affairs reviewed in this chapter underscores the enduring prevalence of sovereignty in the face of weak institutional capacity at the regional level and the preference for the integration of labor markets and security management through bilateral agreements. This preference reflects the low priority and level of trust that migration-related issues muster between states in the region.

A Regional Migration-Development Challenge?

Capital accumulation in Southern Africa was built largely on a subregional migration system that favored mining, manufacturing, and commercial farming and the export of surplus labor in exchange for currency through remittances. Governments have not yet fully acknowledged the development implications of the disappearance of such a migration system and of the parallel emergence of "mixed" regional migration. The interdependencies created by migration within Southern Africa have yet to be fully assessed.

Migration could play a developmental role in at least three areas. First, migration has historically played an important role in times of crises as a survival strategy in a region that has very limited disaster management or social protection systems. Second, migration plays a role in mitigating some of the shortcomings of regional labor markets with regard to the gap between the number of new labor market participants and the number of new jobs created, cyclical financial shocks, and the poor performance of some education and training systems. Although it may be marginal at the national level, migration can prove significant at the micro level of hosts and sending localities or in specific sectors, such as construction, retail, security, and mining. Although addressing the root causes of labor imbalances should be a longer-term development goal, ensuring that governments' core regulatory function in managing labor markets is facilitated rather than complicated by migration legislation and practices would make a substantial difference. Third, migration represents a crucial link between dying rural economies and ever expanding urban areas through monetary, informational, and in-kind transfers. This interconnectedness within countries (between the Eastern Cape and the Western Cape in

South Africa, for instance) as well as between neighboring provinces across borders (between the Mpumalanga Province in South Africa and the Gaza region in Mozambique, for instance) is another key aspect of more integrated, economically sound regional development.

The SADC Protocol on the Facilitation of Movements of Persons is not intended to become a regional instrument on which member states can rely to improve the management of migration in fields such as labor market needs assessments or social protection portability. Bilateral initiatives, mainly between South Africa and its neighbors, focus on visas and documentation and rarely venture into other dimensions of migration. This study attempts to document and analyze the approach to regional migration (in terms of both rhetoric and practice) that has informed South Africa's migration policies in the postapartheid period.

Organization of This Volume

The book consists of five chapters and four appendixes. Chapter 1 describes the historical experience of migration in South Africa. It analyzes the changes in official attitudes throughout the 20th century, indicating the roots of contemporary ideas and dilemmas. The chapter sheds light on the policy transformation process, particularly on the passage from a formal migrant labor system to postmigrant labor dynamics since the end of apartheid.

Chapters 2–5 complement this analysis by looking at four often neglected dimensions of migration. Chapter 2 explores skilled labor, a crucial issue given the unbalanced structure of the South African labor market and one that is particularly sensitive in a region characterized by high levels of brain drain. Chapter 3 examines the impact of migration on local government in South African cities, with an emphasis on the importance of local government responses, failures to respond, and the implications for urban planning and service delivery. Chapter 4 examines undocumented migration, one of the main outcomes of the transition from formal labor migration to a mixed system, and the ways in which both state and nonstate actors have responded to it. Chapter 5 examines the health implications of migration. It makes the case for the need to develop and implement "spatially sensitive" health system responses within South Africa and the SADC region.

The main text is supplemented by four appendixes. Appendix A presents a chronology of immigration legislation and policy in South Africa and other SADC countries from 1986 to 2010. Appendix B discusses methodological issues in understanding migration in South Africa. Appendix C presents migration statistics for Southern Africa. Appendix D presents statistics on urbanization in Africa.

Notes

1. A great number of articles were published following the attacks in an attempt to make sense of them. Only a few were academic and evidence-based. References to these events in this volume draw mainly on Bekker and others (2008); Crush and others (2008); Human Sciences Research Council (2008); Misago, Landau, and Monson (2008); CoRMSA (2009); and Landau (2011).
2. The data used in this section are from UN (2009a, 2009b).
3. See www.queensu.ca/samp.
4. See www.migration.org.za.
5. All statistics in this section are from UN (2009a).
6. Some countries in Western and Northern Africa remain more significant host countries than Botswana, Namibia, or South Africa in absolute numbers. Despite the return of the Burkinabe following the Ivorian crisis, Côte d'Ivoire, with a population half the size of that of South Africa, still hosted an estimated 2.4 million international migrants in 2010 (UN 2009a). http://esa.un.org/migration/p2k0data .asp.
7. This discussion draws heavily on Wade Pendleton's (2004) synthesis of the Migration and Remittances Survey, the Migration and Poverty Study, and the Potential Skills Base Survey.
8. Tshwane has been the official new name of the Greater Metropolitan Municipal Area around Pretoria, the administrative capital, since 2010. The boundaries of the City of Pretoria, one of its subdivisions, remained almost unchanged.
9. Taking into account the post–2005 influx from Zimbabwe, migrants probably represent about 2.5–3.7 percent of South Africa's population. A 2009 estimate drawn from 2001 census data and estimates of Zimbabweans who have entered the country since 2005 put the total number of foreigners in South Africa at 1.6–2.0 million people (Forced Migration Studies Programme 2010). There are no reliable estimates of the percentage of foreigners in the South African labor market.
10. For a detailed review of these agreements, see Crush and Tshitereke (2001) and Williams (2009).

References

Altman, M. and I. Valodia. 2006. "Introduction: Where to for the South African Labour Market? Some 'Big Issues.'" *Transformation: Critical Perspectives on Southern Africa* 60: 1–5. East Lansing, MI: Michigan State University Press.

Anseeuw, W., and N. Pons-Vignon. 2007. "Le paradoxe sud-africain: les conditions de travail depuis la fin de l'apartheid." *Politique africaine* 106 (6): 149–64.

Araia, T. 2011. *Migration and Employment Trends in the Gauteng Hospitality Sector (Food and Beverage).* Johannesburg: African Centre for Migration and Society.

Araia, T., T. Polzer, and S. Kola. 2010. *Migration and Employment in the Construction Industry: Pilot Study.* Forced Migration Studies Programme, University of the Witwatersrand, Johannesburg, and South African Department of Labour, Pretoria.

Bach, D. 2008. "The European Union's 'Strategic Partnership' with the African Union." In *The African Union and Its Institutions,* ed. J. Akokpari, T. Murithi, and A. Ndinga-Muvumba, 355–70. Auckland Park and Cape Town: Fanele & CCR.

Barker, F. 2003. *The South African Labour Market*, 4th ed. Pretoria: Van Schaik Publishers.

Baxter, R. 2008. *The Global Economic Crisis and Its Impact on South Africa and the Country's Mining Industry*. South African Reserve Bank, Pretoria. http://www.reservebank. co.za/internet/Publication.nsf/LADV/21EFDE8DEE82935342257601003680B6/$File/ Roger+Baxter.pdf.

Bekker, S., I. Eigelaar-Meets, G. Eva, and C. Poole. 2008. "Xenophobia and Violence in South Africa: A Desktop Study of the Trends and a Scan of Explanations Offered." University of Stellenbosch, Department of Social Anthropology.

Crush, J., D. MacDonald, V. Williams, K. Lefko-Everett, D. Dorey, R. Taylor, and R. la Sablonnière. 2008. *The Perfect Storm: The Reality of Xenophobia in Contemporary South Africa*. SAMP Migration Policy Series No. 50, Southern African Migration Programme, Queen's University, Kingston, Canada, and IDASA (Institute for Democracy in South Africa), Cape Town, South Africa.

Crush, J., and C. Tshitereke. 2001. "Contesting Migrancy: The Foreign Labor Debate in Post-1994 South Africa." *Africa Today* 48 (3): 49–70.

Crush, J., T. Uliki, T. Tseane, and E. Jansen Van Vuuren. 1999. *Undermining Labour: Migrancy and Sub-contracting in the South African Gold Mining Industry*. SAMP Migration Policy Series No. 15, Southern African Migration Programme, Queen's University, Kingston, Canada, and IDASA (Institute for Democracy in South Africa), Cape Town, South Africa.

Crush, J., and V. Williams. 2010. *Labour Migration Trends and Policies in Southern Africa*. Southern African Migration Programme, Queen's University, Kingston, Canada, and IDASA (Institute for Democracy in South Africa), Cape Town, South Africa.

CoRMSA (Consortium for Refugees and Migrants in South Africa). 2009. *Protecting Refugees, Asylum and Immigrants in South Africa*. Braamfontein.

Forced Migration Studies Programme. 2010. *Population Movement in and to South Africa*. FMSP Migration Fact Sheet. University of the Witwatersrand, Johannesburg. http://www.migration.org.za/report/population-movements-and-south-africa.

Forced Migration Studies Programme, and Musina Legal Advice Office. 2007. *Special Report: Fact or Fiction? Examining Zimbabwean Cross-Border Migration into South Africa*. Forced Migration Studies Programme. University of the Witwatersrand, Johannesburg.

Gallo-Mosala, S., ed. 2008. *Migrants' Experiences within the South African Labour Market*. Scalabrini Centre of Cape Town.

Gindrey, V. 2011. Map in L. Landau, A. Segatti, and J. P. Misago, *Governing Migration and Urbanisation in South African Municipalities—Developing Approaches to Counter Poverty and Social Fragmentation*. Johannesburg: ACMS, University of the Witwatersrand, and Pretoria: South African Local Government Association.

Human Sciences Research Council. 2008. *Citizenship, Violence and Xenophobia in South Africa: Perceptions from South African Communities*. Democracy and Governance Programme. Pretoria. www.hsrc.ac.za/Research_Publications_7394.phtml.

Landau, L. B. 2008. *The Humanitarian Hangover: Displacement, Aid and Transformation in Western Tanzania*. Johannesburg: University of the Witwatersrand Press.

———, ed. 2011. *Exorcising the Demons Within: Xenophobia, Violence, and Statecraft in Contemporary South Africa*. Johannesburg: University of the Witwatersrand Press.

Marais, H. 2010. "The Impact of the Global Recession on South Africa." *Amandla*, September 30. http://www.amandlapublishers.co.za/home-menu-item/156-the-impact-of-the-global-recession-on-south-africa.

Misago, J. P., L. B. Landau, and T. Monson. 2008. *Towards Tolerance, Law and Dignity: Addressing Violence against Foreign Nationals in South Africa*. International Organization of Migration, Pretoria.

Oucho, J. 2006. "Cross-Border Migration and Regional Initiatives in Managing Migration in Southern Africa." In *Migration in South and Southern Africa: Dynamics and Determinants*, ed. Pieter Kok, Derik Gelderblom, John Oucho, and Johan van Zyl, 47–70. Pretoria: Human Sciences Research Council Press.

Oucho, J., and J. Crush. 2001."Contra Free Movement: South Africa and SADC Migration Protocols." *Africa Today* 48 (3): 139–58.

Pendleton, W. 2004. *Migration and Xenophobia in Southern Africa*. http://www.iiz-dvv.de/index.php?article_id=725andclang=1.

Posel, D., and D. Casale. 2003."What Has Been Happening to Internal Labour Migration in South Africa?" *South African Journal of Economics* 71: 455–79.

Southern Africa Resource Watch. 2009. *Impact of the Global Financial Crisis on Mining in Southern Africa*. Johannesburg.

Statistics South Africa. 2001. Census. Pretoria: Statistics South Africa.

———. 2003. *Documented Migration 2003*. Report No. 03-51-03. Pretoria.

———. 2007. Community Survey. Pretoria: Statistics South Africa.

UN (United Nations). 2009a. *Trends in International Migrant Stock: The 2008 Revision*. Department of Economic and Social Affairs, Population Division, New York.

———. 2009b. *World Urbanization Prospects: The 2009 Revision*. Department of Economic and Social Affairs, Population Division, New York. http://esa.un.org/wup2009/unup/.

UNHCR (United Nations High Commissioner for Refugees). 2010. *2009 Global Trends: Refugees, Asylum-Seekers, Returnees, Internally Displaced, and Stateless Persons*. Geneva.

Vidal, D. 2008. "Vivre sur fond de frontières. Les migrants du Mozambique à Johannesburg." *Cultures & Conflits* 72: 101–17.

Williams, V. 2006. "In Pursuit of Regional Citizenship and Identity: The Free Movement of Persons in the Southern African Development Community." *Policy, Issues and Actors* 19 (2): 1–15.

———. 2009. "Facilitating Co-operation and Integration: The SADC Protocol on the Facilitation of the Movement of Persons." Seminar Presentation, University of South Africa, Pretoria, August 18.

Chapter 1

Reforming South African Immigration Policy in the Postapartheid Period (1990–2010)

Aurelia Segatti

One can fully understand the meaning of immigration in South Africa, and of South African attitudes toward it, only with reference to the history of the country and the Southern African region. Although exploitative migration practices have been central to the region for more than a century, the African National Congress (ANC) did not place immigration policy high on its reform agenda in the early 1990s. Despite Ruth First's pioneering 1983 book and a consistent Marxist analysis of the migrant labor system, most evident within the South African Communist Party, there was no clear party line clarifying what the government's position should be in addressing profound, ongoing changes in the region's migratory system. From the initial sociodemocratic Reconstruction and Development Programme (RDP) through the neoliberal turn initiated with the adoption of the Growth, Employment and Redistribution Programme (GEAR) in 1996 to the Accelerated and Shared Growth Initiative (ASGISA) launched in 2006, the government failed to place migration among key issues for reform or to consider it a primary tool in the country's development strategy. Migration consequently remained a largely unacknowledged socioeconomic process on which the region's economy (and South Africa's most competitive sectors) relied.

For policy makers, migration and immigration were not simply about border control and access to jobs in South Africa. Internationally, migration and immigration were embedded in bilateral agreements that sometimes dated back to the colonial era. Although exploitative, these arrangements were deeply ingrained in regional populations' livelihood strategies. Any shift in policy would therefore draw attention to the unequal relations within the region and threaten the welfare of millions of people. Domestically, migration policy had been the product of ongoing, if opaque, negotiations with the private sector. In the postapartheid period, such arrangements were under mounting popular and union pressure for redress of the legacy of unequal education and chronic unemployment among the local workforce. The complexity of the politics surrounding migration almost certainly helped keep it off the front burner and prevented it from being conceptually linked with other pressing developmental concerns.

Although migration remained (and remains) a critical driver of development in the region, the ANC's reluctance to grapple with it reflected patterns across the global South. Across developing countries, especially in Africa, the governments in place during the early 1990s were not particularly proactive on migration issues. Academics and experts were also late to the game, producing few robust databases (quantitative or qualitative) on South-North migration. Data on South-South movements were even scarcer. The reason for this scarcity of data on migration was not only a question of research capacity, a challenge that remains to this day; it also reflected the symbolic and ideological space occupied by migration in developing countries' nation-building narratives. The link between decolonization struggles and immigration policy is particularly evident in former settler colonies (for example, Kenya, South Africa, and Zimbabwe). Despite a profile bearing many resemblances with other "newfound lands," such as the Australia, Canada, and United States in terms of colonial settlement and migration, South Africa did not produce the intellectual migration debate that would give the issue weight among its political elites and enable decision makers to consider it as anything other than a negative legacy of colonialism and apartheid. Somewhat paradoxically, despite the strong awareness of apartheid's inheritance, the South African government and administration continue to find it difficult to move away from a narrowly defined security approach to migration in both legislation and practice. Although this reluctance to envisage migration more innovatively is understandable in a country that was severed from the rest of the continent for almost half a century, such framing further delayed healthy engagement by stakeholders.

Without reform, the obsolescence of the regulatory framework led to continued human rights abuses by the police and immigration services, urging advocacy groups to respond. The result was an adversarial climate that constrained the analysis of migration as a developmental issue. The new constitutional and legislative dispensation put in place in the early to mid-1990s, coupled with human rights activism, created a paradox: advocates' victories helped produce a fairly progressive regime on paper, but these protections and policies stood in stark contrast to recalcitrant police, policy makers, and the population as a whole. The consequences were ongoing human rights abuses and a strong and widespread anti-immigrant sentiment across the country. This chapter documents and explores these contradictory dynamics.

This paralysis continued for more than a decade, even as the Southern African migratory system was changing rapidly in response to shifts in other policy arenas. Events thrust migration into the spotlight. In May 2008, a series of violent attacks against (mostly) foreign dwellers of impoverished urban communities killed 62 people and displaced about 150,000. The attacks came as a brutal wake-up call to many in government who had underestimated the degree to which social tensions had crystallized over the years in the context of a housing crisis, chronic unemployment, poverty, and inequalities.

Despite several announcements made since 2008 by the Department of Home Affairs, the recent Immigration Amendment Act, passed in March 2011, does not address issues of social cohesion and hardens conditions of control and access to South Africa for migrants.[1] Although there is a strong sense, among both state and nonstate actors in South Africa, that the 2008 violence stirred a variety of policy initiatives from within government, the ruling party and its allies, and civil society, these have not transformed into more concrete policy decisions. The renewed interest from local government in particular (analyzed in chapter 3 of this volume), as well as the flurry of educational activities by nongovernmental organizations (NGOs) and community-based organizations, largely happen without any bearing or even linkage with immigration policy as formulated at the national level (Polzer and Segatti 2011). As the South African government's recent reform of its immigration legislation failed to address social cohesion issues linked with migration, it is worth taking stock of what the key challenges have been to previous reform and analyzing the nature of the achievements attained. The transformation of the immigration policy framework should be seen as the product of a triple process: the legacy of apartheid administrations, the constraints created by transition rules, and the introduction into the game of new actors and groups carrying with them new and often competing models of migration management, sometimes in the form of violent anti-foreigner mobilizations, as exemplified by the 2008 attacks.

This chapter unfolds in three directions to shed light on the postapartheid policy transformation process. First, it presents a brief overview of 20th century migration policy in South Africa in order to situate the specificity of the current shift. Second, it outlines the position on international migration developed by the ruling party in the postapartheid period and its capacity (or lack thereof) to affect a system inherited from the apartheid regime and adjust it to the redefined objectives of the country's national and regional development. Third, the chapter considers the role played by nonstate actors in engaging with the South African government on migration issues and examines their impact on the current policy framework. It assesses state and nonstate actors' changing discourses and positioning within the migration policy framework following the 2008 xenophobic attacks.

The chapter draws on primary and secondary data gathered between 1995 and 2010. In particular, it builds on the author's doctoral dissertation, as well as supplementary qualitative research conducted between 2006 and 2010 (see acknowledgments). Research included observation at the national, regional, and local level in various policy processes related to the reform of South Africa's immigration policy; formal and informal interviews with NGO, academic, institutional, and political actors; and archival research.

The Genesis of a Discriminatory Migration System (1910–91)

In the waning days of the apartheid regime, the de Klerk administration instituted a policy framework that would last for a decade of democratic rule. The framework included the 1991 Aliens Control Act, which survived until 2002 with only incremental modifications (despite mounting criticisms from the nongovernmental organization and academic sectors as well as the business community). Examination of how this discriminatory migration system was built over the 20th century, and of how public administrations were reformed (or not), provides insights into the persistence of certain perceptions and administrative practices, particularly within the Department of Home Affairs and by many in the ANC.

The Two-Gate Policy
The specificity of the South African case resides less in the introduction of increasingly drastic selection criteria based on social, racial, and religious prejudices—indeed, a number of countries, including European ones, adopted similar policies.[2] Rather, it comes from the parallel and simultaneous movement of on one hand, denationalization of the indigenous population to serve the political economy of apartheid (the Bantustan system) and on the other, the subsequent reincorporation processes and constantly shifting demarcation lines between citizens and noncitizens (through the vote, the Constitution, the reincorporation of Bantustans and their inhabitants into the Republic) (Morris 1991; Marais 1998; Peberdy and Crush 1998).

Most of the 20th century was characterized by the progressive consolidation of a system known as the "two-gate policy." The front gate welcomed people who corresponded to the criteria of attractiveness defined by the governing minority. The back gate served a double function, preventing unwanted migrants from entering and allowing cheap and relatively docile labor in for temporary periods. Closely connected to the grand apartheid scheme, notably its homelands policy, this system blurred the lines between citizens (specifically, the indigenous population) and foreigners in a way achieved by few other societies.[3] The various laws and regulations on migration passed throughout the 20th century (see appendix A); the proactive white (and Protestant) immigration policy of successive nationalist governments; the relations between the South African state, the agricultural and mining sectors, and labor-sending neighboring countries; and apartheid legislation itself, specifically on residential segregation and preferential job areas, all contributed to mainly coercive migration management practices and stereotyped images of foreigners.

The situation that prevailed under the de Klerk administration reflected 90 years of legislation aimed at creating and preserving a certain racist society. From 1913 to 1937, legal criteria defining foreigners and their access to South African territory were set up and regulated. From 1937 to 1986, legislation was gradually aligned based on the principle of separate economic development and served the objectives of the two-gate policy. From 1986 to 1994, there was a widening gap between the intentions of legislative normalization and deep political transformation. These developments led to a series of deeply entrenched practices, a tension the postapartheid constitutional dispensation would heighten.

In the early 1990s, laws regulating immigration essentially replicated the principles enshrined in the 1937 Aliens Control Act, aimed at restricting the influx of Jewish refugees from Eastern Europe following the rise of Nazi Germany. The act first introduced the term *alien* into legislation and explicitly introduced the "racial" criterion as a condition of entry into South African territory. Section 4(3)(b) of the act stated that all applicants should be 'likely to become readily assimilated' with the European inhabitants of the Union and that they should not represent a threat to "European culture." From 1948 onward, the National Party passed three major laws that closely bound immigration policy, citizenship, and the management of indigenous populations: the 1950 Population Registration Act (on racial classification), the 1962 Commonwealth Relations Act (which ended uncontrolled transborder movements in Southern Africa), and the 1955 Departure from the Union Regulation Act (which required authorization to depart from South African territory).

Although the policy that lasted until the late 1990s was first established in 1937, it was not until 1961 that a proactive white immigration policy was instituted, with the creation of a government department devoted entirely to immigration. Until then, immigration had been effectively outsourced to private initiatives after unsuccessful governmental attempts at the beginning of the century with the Milner administration.

In the 1950s, the (largely Afrikaner) National Party faced a dilemma. By suppressing immigration, at the time largely Anglophone, it exposed the white population to the risk of "sinking into an ocean of color"; by allowing immigration to continue, it risked losing its majority in Parliament.

By the early 1960s, the political context had changed. The politically strengthened National Party decided to set up a proactive (albeit still Protestant) policy to address the increasing scarcity of qualified white labor. Between 1961 and 1991, several programs were implemented. Subsidies and direct state aid allowed for the settlement of tens of thousands of European immigrants. These subsidies—used to fund travel expenses, accommodations, and settlement allowances—reached R 3.6 million ($4.8 million) in 1972–73 and up to R 8 million ($2.9 million), in 1991 when they were eliminated.

Until the democratic transition of 1994, South Africa was widely regarded as a refugee-issuing country. It was endowed with better border monitoring capacity than its neighbors, protecting it from massive inflows stemming from the civil conflicts that affected the region following independence elsewhere. Although South Africa actively protected itself from refugees (except immigrants or often South African returnees from liberated newly independent African countries) and produced a range of refugees and exiles of its own, it was also actively involved in promoting the conflicts that generated refugees in other countries, through the regional destabilization strategy conceived by President P. W. Botha in the early 1980s. Southern Africa was also affected by the major refugee movements experienced elsewhere on the continent in the early 1990s, namely the Angolan and Mozambican and later the Burundian and Rwandan crises.

Although asylum systems had been progressively put in place in neighboring African countries, South Africa entered the 1990s with no system in place. The lack of such a system reflected both the fact that South Africa had fewer refugees than other countries and the isolation of the South African government internationally. Before the 1990s, asylum reflected segregationist immigration policies rather than international agreements. South Africa welcomed different waves of European immigrants, including Huguenots who fled France in the 17th and 18th centuries; Russian and Lithuanian Jews who fled pogroms in the late 19th century and later with the rise of Nazi Germany; Italian prisoners during World War II; Greeks fleeing the dictatorship of the colonels; Belgians and Portuguese fleeing the Congo, Angola, and Mozambique after independence; returnee South Africans from Northern and Southern Rhodesia; and Jews fleeing the Congo. Despite religious and anti-Semitic reservations within the white community, no special status was created for these immigrants, and they were not required to formalize their reasons for coming to South Africa, although acceptance of some groups of immigrants was done gradually and often in a discriminatory way, particularly in the case of the Portuguese. Some communities, such as white expatriates from Rhodesia and Mozambique, formed solidarity networks.

In the 1980s, conditions within the region began to put pressure on South Africa's refugee and asylum policies and practices. The Mozambican conflict created an important inflow of refugees in a difficult period, during which the regional balance was disrupted. The inflow of Mozambican refugees from 1984 onward was the only massive inflow of refugees to South Africa in recent history, except for the inflow of Zimbabweans in 2000, whose acknowledgement as refugees raised specific concerns (discussed in the next section). The Mozambican inflow had major repercussions for the asylum and immigration policies the new postapartheid government developed during the 1990s. Agreements signed between the United Nations High Commissioner for Refugees and the South African government from 1993 onward made it possible (after a laborious process) to afford Mozambican refugees a status. However, despite an official legal recognition of their refugee status, Mozambicans who had sought refuge in South Africa continued to be deported en masse as illegal immigrants and only a few managed to legalize their situation in the late 1990s, early 2000s.[4]

The immigration policy inherited by the de Klerk administration in 1989 bore three characteristics. First, it was based on a classical colonial settlement policy, focusing on the almost exclusive development of the needs of the European minority and its corollary, a cheap black labor force maintained in a precarious position. Second, the management of migration and foreigners was discretionary and often based on opaque practices. Third, the development mode through which this policy was meant to evolve was incremental, very rarely providing enough space for assessment or even public debate. It was thus largely disconnected from both ongoing migration trends and dynamics and actual assessments of skills needs in the economy.

Preparing for Tomorrow's Transformation with Yesterday's Tools: 1986–1991

A fundamental reform occurred, if only in principle, during the height of the political crisis in 1986. An amendment to the Aliens Control Act of 1937 was promulgated that deleted the definition of European from section 4(3)(b). Adopted at a time when South Africa was plunged into a state of emergency at the heart of one of the worst crises in the apartheid system, this amendment met national and international policy challenges. Removing the racial criterion from the 1937 act was meant to show tangible signs of institutional transformation in the system and to enable the influx of qualified yet cheap labor from other African countries into the homelands. J.C.G. Botha, then Minister of Home Affairs, insisted that, "the Government has irrevocably committed itself to removing discriminatory and offensive measures from the Statute book" (Botha 1986). Immigration policy remained a selective policy aimed at "fulfilling the country's labor needs ... bearing in mind the needs and interests of South Africa."

Criticized by the representatives of the Conservative Party as one of the "most dangerous bills which had ever been introduced by the governing party," the 1986 amendment had very little effect on the actual granting of permanent residence. Racial criteria continued to be unofficially applied by the Immigrants

Selection Board, which kept a firm grip on the selection process (interview with P. J. Colyn, Director-General of Home Affairs 1989–97, November 16, 2001). Even if applicants no longer had to be European, they were still supposed to "within a reasonable period of time after entry into the Republic become assimilated with any community of the Republic" (Republic of South Africa 1986). The level of qualifications and applicants' financial resources became, after race, the major criteria for immigrants.

The ascension of F. W. de Klerk to power in 1989, the fall of the Berlin Wall, and the decision to abandon the apartheid system and the regional destabilization policy through negotiations contributed to the adoption of a new immigration law in 1991. The legislation was meant to tackle domestic issues rather than to be a long-term management instrument for regional migration, however. The volatile situation of the early 1990s and the isolation of South Africa from the rest of the continent contributed to the maintenance of a strong security focus on immigration issues despite the post–Cold War context.

At just this time, the question of Mozambican refugees, which was to become one of the thorniest migration issues of the decade, came to the fore. Although the number of Mozambican refugees, who were tolerated only in the homelands, kept increasing, the government opened up the possibility of acknowledging refugee status through the signing of three agreements with the United Nations High Commissioner for Refugees (UNHCR).[5] This partial acknowledgement of refugee status began a highly controversial voluntary repatriation program for Mozambican refugees. Yet almost simultaneously, a policy of systematic and massive forced repatriation was adopted (Wa Kabwe-Segatti 2002). (See appendix A and an update on the issue of repatriation and undocumented migration in chapter 4.)

The 1991 Aliens Control Act, nicknamed "apartheid's last act," was the cornerstone of South African immigration policy throughout the 1990s. Drafted in order to unify and simplify all immigration laws since 1937, as well as to mark a break from the past, this act reflected a fundamental paradox from the advent of the 1994 democratic regime. The intrinsic contradiction between the act and both the interim Constitution and the 1996 Constitution played an important role in the decision to deeply reform immigration legislation with the official opening of a consultation process on the issue beginning in 1996. Since the 1991 Aliens Control Act was declared unconstitutional and liable to constitutional review by 2002, there was no option but to reform the immigration legislation.

However, despite this sword of Damocles hanging over it, the Aliens Control Act survived 12 years into the postapartheid period, despite perpetuating a policing vision of immigration characterized by the suspicion and coercion of migrants. Section 55 established that "no court had any jurisdiction to review, quash, reverse, interdict or otherwise interfere with any proceeding, act, order or warrant of the Minister, a board, an immigration officer or a master of ship" (Republic of South Africa 1991). In the tradition of past laws, undocumented migrants were deprived of even basic rights; their time in detention and the conditions of their deportation or repatriation beyond borders was left almost entirely to the discretion of immigration officers, the police, or the army. The notion of public order (Section 47) permitted restrictions on undocumented migrants' fundamental constitutional rights. For the majority of Mozambicans, refugee status was not acknowledged in urban areas before the mid-1990s. Provisions for appeal in the 1991 act were very limited, exposing some South African citizens to arrest, detention, and deportation.[6] The 1991 act did not modify the 1984 legislation that denationalized citizens from the homelands, who remained foreigners subject to immigration legislation within white South Africa until 1993, when the interim Constitution reintegrating the homelands went into effect. Thousands of these people were deported every year between 1984 and 1993 (Department of Internal Affairs and Home Affairs 1984–93).

The gap between immigration and emigration continued to widen after 1991, with emigration again exceeding immigration as from 1994 (see figure 1.2).[7] The proportion of African immigrants decreased until 1992–93, while the number of Asian immigrants jumped dramatically. The proportion of African, Asian, and European immigrants then stabilized at about one-third from each region (Department of Home Affairs 1995). Quite predictably, the restriction imposed on permanent residence led to an explosion in temporary entries, which rose from about 400,000 a year in 1988 to almost 700,000 in 1992 (Department of Home Affairs 1995). This boom most benefited migrants from Africa, particularly African students, who represented up to 60 percent of foreign students enrolled at South African universities in 1996 (Ramphele 1999). Renewals of temporary work permits consistently diminished between 1993 and 1995. Broadly speaking, there were fewer permanent immigrants to South Africa, and permanent immigrants were no longer exclusively Europeans. The beginning of the 1990s was also the time when increasing numbers of white collar workers from Africa and Asia reached South Africa. Unable to access permanent residence because of weak financial resources (permanent residence fees were prohibitively high at the time), they progressively occupied positions deserted by the white minority, but their position remained precarious, given their status as holders of temporary work permits.

The new regime that came into office in 1994 had to face a rapidly changing migrant situation with a legal instrument focused on a policing and coercive vision of migration management. Although some may have disagreed with this approach, few had the necessary understanding of the broader field of migration to assess pressing issues such as the increasing numbers of asylum seekers, the brain drain/brain gain phenomena, skills needs, or the rights of undocumented migrants. Existing practices, administrations, and institutions

Figure 1.1 Number of Documented Immigrants in South Africa, by Continent of Origin, 1984–2004

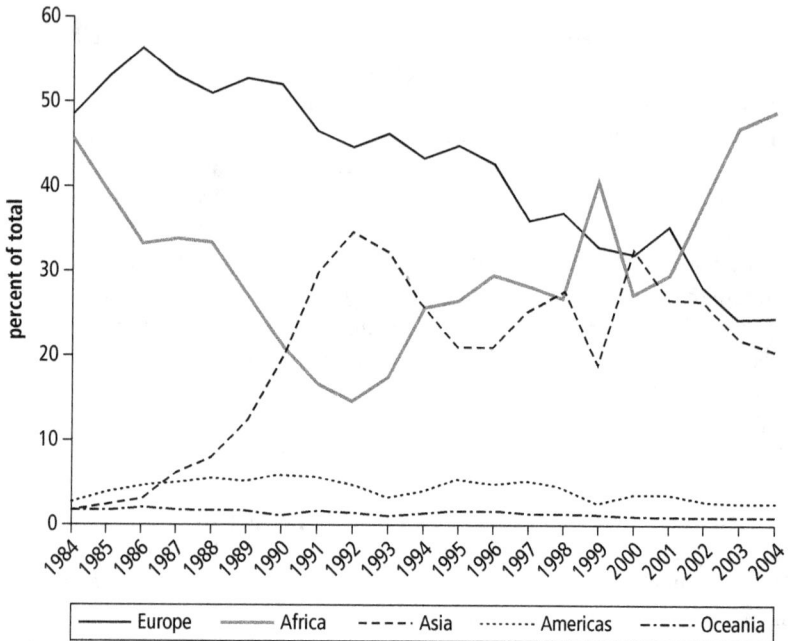

Source: Department of Home Affairs, Annual Reports (1984–2004).

in charge of migration management and the legal apparatus ensured the continuity of a national immigration policy awaiting redefinition.

When the ANC came to power after the April 1994 elections, some political analysts and migrant groups expected a more open immigration policy, having confused the advent of democracy and the change in regime with a change in the definition of core national interests. No such change occurred. In a July 1994 newspaper article, an undocumented Zairian immigrant stated that he believed the new government would give more leeway to people who settled in South Africa illegally because "we should be more welcome by a black government" (Nxumalo 1994). This kind of expectation was widespread at the time among NGOs, particularly among lawyers specializing in asylum claims, and business circles (interviews with Lee Ann de la Hunt, University of Cape Town Legal Clinic; Jacob van Garderen, Lawyers for Human Rights, Pretoria; and Vincent Williams, IDASA and SAMP, Cape Town). As one analyst from the Centre for Policy Studies noted, "There is a crucial moral imperative: the republic is riding a wave of moral legitimacy and it must navigate responses in line with its global

Figure 1.2 Number of Permanent Immigration Permits Granted in and Declared Emigrants from South Africa, 1941–2009

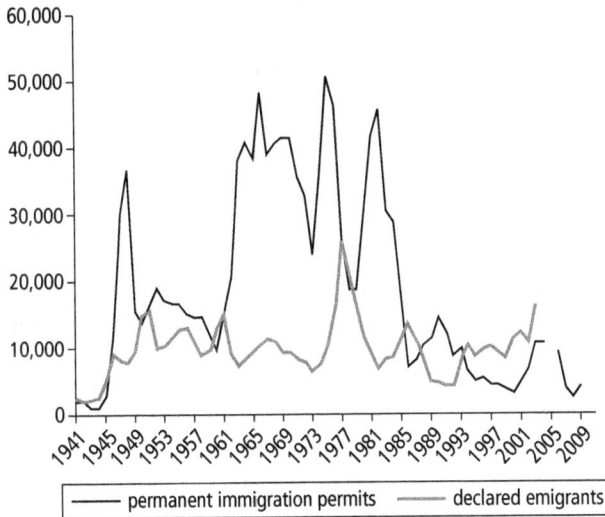

Source: Department of Home Affairs (various years); Statistics South Africa Tourism and Migration Reports, 1973–2010.
Note: Since 2004, departure forms have not been required.

standing; it can ill-afford to turn a blind eye to xenophobia and human rights abuses generally" (Landsberg 1995: 672).

When it discovered that immigration legislation had remained unchanged since 1991, the liberal press in South Africa expressed its surprise at this vestige of apartheid, in direct contradiction with the interim constitution (Koch 1994). Soon, academics, activists, the liberal press, and NGO circles, as well as some ANC politicians, introduced the idea of a moral debt owed by South Africa to the rest of the continent. An editorial from the *Mail & Guardian* in September 1994 warned both the government and South African citizens that "the response [to migration] is taking on an increasingly racial and nationalistic tinge as some political groupings try and whip up xenophobia, presumably to set the ground for a ruthless clampdown. There are good moral reasons to warn against such sentiments. After all, this country, with its previous policy of destabilization, bears a good deal of responsibility for the economic chaos of our neighbors."

It is in this context that the Institute for Democracy in South Africa (IDASA) initiated a fact-finding mission on transborder migration in 1995 with, among others, the chairs of the Parliamentary Portfolio Committee on Foreign Affairs (Raymond Suttner), Home Affairs (Desmond Lockey), and

Minerals and Energy (Marcel Golding). Led by IDASA's director, Wilmot James, this mission concluded that regional solutions should be found, as South Africa could be considered responsible for the imbalances causing migration flows in the region. According to James, "In Mozambique, the morality of our actions became even more stark. South Africa played an integral part in the war that ravaged Mozambique's economy and its officials clearly believe South Africa has a moral responsibility in promoting development there. Unfortunately, that means maintaining the migrant labor system" (Rossouw 1995).

Following this first report, the Department of Home Affairs and its minister, Mangosothu Buthelezi, the leader of the Inkatha Freedom Party, the ANC's historical rival but ally in the government of national unity, decided to appoint a task team in November 1996 to write the Green Paper on International Migration. The consultative process that was initiated would take seven years to be finalized into new legislation and political vision.[8] The consultative process received protracted media coverage and included various complex episodes that created space for activist, business, and academic interest groups to define their positions on migration. The extent to which this consultative ritual affected the actual decision-making process and ongoing management of migration is unclear. The publication of the green paper in 1997 was followed by two white papers, on refugee affairs (1998) and international migration (1999). The White Paper on International Migration was a confusing document that tried to reconcile stringent migration control and the fight on illegal migrants with mechanisms for a new and more open skills-based system. In the words of one analyst of and actor in the process, "There is not a great deal of evidence that this particular consultative process has shaped the new legislation in significant ways" (Crush 2001: 3).

The Emergence of a Democratic Reformist Movement (1991–2003)

Thanks to institutional reforms and because of transformed migration flows from the region and beyond, the postapartheid context played out as a special window of opportunity for different groups intent on reforming South African immigration policy. The combination of former activist networks and new patterns of mobilization helped these groups seize the opportunity of the government-led reform process to push specific agendas, mainly focused on human rights issues. Both government and activists' activity created demand for renewed specialized knowledge serving both genuine efforts to transform policies and media strategies to delay transformation.

Human Rights Activism and Migration as a New Consultancy Market

South Africa has a vibrant human rights and NGO community, a century-long history of fighting discrimination and arbitrariness, and a robust legal and constitutional apparatus that is one of the most advanced in the world in terms of fighting discrimination and protecting basic rights. The attachment to legal traditions goes back much farther than the advent of democracy and was perhaps one of the most paradoxical features of South Africa's racially and socioeconomically divided society throughout the 20th century. With the advent of democracy and the reopening of the African continent to the rest of the world in 1994, South Africa found itself in a very specific situation as far as migration was concerned. In contrast to other African countries, South Africa had a much higher capacity to control its borders and manage migration internally (this capacity would prove rather illusory in the longer term). But its moral commitment to democracy at home and in the region prevented its government from adopting a strictly anti-immigration stance. Looking at South African immigration policy over the century, it is clear that every significant political turn was accompanied by harsher immigration measures; in this sense, the 1994 regime change displays continuity with previous immigration policy. The first impulse of each new government has been to redefine notions of belonging to and exclusion from the national community (Peberdy 2009). Highly restrictionist and conservative discourses on migration control and management were thus adopted in 1910, 1948, 1963, and after 1994.

On the other hand, compared with Organisation for Economic Co-operation and Development member countries, South Africa's capacity to control migration was limited and its land and sea borders were (and remain) porous. Its internal political context was also complex. While the ANC had not developed a position on immigration when it came to power in 1994, human rights activist groups (such as universities' legal aid clinics and the Johannesburg-based Lawyers for Human Rights) had experience in protecting such vulnerable populations and swiftly devised legal strategies around the coercive control and detention practices that continued to prevail. Experience gained in protecting black South Africans from the Bantustans was redeployed toward the protection of international migrants, victims of police abuse, and refugees and asylum seekers caught in the net of inconsistent migration policies. With South Africa becoming a signatory to all international treaties on refugees and asylum seekers by 1994, the adoption of the 1996 Constitution, and national refugee legislation passed in 2000,[9] these groups could now rely on an entirely new rights-based legal apparatus and a favorable institutional context.

In the meantime, another group of actors, scholars, and researchers working on migration, often with close connections to human rights groups, emerged in the debate. They played a prominent role in the consultative process, becoming closer to the government over the period under discussion. The space created by government through rounds of consultations from 1994 onward facilitated the emergence or consolidation of several research structures and think tanks that produced data in a field characterized by a scarcity of knowledge in the early 1990s. In conjunction with business and trade unions, these institutions largely shaped the various policy options elaborated upon in the 1990s and 2000s.[10]

One of apartheid's legacies at the turn of the 1990s—partly the result of ad hoc policy management in a period of vast political upheaval—was a dearth of data on migration. In 1993–94, when the first bouts of xenophobia erupted, little quantitative and qualitative knowledge was available on migration apart from broad statistics on annual legal entries and deportations. The first post-apartheid studies emerged only in 1996 and especially 1997–98. Approaches to migration were very much influenced by past categorizations. Although economic migration from the rest of the subregion and continent was crucial to the region's economy and undergoing major transformations (downscaling, retrenchment, and casualization), migration was looked at strictly from the perspective of existing agreements. In general, South African researchers adopted administrative categorizations uncritically. In the late 1980s and 1990s, migration was increasingly studied as a security threat, with a focus on "illegal aliens," perhaps partly reflecting the concerns of a dying and isolated regime. Data on new trends were almost nonexistent in the mid-1990s. Pro- and anti-immigration actors confronted one another, resorting to outdated data and archetypical situations borrowed from other countries (the U.S.–Mexican border, Europe) without any knowledge of the actual impact of immigration on South Africa.

One of the results of this lack of research was the predominance of state sources in the media and academic publications between 1994 and 1998–99. A 1996 study of the South African press indicated that the three departments in charge of migration—Home Affairs, Security, and Defense—were quoted more often than all other sources (Dolan and Reitzes 1996). As the legal challenge to immigration regulations and practices became more structured, the media began using newly published research data that started appearing after 1998 from the academic and NGO sectors. Reliance on official sources waned as advocacy groups began challenging government statements.

The 10-year period (1994–2004) of the wide consultative process and passage of the new Immigration Act in 2002 and the Immigration Amendment Act in 2004 (box 1.1) was crucial in shaping positions and structuring networks on migration issues. From the idea of in-depth transformation and rupture with the past that animated IDASA, the migration policy framework gradually moved toward a rather narrowly defined agenda, limiting the government's action to incremental amendments and compromise. Three routes were then followed by various clusters of actors:

BOX 1.1

The Immigration Act of 2002 and the Immigration Amendment Act of 2004

The ANC chair of the Parliamentary Portfolio Committee on Home Affairs called the Immigration Act of 2002 "a product that … all of us can live with," a phrase reflecting the heterogeneous character of postapartheid migration legislation. Passed after a seven-year consultative process, the act was amended in 2004 at Thabo Mbeki's request. The final regulations were published in late 2005, bringing to a close a 10-year process, certainly the most cumbersome legislative and policy-making process of the new era in South Africa.

The new legislation reveals much continuity with previous legislation. Indeed, it reflects three options the ANC opted for in 2002. The first is minimal constitutional conformity—that is, alignment with constitutional rights, such as spouses' rights, including the rights of homosexual couples (same sex marriages were legalized in South Africa in 2007). The second is the pursuit of a dual system of limited permanent high-skilled immigration and temporary lower-skilled migration, mainly through corporate permits. The third is the retention of power within central government services and the concentration of power within the Department of Home Affairs, as illustrated in the 2005 strategic plan, which reiterated control and sovereignty as core values guiding immigration policy in South Africa.

The 2002 Act and its subsequent amendment were attempts at accommodating these contradictory trends without questioning the core elements of continuity referred to above. Thus, the Immigration Act of 2002 eliminated prospects of an externalized immigration service and state control over access to the South African labor market. It confirmed the choice of incremental change. This choice shows the ANC's ability to remain both independent from the neoliberal views on which the first immigration bill was premised (it was clearly aligned with the General Agreement on Tariffs and Trade) and the voices of organized labor, whose public comments (mainly on regional socioeconomic development and the cessation of the differential pay system) were largely ignored.

The final regulations adopted in 2005 focus on discouraging illegal immigration. They contain measures facilitating access to permits for the region's workers and students and restrictions aimed at fighting illegal immigration, such as increasing to five years the length of time a person must be married to a South African citizen before being able to apply for citizenship, an attempt to fight fraudulent marriages.

- A neoliberal agenda favoring the withdrawal of the state from migration matters, the subcontracting of administrative processing of control to employers, the establishment of incentives to highly skilled labor and investors, and accelerated policy reform simplifying administrative procedures. This agenda was put forward beginning in 1994 by the then minister of home affairs and supported by business circles and to some extent liberals in the opposition.

- An interventionist approach in favor of balanced migration control, taking into account democratic commitments and state capacity for a flexible, reactive, and transparent migration policy. This approach, shared by advocacy groups and minority constituencies within the ANC and the Congress of South African Trade Unions, called for more profound policy transformation and a regional thrust.
- A security and sovereignty-centered agenda favored by the majority in the ANC and by departments' bureaucratic strata, based on a narrowly defined notion of national interest bearing many resemblances to previous positions.

To a large extent, these orientations still inform dominant approaches to migration and shape public discourses as well as policy analysis within the ruling party. The major change in terms of policy prioritization, if not content and orientation, was forced on political actors by the 2008 xenophobic attacks.

Examination of the legislative reform process in the early 2000s based on interviews with all key actors reveals the low level of consensus over the issue by political parties and other stakeholders. In 2002, when some ANC leaders realized the government was about to adopt a piece of legislation that would continue to favor mining and farming interests and potentially reduce the protection of low-skilled South African labor, a special task group organized an 11th-hour intervention that took the form of the patchwork 2002 Immigration Act, a last-minute effort meant to accommodate all stakeholders, according to the chair of the Parliamentary Portfolio Committee on Home Affairs (Scott 2002: 2702). The wide consultative process of the 1990s was therefore not what eventually gave birth to the final legislation adopted in 2002, but it accomplished a number of tasks: it shaped the policy options (table 1.1), fostered research initiatives from all sides in order to enrich the debate with empirical data, and reorganized the policy framework in such a way that the government soon realized that its every move on migration issues would be subject to scrutiny by legal, human rights, and immigrant and refugee activists. This new state of play led to changes considered as breakthroughs by these groups.

The Reformists' Breakthroughs and Their Impact on the New Migration Agenda

The people most closely involved in the consultative process believe that little was achieved after passage of the 2002 Immigration Act, especially considering the length of the process (12 years) and the number of stakeholders involved (Crush 2001). Yet the situation of foreigners in the mid-2000s differed considerably from what it was in 1994 in at least three respects: refugee matters, public accountability

Table 1.1 Overview of Policy Options within South Africa's Migration Policy Framework, 1994–2010

Approach	Internal control	Border control	Regional cooperation	Migrants' rights	Access to job market	Sanctions on employers
"Securitarian"	Yes	Yes	No; bilateral temporary work contracts	Limited	Limited to highly qualified people and investors	Yes
Neoliberal	Limited	Yes, but ought to disappear eventually	Yes, maximum regional integration; suppression of tariff barriers and limiting of regulations governing access to foreign labor; hegemonic vision favoring bilateral contracts	Limited	Free access, restrictions only to combat terrorism and crime syndicates	None or very limited
International human rights	Limited	Yes, but limited	Yes; proactive migration policy; regional integration/cooperation; specific visas and quotas for unskilled workers	Pragmatic version of universal basic human rights in which negative rights (that is, the right not to be subjected to an action) are constitutionally defined	Free access, restrictions only to combat terrorism and crime syndicates	Yes
Bureaucratic/interventionist	Yes	Yes	Moderate, largely bilateral	Yes, within limits of state sovereignty and "national interest"	Under state control (Department of Employment), strictly restricted to needs of the economy	Yes

Source: Authors' compilation.

and due process of migration policy, and the government's position on xenophobia. This section briefly describes the progress made in each area.

The refugee area was the one area in which immediate progress occurred. Just one year after the publication of the Green Paper on International Migration (1997), new legislation was passed incorporating the standards of international conventions. The Refugee Act was adopted in 1998 and came into effect in 2000. South Africa had to honor its obligations as a signatory of international conventions. With growing instability in the Horn of Africa and the Great Lakes region, it was facing unprecedented arrivals of asylum seekers. Despite widely acclaimed progress in refugee protection, the 1998 Refugee Act and the discussion to which it gave rise illustrate the confrontation between two discourses: that of international human rights law and that of the sovereign state, supported by the Department of Home Affairs and the cabinet. The Department of Home Affairs tried to implement the most regressive parts of the act and to amend it to make it more restrictive. Each time it did so, human rights groups fought back in the courts; to date, they have succeeded in preventing major amendments, including amendments creating refugee camps and disallowing third-country applications. Yet despite legal progress in favor of refugees, the Department of Home Affairs lacks the capacity to honor its commitment to refugee protection, as indicated by the backlog in asylum seekers' applications. South Africa has the largest backlog of pending asylum applications in the world. In 2009–10 alone, 364,638 new applications for asylum were issued, of which 9,000 were approved and 131,961 were rejected (Department of Home Affairs 2009–10). Massive corruption and abuse of the system plague the section of the Department of Home Affairs responsible for handling these applications. The asylum process is in need of profound reform, which cannot be undertaken independently of immigration reform, given the interdependency between the two. The government is thus left with the paradox that one of the most progressive asylum regimes in Africa is so poorly implemented that it has become discredited and no longer protects the people it is supposed to protect.

The second major change is that of public awareness and due process. Migration policy—once crafted only with input from the business community—is now subject to public scrutiny, with an important role played by the media, advocacy groups, and a larger group of stakeholders.[11] The interdepartmental commission appointed in 1999 is an example of this change, as is the immigration advisory board appointed following adoption of the new act. The ongoing dialogue platforms between different sectors of government and civil society proved disappointing, however, largely because of poor management. In other areas, such as communication between spheres of government (in particular between the provincial and local levels) on migration management issues, communication is nonexistent. In terms of due process, constitutionalism enabled the NGO sector to protect migrants and refugees from state abuses and to preempt government attempts at changing asylum legislation. However, despite a robust body of jurisprudence cases protecting migrants' rights, particularly in relation to family life and unfair treatment, only the few migrants with access to the justice system and connections with NGOs have benefited. By and large, the protection of migrants, particularly those without documents, is ineffective and left to the discretion of local leaders. In addition, the regular recourse to constitutionalism and the courts by the NGO sector created a situation in which dialogue between the department and civil society organizations is almost constantly the result of litigation and media pressure. Although this has increased transparency, it has also revealed the failures of constructive engagement by government and civil society on policy reform and monitoring.

The policy changes induced by the xenophobic violence of 2008 have not been fully assessed. The humanitarian toll paid is a sign of the failure of the anti-xenophobia campaigns rolled out since 1998, as well as, to some extent, the strategies adopted by advocacy groups in their relations with government. For some this failure is also emblematic of the ruling party's schizophrenia, which leads it to condemn xenophobia in public and international forums while tolerating it in its own ranks, denying its scope and seriousness, and failing to take significant action. The difference between results and expressed sentiments is striking. On the one hand, South Africa is characterized by extremely high levels of anti-immigrant sentiment, regularly documented by opinion polls; it is highly territorialized, with a consistent potential for violence.[12] On the other hand, xenophobia is strongly condemned publicly and in policy documents of the ruling party and combated through several government sensitization campaigns; it has not been used as a populist card in elections (at least not officially in national elections). The ANC or opposition parties may issue grossly inaccurate statements on migration and migrants, but it does not openly condone xenophobic statements, and there has been much more controlled communication on migration-related issues at the national level since the mid-2000s. Yet neither the breakthroughs in legislation nor constitution-based jurisprudence nor anti-xenophobia campaigns have fundamentally transformed the deeply rooted structural characteristics of immigration management in postapartheid South Africa. The reformist circles found their expectations crushed by the challenge posed by institutionalized and reactionary interests, to which this chapter now turns.

Overcoming Institutionalized and Reactionary Interests (1994–2008)

More structural challenges prevented the formulation and implementation of the new policy that different constituencies called for. As in other sectors, immigration policy was affected by general constraints related to bureaucrats' resistance to change in vision, direction, and methods imposed by the new political leadership. The tension within the government of national unity between the ANC president and the Inkatha Minister of Home Affairs further complicated an already deteriorating atmosphere within the Department of Home Affairs. In addition, two elements exacerbated the narrowing of opportunities for transformation more than in other areas of public policy. One is the difficulty with which the ANC came to define a long-term position and plan of action on the issue, both internally and officially. The other is the autonomy of bureaucratic practices and their impact on policy making.

Thanks to the ANC's tradition of secrecy and extremely tight internal discipline, little is known about policy-making processes within the party. The great majority of policy changes have been directed from within the party, not from the new consultative and legislative institutional framework. This does not mean that the ANC is a monolithic entity. Different streams of thought, internal institutional mechanisms, and external spheres of influence coexist in the production of ANC policy positions. In the case of immigration, this process proved particularly cumbersome. In the words of one researcher involved in the reform of the Immigration Act:

> To argue that the new government has been actively hostile to immigration would be an overstatement. Benign indifference would be a better description. There is little evidence that the ruling African National Congress (ANC) saw any role for immigration in its social and economic transformation plans. Even the growing acceptance of neoliberal economic doctrine and the scurry for foreign capital did not produce any shift in thinking about the potential value of immigration. Only in 2001, in response to perceptions of a massive brain drain and the entreaties of the private sector, has the ANC suddenly declared a new policy direction, an aggressive international hunt for skilled immigrants (Crush 2001, 33).

In fact, since its accession to power in 1994, the ANC seems to have grappled with the multiple dimensions of the issue. Both the Reconstruction and Development Programme and the Growth, Employment and Redistribution Programme were silent on migration in general, but they gave indications that a new framework should rectify policies that perpetuate apartheid's economic and racial imbalances. The 1996 presidential commission to investigate labor market policy heightened these expectations, as it gave clear indications of directions to be followed to reform the South African immigration system (Department of Labour 1996). However, the emergence of immigration as a structured policy issue within the ANC occurred only in late 1997. Before that, there is no evidence of an internal study group devoted to the issue within the party's National Executive Committee or its subsections. Observers refer to the emergence of a more formal discussion of immigration after 1997, with the creation of the Policy Coordination and Advisory Services and a study group on the topic within the ANC parliamentary group. After 1994 only a few public statements were made by ANC officials on the occasion of official events: the passage of the 1995 Amendment to the Aliens Control Act of 1991; the ANC national policy conferences of 1995, 1997, 2002, and 2007; the ANC National General Council of 2010; and passage of the 1998 Refugees Act and the 2002 Immigration Act. Xenophobic violence also triggered immediate reactions, not just in 2008 and subsequently but as early as 2001, after the lynching of African immigrants on a Pretoria train, when then President Thabo Mbeki released a strong and lyrical condemnation in the name of pan-Africanism in *ANC Today*.

Analysis of official comments and policy documents reveals a timid although increasingly consistent political line over time. It also bears witness to dissenting voices within the party. Between 1997 and 2004, the position of the ANC consisted of distancing itself as much as possible from that of the minister of home affairs. When it came to power in 1994, the ANC was divided on immigration. Some of its members appealed to the rank and file by using xenophobic terminology; they favored the reinforcement of control and the adoption of more stringent measures to access South African territory and the curtailment of both permanent and temporary permits. In 1995, during the parliamentary discussion of the Amendment Act, two trends emerged. Robert Davies—an ANC economist in exile in Mozambique who had chaired the Parliamentary Portfolio Committee on Foreign Affairs at the time of the legislative reform and later served as deputy minister of trade and industry—criticized the policy of the Department of Home Affairs. He highlighted the prominent role played by immigration on the foreign affairs agenda by reminding Parliament of the official ANC position on immigration, as expressed during the 1995 ANC National Conference. That policy recognized:

- The historical role played by South Africa in creating the causes of immigration and the need for a discussion of South Africa's new regional role.
- The need to distinguish between categories of irregular migrants by acknowledging the responsibility of the previous regime's discriminatory policy in creating their situation.
- The necessity to take into account the repercussions of any decision taken by South Africa on its neighbors.

Davies openly criticized the debate on migration on two grounds: the excessively unilateral vision of South Africa and the neglect of long-term solutions in favor of actions based on control (Davies 1995). Penuell Maduna, the then ANC deputy minister of home affairs, condemned xenophobia and defended the following points:

- Legal immigration as a source of income for South Africa.
- Concern for the national interest at the economic, social, and security levels.

- Respect for undocumented migrants' constitutional rights.
- The need to align the Aliens Control Act on constitutional demands before a more comprehensive reform (Maduna 1995).

In 1997, at the next ANC Congress, regional and historical dimensions were abandoned in favor of discussions of asylum policy and undocumented migration. The role of legal immigration in postapartheid socioeconomic transformation was not discussed. The final document cited the pressure placed on certain sectors of the South African economy by illegal immigration. According to the document, it was the competition for scarce resources that caused xenophobia. Although long-term strategies were alluded to, the fight against illegal immigration was identified as a priority, with resolutions passed on tightening border security, improving cooperation between the Departments of Home Affairs and Security, and fighting corruption within the Department of Home Affairs (ANC 1997).

Despite the dearth of data on the socioeconomic impact of undocumented migration on the South African economy, the ANC considered that the effect was by and large negative. The interdepartmental cooperation proposed reflected the predominantly security-oriented approach that had carried over from the previous regime. In 1998, a press conference given by Lindiwe Sisulu, the next ANC deputy minister for home affairs, confirmed this trend. The adoption of a clearer position on asylum with the passage of the Refugees Act was used to justify harsher policy on undocumented migration and a refocus on security dimensions. Sisulu (1998) thus explained:

> The refugee policy is premised upon two sets of interrelated threshold considerations. On the one hand, the policy is constructed so as to reflect but also to enable the fulfillment of the international and constitutional obligations, and on the other hand, it touches upon a number of other directly and indirectly state and national interests and priorities. . . . It does not consider refugee protection to be the door for those persons who wish to enter South Africa by the expectation for opportunities for a better life or brighter future. . . . The most important priorities of these concern the migration control objectives, law and order, concerns over gun-running, drug trafficking and racketeering, money laundering and international crime syndicates, and cartels, various other aspects of national and state security, social and economic interests, as well as bilateral, regional and international relations.

The ANC Congress of 2002 devoted even less attention to the topic of immigration than the previous congress had. Only two resolutions were adopted in an attempt to reconcile the two tendencies:

1. The ANC and government revisit and deal with necessary amendments of the Immigration Act, which must include measures to deal firmly with illegal immigration.

2. We remain committed to accelerate the economic growth of countries in Africa, within the framework of NEPAD [New Partnership for Africa's Development] as the economic prosperity of these countries will contribute to the reduction of the number of so-called economic refugees (ANC 2002).

These quotations reflect the difficulty for the party in power to find a consistent position that reflected both the country's national democratic struggle and the black consciousness movement and pan-Africanism. The period 2001–08 was emblematic of this difficulty to makes its public discourse consistent while part of its constituency—including both rank and file members and elites—shared xenophobic ideas. President Mbeki's strong reaction to the 2001 lynching was soon forgotten and his pan-African stance often misunderstood. He was much criticized by the international media as well as the South African humanitarian sector for his belated reaction in 2008, by which time his unpopularity was such that he was often associated with an overly lenient approach to migration and border control. Mbeki did not manage to channel his own personal feelings about migration into the ANC policy mechanisms; subsequent party policy conferences reflected a very cautious and narrow approach.

The 2007 Polokwane Conference briefly mentioned migration and xenophobia. Resolutions 48 and 49 of the Peace and Stability chapter note that "immigration control and the management of refugee affairs pose a challenge to the state" and that "the Immigration Act be revised to make it more comprehensive to ensure that while it promotes development, national and regional security concerns are addressed" (ANC 2007). Migration and xenophobia were flagged as areas requiring "policy review, strengthening and reinvigorating" in the International Relations chapter, with an emphasis on "taking on board the new decisions on the free movement of people and regional economic communities" and the "need to work closely with SADC [Southern African Development Community] countries to harmonize immigration policies with particular reference to combating of crime associated with illegal immigrations." Xenophobia triggered practical recommendations (one year before the riots), consisting of "work(ing) on improving the relationship between South African communities and foreign nationals; conduct(ing) awareness campaigns amongst our communities to prevent incidents resulting from xenophobia; acknowledg(ing) the valuable skills many immigrants bring to the country, while preventing exploitation; and ensur(ing) that our policy formulation is guided by the resolutions of the World Conference against Racism, Xenophobia and other Intolerances" (Resolutions 39–42). However, at the September 2010 National General Council of the ANC, recommendations remained extremely vague, albeit acknowledging the importance of the 2008 events.[13] From a policy perspective, these resolutions point to a firming up of the more regionalist, interventionist approach, with a clear connection between migration and development. The position on xenophobia was directed to community awareness and governance. Although this may be a sign of changes in the ruling party's internal line, the newer dimensions (recognition of the migration challenge, link with development and labor issues, fight against xenophobia needed at the local level, role of local government) have largely gone unheeded to date.

Within the Department of Home Affairs, changes in policy vision percolated slowly. In May 2005, a strategic plan for 2005–10 was presented to the cabinet. The plan began by stating that "immigration is a critical element in maintaining the integrity of the Republic of South Africa as a sovereign state" (Department of Home Affairs 2005). The plan formally linked immigration policy to two dimensions: South Africa's shortage of skills and its regional policy within the frameworks of SADC, NEPAD, and the African Union. Thus, although the core understanding of what immigration management is about had probably not reached the new National Immigration Branch of the Department of Home Affairs (inaugurated in 2005), it is evident that mindsets at the policy-making level were already more sensitive to the developmental dimension of migration, both domestically and regionally. The two dimensions put to the fore in the 2005 strategic plan were taken up and illustrated in the minister's 2006 budget speech, in which she insisted on the fact that the amendments to the Immigration Act sought to meet South Africa's foreign policy objectives in the region. Two examples were changes in favor of traders (in particular women) and the relaxation of the requirement that African students pay repatriation deposits. The Department of Home Affairs' annual reports for 2007–10 reiterated the three pillars of South African migration policy: the link to regional development policies, the commitment to a human rights–based approach, and the sovereignty of South Africa in the fight against illegal migration and the promotion of border security.

The Resilience of Policing and Administrative Practices in the Post–1994 Era

However, rather than moving toward firmer integration of migration into domestic and regional development policies, the approach to immigration that shaped policy after 1994 drifted toward a mix of laissez-faire and mismanagement, related to both chronically weak administrative capacity and coercive and abusive practices inherited as a result of the low human rights standards of police and immigration personnel. This section shows how the tightening of entry and control as well as access to South African citizenship, and the failure to transform the Department of Home Affairs, have hampered the transformation of immigration policy beyond legislative changes. (As the issue of undocumented migration is dealt with in chapter 4, this section focuses on the other dimensions.)

Tightening Entry and Control

The constitutional problems raised by the 1991 Act triggered legislative reform in the form of the Aliens Control Amendment Act, voted on shortly after the ANC took office in 1995. Section 55 of the 1991 Act, problematic for the lack of appeal procedures it offered, was excised in the 1995 text and the protection of certain fundamental constitutional rights introduced (section 54(6) on dignity, freedom, the security of persons, and the right to private property). Yet by and large, the 1995 amendment was meant to confirm the political hardening of immigration initiated in 1991. A protectionist approach to employment and subsidized education, selection according to qualifications, and the strengthening of measures against undocumented migrants (and the internal monitoring of foreigners) became the overall objectives of the Department of Home Affairs headed by Mangosuthu Buthelezi, the leader of the Inkatha Freedom Party.

Among other changes, the time spent in detention without trial by people suspected of being "prohibited" (that is, undocumented migrants) was increased to 48 hours, renewable up to 30 days and then 90 days without judgment. Workers in the mining and agricultural sectors remained exempt from these changes, as their periods of contract were not even considered temporary work, which prevented them from applying for permanent residence. This situation was denounced by unions and human rights organizations until the Department of Home Affairs agreed to take contract periods into consideration in applications for permanent resident status beginning in 1996.

Three amnesties for undocumented migrants were implemented between 1996 and 2002 (for a global assessment of these amnesties, see Handmaker, Johnston, and Schneider 2001). Addressing the situation of citizens from neighboring countries (migrant workers and ex-Mozambican refugees), these measures were designed as evidence of South African good will within the wider framework of the country's incorporation into SADC. Implementation of these measures was not always satisfactory, however, and the measures did not provide for legal access to the South African labor market for low-skilled workers, the issue at the heart of regional migration flows.

A fourth regularization or documentation process, restricted to Zimbabwean nationals, took place in 2010. Large numbers of documented and undocumented Zimbabwean migrants took refuge in South Africa in the first decade of the 21st century. Depending on their socioeconomic and personal situations, Zimbabwean migrants then either remained undocumented or applied for asylum. Some of these people were, and are, in South Africa legally. After more than four years of lengthy and unproductive consultations with the Immigration Advisory Board over the granting of different statuses to Zimbabweans, no decision was reached, leaving them in an uncertain situation. In some localities, such as the border town of Musina, large influxes of Zimbabwean migrants resulted in humanitarian situations that rapidly overwhelmed South African authorities (Polzer, Kiwanuka, and Takabvirwa 2010). Between 2005 and 2009, Zimbabweans were subject to massive deportations and abuses at the hands of smugglers and the police. They also faced great difficulties accessing asylum. Under pressure from NGOs, the government announced a moratorium on the deportation of Zimbabweans in April 2009, in order to set up a "special dispensation"—a subsection of the Immigration Act that could allow the minister of home affairs to grant temporary permits to certain categories of foreigners for a period of two years. In the meantime, Zimbabweans were no longer deported and were given authorization to work, although they were not given work permits.

After more than a year of procrastination, on September 2, 2010, the Department of Home Affairs announced that deportations of Zimbabweans would resume January 1, 2011, a reversion to pre-2009 practice. In the meantime, measures were put in place to allow certain categories of Zimbabweans to regularize their situation through the distribution of passports by Zimbabwean authorities and examination of cases by the South African Department of Home Affairs, a process which raised numerous issues in terms of implementation capacity and the safety of asylum seekers (see CoRMSA 2010). Between September 20 and December 1, 2010, the Department of Home Affairs accepted 99,435 applications and eventually acknowledged reception by January 2011 of 255,000 applications, a total that corresponds to a small fraction of the 1.5–3 million Zimbabweans government officials claim illegally reside in South Africa (Forced Migration Studies Programme 2010).[14] Despite thousands of people queuing outside the Department of Home Affairs in December 2010, the department and its minister, Nkosazana Dlamini-Zuma, were adamant that no extension would be granted; the administrative capacity of the department to process all potential applications was clearly lacking.

Ten years after the previous regularization procedure, the 2010 Zimbabwean Documentation Project is emblematic of the Department of Home Affairs' persistent ad hoc management of crises, poor communication and strategic skills, appalling lack of organization, and bad relationship with the NGO sector. The project also reflects the type of nontransparent bilateralism that governments in the region still favor over more open and inclusive crisis-resolution mechanisms.

Despite being constantly denounced, the systematic deportation policy of the Department of Home Affairs largely intensified: about 2.5 million people were deported between 1988 and 2010, mostly to neighboring countries (see appendix B).[15] The scope of this policy allows a de facto labor market regulatory mode to operate. It is unclear to what extent the police, the government, and the business sector communicate, but periods of "tolerance" and "crackdowns" alternate conveniently with periods of labor needs and labor surplus, as exemplified by the relaxation of restrictions on Zimbabwean migrants when South Africa needed their labor in preparation for the 2010 Soccer World Cup (see chapter 4 on undocumented migrants).

Restricting Access to Citizenship

Under apartheid, immigration and citizenship were closely associated. When the National Party came to power in 1948, it immediately passed the South African Citizenship Act of 1949, which was amended in 1961, 1973, 1978, 1981, 1984, 1991, and 1993. In the postapartheid period, citizenship was not associated with the consultative and legislative processes on international migration. Yet the Green Paper on International Migration did advise replacing the Aliens Control Act of 1991 with a law on immigration, naturalization, and migration, without specifying the content of the naturalization dimension (Task Team on International Migration 1997). In 1993 the Restoration and Extension of South African Citizenship Act partly settled the issue of homeland citizens and exiles. The reform of citizenship was completed by the South African Citizenship Act of 1995, the first postapartheid piece of legislation that unified all South African legislation on citizenship. This law established three types of citizenship: citizenship through birth in South African territory, citizenship through birth by virtue of having at least one South African parent, and citizenship through naturalization after at least five years of permanent residence (two years for people married to South African citizens).

In this new context, permanent residency became the paramount condition to access South African citizenship, which de facto linked citizenship through naturalization to immigration policy and legislation. On average since 1994, 13,000–15,000 people have become South Africans every year. Although these numbers increased to 19,888 in 2006, 24,671 in 2007, 32,627 in 2009, and 37,522 in 2010 (Department of Home Affairs 1994–2010), they remained very low, despite three amnesties and the granting of permanent residence permits to about 200,000 people in the late 1990s.[16] The current policy on legal immigration and naturalization has therefore had minimal impact on the transformation of South African demographics: only about 20,000–25,000 people become South African citizens or permanent residents combined every year for a population of 50.4 million compared with 200,000 people a year with comparable status in France with a population of 65 million. These low figures reflect the fact that for most migrants in the region, permanent immigration is not a goal, especially if it means renouncing the mobility that allows many to survive. Given the precariousness of many migrants in South Africa and the very limited possibilities of their remaining legally for extended periods of time, they are unable to meet the conditions required to apply for permanent residence, making citizenship unattainable.

Home Affairs: "A Department Coming Apart at the Seams"

The incapacity of the Department of Home Affairs has earned it the nickname of the Department of Horror Affairs from the *Daily Sun*.[17] In 2003 a former director-general, Barry Gilder, called the department's service delivery "a joke" (BBC 2003).

In 2004, with the appointment of an ANC minister following Mangosuthu Buthelezi's departure from government, an administrative reform strategy known as the Turnaround Strategy was adopted. Focused on the development of information and communication technology support, the reform had mixed results. It improved civic affairs services (the issuance of identity documents, the fingerprint database, and information to the public), an achievement that earned it international recognition in the form of the public service delivery to citizens award at the biannual Technology in Government in Africa Award ceremony held in Addis Ababa on April 30, 2009 (Department of Home Affairs 2009). On the immigration services side, however, the results have been disappointing.[18]

The Department of Home Affairs is poorly endowed compared with other government departments.[19] It is also reportedly seriously mismanaged. In 1996, writing on the Immigrants Selection Board, the Labor Market Commission indicated that "development is severely hampered by a lack of accurate and comprehensive data. . . . Labor shortages are thus determined in a rather ad hoc manner. It is vitally important for the development of a coherent labor migration policy [so] that current methods of data collection be reviewed, expanded and updated" (Edmunds 1996). In 2001 a report from the auditor-general pointed to a number of instances of gross mismanagement, including the costly repatriation system. In April 2001, the auditor-general's report was followed by a report from the Public Service Commission that condemned the management of the department (South African Press Agency 2001).

Home Affairs officials have regularly been arrested and condemned for corruption and fraud. In 1998 the large number of corruption and fraud cases reported in the press pushed the department to set up an anticorruption unit, with the help of the National Intelligence Agency. In its first year of activity, the unit investigated 225 cases of fraud; 69 people were convicted (104 were convicted in 2000). However, the impact of the underfunded anticorruption unit remains limited to date. Numerous research reports on the asylum process, as well as on the 2010 Zimbabwean Documentation Project, reveal continued widespread corruption (Amit and others 2009).

Since 2004 and the change in ministers, the management style of the department has evolved toward more control and transparency. A 2006 speech by Minister Nosiviwe Mapisa-Nqakula highlighted the need for profound transformation and a rupture with past practices, including financial management practices.

The department's administrative reform, the Turnaround Strategy, was officially launched in 2007. At that time, it was presented as "a comprehensive long-term programme for the rebuilding of a new and different Home Affairs" (Mapisa-Nqakula 2008a) in order to "[put] in place fundamental changes in the culture and organization of Home Affairs and the way we do our business" (Mapisa-Nqakula 2008b). The then newly appointed director-general, Mavuso Msimang, immediately highlighted both the leadership fragmentation and the central cultural dimension he saw as the key challenges to that reform process:

> Some people in the current leadership in the department have no appreciation of the extent of the rot. They believe others are being too hard on them. ... A total culture change is a sine qua non for the overhaul of the prevailing situation that has deteriorated to a point where not fixing it would certainly be a catastrophe (Robinson in *Mail & Guardian* 2007).

Another observer notes, "This lack of transformation is not about race and colour—it's about administrative practice and a prevailing institutional culture of indolence, lethargy and arrogance" (Robinson in *Mail & Guardian* 2007). Sven de Kock, the chief executive officer of Fever Tree Consulting, AT Kearney's local branch, the company that was commissioned by Home Affairs to undertake the preliminary research and design the strategic plan of the turnaround, confirmed that a culture change in Home Affairs had to be the driver of the strategy, with the implementation of new technology and infrastructure the enabler of change (*Mail & Guardian* 2007). Fully supported by the cabinet and the treasury, an important dimension given the substantial budget implications of the strategy, the Department of Home Affairs was allocated R1 billion over the period 2008–10 for implementing the strategy (Robinson in *Mail & Guardian* 2007).

Building on the core precepts of neoliberal public administration reform, the Turnaround Strategy thus represents a balanced design, placing organizational cultural changes at the heart of its approach, in a broader plan that focuses primarily on increased professionalism. Very little of this strategy was conveyed to lower management or staff on the ground. Even the most thoughtful dimensions, introducing elements of immediate change in service delivery in order to boost staff morale and gain public confidence in the process, were not communicated in way that allowed them to be understood at the office level. The turnaround strategy was not accompanied by an internal communication strategy able to keep staff updated on its development. As a result, ownership of the reform was weak, particularly among immigration staff (Wa Kabwe-Segatti, Hoag, and Vigneswaran 2009). The fiasco of the Zimbabwean Documentation Project is only one illustration of embedded administrative challenges coupled with political unpreparedness.

Conclusion: The Aftermath of the 2008 Events

To many migrants' rights activists in South Africa, there should have been a pre– and a post–May 11, 2008: the tragedy should have effected a profound change in migration policy. They hoped the crisis could be turned into an opportunity for renewed engagement.

The xenophobic violence did trigger a plethora of governmental forums at different levels.[20] However, many of the *imbizos* and *legotlas* (consultative meetings) called to discuss the causes of the violence and "learn lessons" from it had few substantive or programmatic impacts. Several migrant leaders were invited to meetings with the mayor of Johannesburg and provincial ministers, a level of access previously unimaginable for them.[21] The crisis also led to strengthened individual contacts and informal consultation between the humanitarian sector (disaster management), the research sector, the police, and the Department of Cooperative Governance and Traditional Affairs (the department responsible for local government).

The fact that the crisis did not result in more substantial institutionalization or mobilization between civil society and government is perhaps revealing of the fact that the xenophobic violence expressed in 2008 did not affect the core elements structuring the migrant system. Claims made on the basis of refugees, migrants, or other "foreign" identities continue to be met with strong resistance and defensiveness by governmental and nongovernmental institutions.

Two major conclusions emerge from this review of postapartheid migration policy in South Africa. First, despite changes in the economy and the adoption of constitutionally sound legislation, regulations governing low-skilled labor have remained largely unchanged and the mobility of skilled professionals has not been addressed. Second, policy developments by the ruling party and the government reflect increasing consistency over time as well as engagement with research and advocacy groups on issues such as human rights and a more regional vision of migration. These groups' appeals have remained largely unheeded in terms of substantial changes in management and implementation practice, however.

This tension, and the resulting policy silos, stems from three main challenges:

- Fundamental (and yet opaque) disagreements between government, business, and unions on access to the South African labor market and the role to be played by the state and the market in the control and management of migration;
- The leadership deficiencies of the Department of Home Affairs, which reduce the policy agenda to strictly administrative and mostly documentation issues disconnected from other issues, such as the role of migration in development and economic growth, local government, foreign policy, and social cohesion;

- The absence of a functional platform of engagement between stakeholders, including migrants' organizations, rights advocacy groups, research, business, unions, and different government departments. Both institutionally and politically, the constitutional claims and nation-building discourses about a cosmopolitan or inclusive democracy have serious limitations insofar as giving political space to noncitizens is concerned.

The major obstacles to a modernization of South African immigration policy lie in the transformation of the ANC's vision of (and divisions over) the role migration should play in South Africa's development. The following chapters document the fact that changes at the macro level and in elites' perceptions are not synonymous with profound transformation in the daily treatment of foreigners in South Africa. Stumbling blocks remain within the Department of Home Affairs and the public services in charge of controlling migration, as well as government's overall incapacity to manage migration policy across departments and in relation to civil society, organized labor, and the private sector. These three points need to be addressed in order of priority for any positive change to occur and trickle down to the levels at which migration affects society.

Notes

1. The Immigration Amendment Act that was passed in March 2011 tightened conditions of admission to South Africa and introduced a number of changes to the administration of permit applications.
2. In 1901 the Immigration Restriction Act founded the White Australia policy, which was officially terminated only in 1973. In 1902, the Chinese Exclusion Act (1882) was reinforced and a permanent ban enacted, marking the first time the United States restricted immigration on the basis of race or national origin. In 1910 racial criteria on entry to Canada were made explicit. In 1921 the first quota laws based on national origin were implemented in the United States; in 1924 the Johnson-Reed Act was adopted in order to preserve the racial composition of the U.S. population. In 1974 France officially put an end to all non-European immigration apart from family reunification.
3. For a detailed account of South African immigration policy formation, see Peberdy (2009).
4. For a detailed critical study of the voluntary repatriation program for Mozambican refugees in South Africa, see Wa Kabwe-Segatti (2002). Between 1998 and 2003, South Africa expelled about 1.3 million Mozambicans as irregular migrants (South African Home Affairs Department 1988–2003). For an overview of the regularization of Mozambican refugees in South Africa, see Johnston (2001).
5. The agreements included the Memorandum of Understanding between South Africa and the UNHCR (1991); the Basic Agreement between the UNHCR and the South African Government (September 6, 1993); and the Tripartite Agreement signed by South Africa, Mozambique, and the UNHCR (September 15, 1993).
6. For a detailed account of these situations, see Crush (1998).

7. High subsidies to European immigration ended in 1991, when more than R 8 million ($22 million) was spent directly on European immigration and support to organizations welcoming immigrants. That year, immigration exceeded emigration by more than 10,000 people (Department of Home Affairs 1992).

8. For a chronology of the transformation of immigration policy in relation to other major political South African and international events, see appendix A.

9. For an account of migrants' rights activism in the postapartheid period, see Handmaker (2009).

10. The main organizations were the IDASA–based Southern African Migration Programme (funded by the Department for International Development) and the following Johannesburg-based think tanks: the Centre for Policy Studies, the Centre for Development and Enterprise, the Centre for the Study of Violence and Reconciliation, and (beginning in 2001) the Forced Migration Studies Programme at the University of the Witwatersrand.

11. Media coverage of immigration issues in South Africa remains problematic in terms of methodologies (uncritical use of statistics, stereotyping of categories of migrants, bias in favor of official sources). However, each stage of the policy-making process has been covered extensively, with investigations even enabling human rights NGOs to prevent abusive treatments, such as illegal deportations. The financial press (particularly the *Financial Mail* and *Business Day*) regularly denounces mishandling of company and investors permits by the Department of Home Affairs.

12. SAMP has regularly documented anti-immigrant sentiment in South Africa's population since 1998 (Crush and others 2008). For a discussion of the territorialized dimension of xenophobic sentiment and its violence potential, see Misago, Landau, and Monson (2008).

13. The National General Council report noted that "the violence against foreigners of 2008 reminded us of the need to build a caring and prosperous nation, one that is tolerant of all people. The grievances registered during this period related to growing disparities between South Africans with respect to material possessions, standards and living conditions" and recommended that the ANC "lead dialogues on race, culture and identity to erode all forms of prejudice and promote tolerance including toward fellow Africans and foreign nationals" (ANC 2010: 47).

14. These estimates are unsubstantiated; the Department of Home Affairs has never provided a source or methodology to explain the origin of the estimates it cites.

15. This figure is based on data from the Department of Home Affairs for 1988–2009. Although it is likely that the same people were arrested and repatriated several times, the figure nevertheless remains high by international standards. Even the massive deportations of Mexicans from the United States in the 1930s involved a much smaller number of people (about 500,000).

16. For accounts of the three amnesties, see Crush and Williams (1999) and Handmaker, Johnston, and Schneider (2001).

17. On one occasion, a South African man used a toy gun to leverage the life of a department official against the issuance of his identity document, which had been some six years in the processing (Burger 2008).

18. For a review of the reform as well as an anthropological approach to its impact on migration officials' perceptions, see Wa Kabwe-Segatti, Hoag, and Vigneswaran (2009).

19. The department has been allocated substantial budget increases since 1999, especially since 2003–04: its budget rose from R 433 million ($100 million) in 1996–97 to R 1.3 billion ($209 million) in 1999–2000 and R 2.9 billion ($460 million) in 2005–06. For migration alone, the budget rose from R 106 million ($24.6 million) in 1996–97 to R 127 million ($19.8 million) in 1998, R 171 million ($27.4 million) in 2001–02, R 281 million ($31.2 million) in 2002–03, and R 339 million ($50.6 million) in 2003–04. Since 2005 immigration has received the smallest budget within the department. This limitation on funding translates into poor human resources, characterized by the lack of middle management resources, the lack of competence at the basic staff level, and widespread corruption and patronage.

20. Examples include the Department of Home Affairs' Social Dialogue on Promoting Diversity in South Africa (August 18–19, 2008, South African Reserve Bank, Pretoria) and its follow-up with the Dialogue on Xenophobia organized at the Gordon Institute of Business Sciences (October 10, 2008, Johannesburg); the launch of the Johannesburg Migration Advisory Committee by the city of Johannesburg (October 6, 2009); the hosting of the Development Chamber: Xenophobia Task Team Meeting by the National Economic Development and Labour Council (July 15, 2009, Johannesburg); and the Conference "Toward Defining Service Delivery Implications of Migration in Gauteng Province" convened by the Gauteng Department of Local Government, Johannesburg (January 22, 2009).

21. Some organizations had avenues for engaging with high-level government actors (the Somali Association of South Africa had already given a presentation on Somali migrants and xenophobia to President Thabo Mbeki in 2007) (interview with Ahmed Dawlo, Somali Association of South Africa, May 5, 2009); others did not have such access.

References

Amit, R., T. Araia, T. Monson, D. Vigneswaran, and G. Mukundi Wachira. 2009. *National Survey of the Refugee Reception and Status Determination System in South Africa*. Forced Migration Studies Programme, University of the Witwatersrand, Johannesburg.

ANC (African National Congress). 1997. Fiftieth National Conference. Johannesburg, December.

———. 2002. *Resolutions Adopted by the 51st National Conference of the African National Congress*. Stellenbosch. http://www.anc.org.za/documents.

———. 2007. *Resolutions Adopted by the 52nd National Conference of the African National Congress*. Polokwane. http://www.anc.org.za/documents, Peace and Stability chapter.

———. 2010. *Report of the Third National General Council*. Durban, September 20–24. http://www.anc.org.za/docs/reps/2010/3rdngcx.pdf.

BBC (British Broadcasting Corporation). 2003. "SA Immigration Service 'a Joke.'" November 6. http://news.bbc.co.uk/2/hi/africa/3247767.stm.

Botha, J. C. G. 1986. *House of Assembly Debates*, April 29. Hansard, vol. 8, 4429.

Burger, S. 2008. "Dept. of Home Affairs Criticised at Toy Gun Case." *Mail & Guardian* online. July 9. http://www.mg.co.za/article/2008-07-09-dept-of-home-affairs-criticised-at-toygun-case.

CoRMSA (Consortium for Refugees and Migrants in South Africa). 2010. "Civil Society Responds to Home Affairs Zimbabwe Documentation Project and End of Special Dispensation for Zimbabweans." Press release, September 7.

Crush, J. ed. 1998. *Beyond Control: Immigration and Human Rights in a Democratic South Africa.* Cape Town: Institute for a Democratic South Africa, and Queens, Canada: Southern African Migration Programme.

———. 2001. "Immigration, Xenophobia and Human Rights in South Africa." SAMP Migration Policy Series 22, Southern African Migration Programme, Queen's University, Kingston, Canada, and IDASA (Institute for Democracy in South Africa), Cape Town, South Africa.

Crush, J., D. MacDonald, V. Williams, K. Lefko-Everett, D. Dorey, R. Taylor, and R. la Sablonnière. 2008. *The Perfect Storm: The Reality of Xenophobia in Contemporary South Africa.* SAMP Migration Policy Series 50, Southern African Migration Programme, Queen's University, Kingston, Canada, and IDASA (Institute for Democracy in South Africa), Cape Town, South Africa.

Crush, J., and V. Williams. 1999. *The New South Africans? Immigration Amnesties and Their Aftermaths.* Southern African Migration Programme, Queen's University, Kingston, Canada, and IDASA (Institute for Democracy in South Africa), Cape Town, South Africa.

Davies, R. 1995. "Debate on Vote No.16, 18/05." *Proceedings of Extended Public Committee,* vol. 5, 1476. Cape Town.

Department of Home Affairs (and Internal Affairs). 1988–2003. *Annual Reports.* Pretoria.

———. 2005. *Strategic Plan 2005/06–2009/10.* May. Chief Directorate, Strategic and Executive Support Services, Office of the Director-General, Pretoria.

———. 2009. *Strategic Plan 2010/2011–2012/2013.* Pretoria.

Department of Labour. 1996. *Restructuring the South African Labour Market: Report of the Presidential Commission to Investigate Labour Market Policy.* Cape Town.

Dolan, C., and M. Reitzes. 1996. *The Insider Story? Press Coverage of Illegal Immigrants and Refugees.* Research Report 48, Centre for Policy Studies, Johannesburg.

Edmunds, M. 1996. "Immigration Policy Needs an Overhaul." *Mail & Guardian,* June 28.

First, R. 1983. *Black Gold: The Mozambican Miner, Proletarian and Peasant,* Palgrave MacMillan, Basingstoke, United Kingdom.

Forced Migration Studies Programme. 2010. "Many Individuals Will be Unable to Access the Zimbabwe Documentation Process before the Deadline, Says Wits Research." Press release. December 13. http://www.migration.org.za/press-statement/2010/fmsp-2010-many-individuals-will-be-unable-access-zimbabwe-documentation-process.

Handmaker, J. 2009. *Advocating for Accountability: Civic-State Interactions to Protect Refugees in South Africa.* Intersentia, Antwerp.

Handmaker, J., N. Johnston, and J. Schneider. 2001. *The Status Regularisation Programme for Former Mozambican Refugees in South Africa.* Lawyers for Human Rights/University of the Witwatersrand Refugee Research Programme, Johannesburg.

Johnston, N. 2001. "The Point of No Return: Evaluating the Amnesty for Mozambican Refugees in South Africa." *Migration Policy Brief 6*, Southern African Migration Programme, Queen's University, Kingston, Canada, and IDASA (Institute for Democracy in South Africa), Cape Town, South Africa.

Koch, E. 1994. "The Pass Laws Keep on Prowling." *Mail & Guardian*, July 15.

Landsberg, C. 1995. "Accepting the 'Aliens.'" *West Africa* 1 (07/05): 672.

Maduna, P. 1995. "Proceedings of Extended Public Committee, Aliens Control Amendment Bill, Second Reading Debate, 13/09." *House of Assembly Debates*, Hansard, vol. 6, 4225–39.

Mail & Guardian. 1994. "Take Back Your Tired, Your Poor Huddled Masses. . . ." September 23.

Mapisa-Nqakula, N. 2006. *Address for the 2006 Budget Vote of the Department of Home Affairs (Budget Vote 4)*. May 30. National Assembly, Cape Town.

———. 2008a. *Opening Remarks on the Occasion of the Presentation of the 2006/7 Annual Report of the Department of Home Affairs to the Parliamentary Portfolio Committee.* February 12. Cape Town.

———. 2008b. "Preface." In *Department of Home Affairs, Strategic Plan 2008–2009 and 2010–2011*. Pretoria.

Marais, H. 1998. *South Africa. Limits to Change: The Political Economy of Transformation*, Cape Town: University of Cape Town Press and Zed Books.

Misago, J. P., L. B. Landau, and T. Monson. 2008. *Towards Tolerance, Law and Dignity: Addressing Violence against Foreign Nationals in South Africa*. International Organization on Migration, Pretoria.

Morris, M. 1991. "State, Capital and Growth: The Political Economy of the National Question." In *South Africa's Economic Crisis*, ed. S. Gelb, 33–58. Cape Town: David Philip.

Nxumalo, S. 1994. "The Invisible Fugitives for Whom Joburg Is Paradise." *Mail & Guardian*, July 15.

Peberdy, S. 2009. *Selecting Immigrants: National Identity and South Africa's Immigration Politics, 1910–2008*. Johannesburg: University of the Witwatersrand Press.

Peberdy, S., and J. Crush. 1998. "Rooted in Racism: The Origins of the Aliens Control Act." In *Beyond Control: Immigration and Human Rights in a Democratic South Africa*, ed. J. Crush, 18–36. Southern African Migration Programme, Queen's University, Kingston, Canada, and IDASA (Institute for Democracy in South Africa), Cape Town, South Africa.

Polzer, T., M. Kiwanuka, and K. Takabvirwa. 2010. "Regional Responses to Zimbabwean Migration, 2000–2010." *Open Space: On the Move: Dynamics of Migration in Southern Africa* 3 (3): 30–34.

Polzer, T. and A. Segatti, 2011. "From the Defense of Migrants' Rights to New Political Subjectivities: Gauteng Migrants' Organisations After the May 2008 Crisis." In *Exorcising the Demons Within: Xenophobia, Violence, and Statecraft in Contemporary South Africa*, ed. L. B. Landau. Johannesburg: University of the Witwatersrand Press.

Ramphele, M. 1999. "Immigration and Education: International Students at South African Universities and Technikons." SAMP Migration Policy Series 12, Southern African Migration Programme, Queen's University, Kingston, Canada, and IDASA (Institute for Democracy in South Africa), Cape Town, South Africa.

Republic of South Africa. 1986. "Matters Concerning Admission to and Residence in the Republic Amendment Act No. 53 of 1986." *Government Gazette*, Vol. 252, No. 10277, June 13.

———. 1991. Aliens Control Act No. 96 of 1991, Section 55. *Statutes of the Republic of South Africa, Aliens and Citizens*, June 27.

Robinson, V. 2007. "Can Home Affairs Be Saved?" *Mail & Guardian*, May 28. http://mg.co.za/article/2007-05-28-can-home-affairs-be-saved.

Rossouw, R. 1995. "SA's 'Moral Duty' to Migrants." *Mail & Guardian*, June 23.

Scott, M. I. 2002. "President of the Parliamentary Portfolio Committee on Home Affairs in the Republic of South Africa." Hansard: House of Assembly Debates, 4th session, Cols. 2313–2810, May 14–17, p. 2702.

Sisulu, L. 1998. "Four Years of ANC Governance." ANC press conference, August 19. http://www.home-affairs.gov.za/speech98/0W86098.820.

South African Press Agency. 2001. "UDM Calls on Mbeki to Fire Buthelezi." April 6. Cape Town.

Statistics South Africa. 1973–2010. *Tourism and Migration Reports*. Pretoria.

Task Team on International Migration. 1997. *Draft Green Paper on International Migration*. 13 Government Gazette No. 18033, May 30.

Wa Kabwe-Segatti, A. 2002. "Du rapatriement volontaire au refoulement dissimulé: les réfugiés mozambicains en Afrique du Sud." *Politique africaine* 85: 75–92.

Wa Kabwe-Segatti, A., C. Hoag, and D. Vigneswaran. 2009. "The Turnaround Strategy from Below: Public Sector Reform among South African Home Affairs Migration Officials in Johannesburg." Working Paper 109, Department of Anthropology and African Studies, University of Mainz, Germany.

Chapter 2

The Role of Skilled Labor

Stephen Ellis and Aurelia Segatti

From 1994 until 2002, South Africa generally opposed the immigration and emigration of skilled labor. Despite liberal views espoused by the former minister of home affairs Mangosuthu Buthelezi and leading voices in the private sector, the government focused on stimulating employment among South African citizens. It was particularly concerned with reversing the historical discrimination against black South Africans through employment equity measures broadly falling under the rubric of black economic empowerment.[1] Although there was no legal impediment to South Africans, skilled or unskilled, emigrating in search of work, ministers, and even former president Nelson Mandela, sometimes expressed views that South Africans who emigrated were either unpatriotic or unwilling to accept the postapartheid dispensation. The issue was hardly ever framed in regional terms or as part of a more comprehensive development strategy.

The combination of a poor education system under apartheid and the emigration of significant numbers of skilled workers during and after 1994 has created significant development challenges for South Africa, as discussed below. Some observers believe that the national skills shortage may account for South Africa's failure to reach its target economic growth rate of 6 percent a year. Others blame poor growth on persistent racial bias within the private sector, which prevents black graduates from being incorporated into the labor market. What almost all debates over labor issues neglect is the skilled labor surplus in the region. This factor is often ignored in favor of a focus on the educational system and the private sector's willingness (or unwillingness) to invest in remedial education programs in the sciences and vocational training. Although the importation of skilled labor is ignored at the policy level, the private sector and even some government departments rely on substantial numbers of foreign skilled workers from the region and beyond. These recruitments take place outside of government-to-government agreements on a demand-driven basis. Despite this need, there is widespread political reluctance to recruit highly skilled Africans from outside South Africa. The lack of a regionally institutionalized approach only widens this policy gap. The lack of data on foreign workers in all sectors except mining helps explain the research gap.

This chapter unpacks the complexities of the "skills problem." It begins by exploring its definition by South African policy actors. It then examines labor market imbalances by looking at the departure of highly skilled workers, the availability of skilled professionals from the region and beyond, and the employability of black South African graduates. The chapter then outlines the anti–brain drain positions of the Southern African Development Community (SADC) and examines why there is resistance from certain constituencies, such as trade unions, to building an institutionalized regional labor market. The chapter ends by assessing obstacles to improving the management of skilled labor migration, particularly within the Department of Home Affairs.

The "Skills Problem"

After considerable reluctance to embrace skilled migration as a development driver, the government has slowly begun to change its position. Its shifting views on the international movement of skilled labor have been informed by far more than an appreciation of immediate skills and revenue losses. The redefinition has been accompanied by a broader change in the character of the South African economy and the international labor markets into which it is integrated.

There is fierce international competition for skilled labor, particularly in information technology, engineering, and medicine. South Africa has expertise in these areas, but it produces only small numbers of people with the highest levels of skill. The largest sector in the South African economy in terms of value added is finance, which now far surpasses mining, a traditional employer of foreign labor on a massive scale, almost all of it low skilled or semi-skilled. (Manufacturing is currently South Africa's second-largest sector; retail is the third-largest sector.)

This problem is not new: by 1999 the service sector already employed more skilled workers (as a percentage of total workers) than the old job-creating staples of manufacturing and mining. The most skills-intensive sectors were computers and information technology (where 57 percent of those employed were skilled), business services (47 percent), education and health (41 percent), and banking and finance (29 percent) (Southern African Migration Programme 2000). Market-based services accounted for some 47 percent of employment, direct or indirect. Manufacturing accounted for only 14 percent of total formal employment, having declined by 1.2 percent between 1994 and 2004 (Southern African Migration Programme 2000).

As South Africa has become further integrated into the global economy, companies working in internationally competitive fields have felt the shortage

of skilled labor acutely. Business lobbies have tried to draw government attention to the difficulties in securing permits for foreign workers, even in sectors
where there are undisputed shortfalls in qualified personnel. Major corporations complain of delays of up to a year in obtaining work permits for staff
recruited abroad for highly specialized positions, even when they employ local
law firms or other professional intermediaries to facilitate the procedure. Immigration lawyers claim that insufficient administrative capacity at the Department of Home Affairs has created a backlog of tens of thousands of work and
residence permits. Frustration at acquiring legal documentation is a recurring
theme among business executives, representatives of business organizations,
and recruitment agencies. The British Chamber of Business in South Africa
claims that immigration problems have a "detrimental impact on the short-term
effective running of local and international business in South Africa" (*Financial
Times* 2006). The executive director of the Centre for Development and Enterprise, a pro-business think tank, wrote in a 2007 *Business Day* editorial:

> These false beliefs about our skills shortage combine to ensure that:
>
> - we underestimate the sheer breadth of our skills shortages;
> - overestimate the potential of resources such as skilled retirees and return-
>   ing South African emigrants to fill our skills shortages;
> - vastly underestimate how long it will take to make better use of our own
>   human capital through improved education and training;
> - and ignore what is potentially the quickest and most effective way of alle-
>   viating our skills shortages: aggressively recruiting foreign skills to come
>   and help South Africans to build a great country (Bernstein 2007: 15).

According to the Southern African Migration Programme (2000), before the
election of 1994, only 2 percent of companies rated South Africa's brain drain as
significant, with the rest considering emigration to be having little or no impact
on them. By 1998–99, one-third of enterprises surveyed regarded the problem
as significant. The sectors most affected by the brain drain were reported to be
education and health (59 percent), business services (47 percent), banking and
finance (43 percent), information technology (35 percent), and industrial high
tech (35 percent). A similar survey conducted today would most likely find that
perceptions of the impact of the shortfall of skilled personnel, in part caused by
the loss of skilled labor to emigration, are even more significant.

Government sources claim to have redressed the imbalances flagged by business owners and managers through a series of efforts, including revisions to
immigration legislation that came into effect in July 2005. However, businesses
continue to complain that foreign executives working under intracompany
work permits have been refused extensions to their two-year documentation.

Difficulties in securing work permits for intracompany movements are shared by companies of all origins. The consensus among business and professional staff seems to be that the system for allocating work permits has, if anything, become less flexible than ever. The government has established a quota system for work permit applications in regard to certain skills and professions, but business operators complain that the quotas were drawn up without proper consultation and that they do not correspond to businesses' actual needs. The problem is particularly acute for multinational companies, which rely on the rapid rotation of personnel across offices.

One reason why policy frameworks are weak is that there are disagreements over the calculation of skills shortages per sector. In a 2009 study undertaken for the South African Department of Labor, the Human Sciences Research Council found huge discrepancies between official estimates of skills shortages and the quota lists issued by the Department of Home Affairs, even in sectors identified by the government as in crisis (Erasmus and Breier 2009).[2] Whether the result of political priorities or bureaucratic neglect, these discrepancies indicate that the government ascribes only a limited role to immigration in countering skills shortages within the country. For 2006 the national scarce skills list indicated a shortage of 205,370 workers—almost nine times the quota of 24,100 set by the Department of Home Affairs for 2007 (Erasmus and Breier 2009). Discrepancies at the sectoral level are extremely high, especially in fields that require extensive professional training. In the health sector, for example, the Department of Home Affairs' quota cited the need for only 300 research and development pharmacologists in 2007—a fraction of the 25,895 health professionals (including 14,000 nurses) identified by the national scarce skills list for 2006 (Erasmus and Breier 2009).

The most acute shortages (engineers, artisans, and town planners) are not given priority by the Department of Labor, the Joint Initiative on Priority Skills Acquisition (JIPSA), or the Department of Home Affairs (Erasmus and Breier 2009). The discrepancies between the three institutions and the lack of clarity on the government's strategy led Erasmus and Breier to conclude that "if we do not review our policies of affirmative action, particularly in the engineering sector, then we might end up with a permanent reliance on foreign skills, while our own graduates, many of them African, remain un- or underemployed" (2009: 20). The loss of South African white skilled workers through affirmative action plans combined with the difficulties young black graduates have had entering the labor market makes the hiring of foreigners unavoidable as a short-term fix but undesirable politically.

The "problem" is therefore construed along very different lines depending on the constituencies. Business insists on acute shortages of scarce and critical skills in many sectors and calls for policy changes liberalizing the hiring of highly skilled foreign personnel (at least as a temporary solution). The government accuses business of refusing to see the long-term negative effects of liberalization on local workers and of discriminating against young black graduates. The reality is a combination of factors. As Erasmus and Breier underscore, at least four main factors contribute to South Africa's skills shortages:

- The legacy of apartheid's Bantu education system, which resulted in under-representation of Africans in the scientific professions.
- The decline in apprenticeships and the failure of postapartheid policies in this area.
- The loss of senior capacity as a result of affirmative action.
- Poor working conditions in specific sectors, particularly health.

Political debates often present immigration as an option governments may choose or prevent. The reality is quite different. Semi- to highly skilled professionals from the region, motivated to move by conflict and chronic instability as well as by opportunities in South Africa, Botswana, and Namibia, actively try to define niches for themselves in the local labor markets. The labor market they are helping create is being shaped by a combination of immigration legislation and efforts to subvert or circumvent it. Without a more comprehensive and realistic policy framework that considers regional needs, skills gaps, and emigration along with immigration, South Africa is unlikely to generate the kind of labor market it needs to meet its development objectives. Failure to build a prosperous and sustainable economy will have enormous repercussions not only for South Africa but for the region as a whole.

Where Do Skilled Southern Africans Emigrate?

Too often, observers envisage Southern Africa only from the perspective of regional migration systems in which Botswana, Namibia, and South Africa stand at the receiving end of a chain of labor supply and transit from the rest of the subregion. In fact, a substantial part of regional mobility consists of the emigration of Southern Africans overseas, mostly to the European Union, North America, Australia, and New Zealand. Too often, this emigration is captured under the category of "brain drain," the permanent emigration of highly skilled professionals. This characterization oversimplifies complex and poorly understood forms of mobility that include, among others, the short-term migration of young South African professionals in search of international experience, the permanent relocation of white commercial farmers from Zimbabwe to the United Kingdom as refugees, the protracted stay of Mozambicans in Germany as a legacy of government agreements, and the undocumented migration of low- to semi-skilled Angolans to Portugal. Some migrants from Malawi,

Zambia, Zimbabwe, and (particularly) the Democratic Republic of Congo often pass through South Africa en route to Europe and North America.

Although there is no comprehensive survey of Southern Africans overseas, migration data from Eurostat and destination countries provide some sense of the extent of emigration. According to Eurostat, 453,920 Southern Africans legally resided in the European Union in 2008 (226,050 in the United Kingdom) (see appendix C, table C1). Southern African migrants in Europe were dominated by South Africans (126,065), Zimbabweans (86,075), Congolese (73,905) and Angolans (49,645). Undocumented migrants, as identified by European immigration services, are negligible in number: in 2008, fewer than 19,000 Southern Africans (including 4,905 Zimbabweans, 4,340 South Africans, and 2,770 Angolans) were refused entry, found to be illegally present, or returned to their countries of origin (see appendix C, tables C2–C4). Estimates place the total number of South Africans in other OECD countries at about 280,000–300,000. Australia hosted 104,134 South Africans (2006 census), the United States 68,290 (2000 estimate), Canada 37,680 (2001 estimate), and New Zealand 55,000 (2010 estimate) (OECD n.d.).

About 1.5–2 percent of South Africa's 50.4 million people may reside outside South Africa (authors' estimate based on Eurostat and other official government figures from OECD countries). This diaspora is small, particularly when compared with the largest migrant communities worldwide. Though small by international standards, emigration to OECD countries is of importance to the region's development and labor markets. Despite its significance—and the acknowledgement of its critical importance in the JIPSA policy of promoting the return of skilled emigrants—there has yet to be a systematic survey of emigration from South Africa and its effect on development.

Emigration from South Africa is nothing new: tens of thousands of South Africans officially left during the apartheid era (and many more probably left unofficially), substantial emigration took place immediately before and after the political transition of 1994, and emigration has continued since then. Between 1989 and 1997, 233,000 South Africans emigrated to just five countries: Australia, Canada, New Zealand, the United Kingdom, and the United States (Southern African Migration Programme 2000). The emigrants of these years included a disproportionate number of white South Africans. They also included a disproportionate number of highly skilled people: the proportion of Ph.D. holders among South Africans living abroad may be twice that of those remaining in South Africa (Southern African Migration Programme 2000). Some experts estimate that 23,000 university graduates and 50,000 executives leave Africa every year; according to the World Bank, some 40,000 African Ph.D. holders lived outside the continent (Southern African Migration Programme 2000)]. The International Organization for Migration estimates that 20,000 professionals have left Africa every year since 1990 (Southern African Migration Programme 2000).

Much of the emigration in the period 1990–2000 was of whites; this pattern is changing rapidly. In 2000 more than two-thirds of the sample of highly skilled people surveyed (including 68 percent of black people) by the Southern African Migration Programme reported having given some thought to emigration, and 25 percent of people surveyed thought it likely or very likely that they would leave in the next two years. Only 2 percent of the sample of skilled workers were categorized as having very high emigration potential, with another 10 percent having a high emigration potential.

The reasons why highly skilled people think about emigrating are complex and include concerns about the cost of living, high taxes, crime, and the low standard of public and commercial services in South Africa. Among the skilled workers polled for the 2000 study, 74 percent reported being dissatisfied with the level of taxation, 71 percent were dissatisfied with the cost of living, and 68 percent were concerned about their safety or that of their families (Southern African Migration Programme 2000). The preferred destinations for emigration were the United States (24 percent), Australia (22 percent), the United Kingdom (15 percent), New Zealand (12 percent), and Canada (11 percent).

Interest in emigration appears even stronger among younger skilled workers. In a 2005 study by the Southern African Migration Programme, 4 out of 10 final-year students interviewed indicated giving emigration a "great deal of consideration" (Mattes and Mniki 2005).

It is in connection with these factors that government officials and leaders of the ruling party acknowledge that South Africa should prioritize skills acquisition as part of the national development strategy, including by considering repealing or limiting affirmative action where it widens the skills gap and acquiring skilled labor from abroad. Numerous stumbling blocks stand in the way of transforming these weaknesses in skills policy into effective policy implementation, particularly given the unpopularity of resorting to foreign skilled labor.

Current Government Policy on Skilled Labor Migration

ANC governments have never seriously considered resuming an aggressive immigration recruitment policy or even a consistent reverse brain drain policy. The Immigration Act of 2002 and the establishment of quota lists were supposed to address, albeit passively, the skills issue by improving the administrative management of the recruitment of foreigners. Official figures for documented immigrants with high-level skills, however, have remained very low. In 2003, for example, the government recorded just 1,011 new immigrants it described as economically active, less than half of which were in professional, semi-professional, or technical occupations (Statistics South Africa 2003).

There was a net loss of 9,529 economically active people in 2003, including 703 accountants, 693 medical personnel, 547 industrial and production engineers, and 542 natural scientists. Among economically active immigrants from Africa officially recorded in 2003 were 1,698 Nigerians and 959 Zimbabweans. Skilled Zimbabwean immigrants represented a large share of total immigrants, especially in the managerial, executive, and administrative category.

A study of 200 large firms conducted by the Southern African Migration Programme in 2000 throws light on the nature of skilled workers in South Africa. At the time of the survey, these companies employed a remarkably small number of non–South Africans (2,000–3,000 out of the 101,000 employees in the companies polled). The report, based on research carried out in the preceding two years, revealed that 50 percent of the companies surveyed employed a skilled workforce consisting only of South African nationals or permanent residents; 46.5 percent employed some foreign workers, most of them from Europe, in positions demanding high skills. The number of skilled workers recruited from other African countries was very small, with the main providers Ghana and Zimbabwe. If similar research were done today, it would quite probably reveal a higher number of skilled workers coming from outside South Africa, and a higher proportion from Zimbabwe and other African countries than from Europe.

There are almost certainly more skilled workers from the rest of Africa residing in South Africa than suggested by survey figures from 10 years ago. The government hoped that the creation of six new modes of entry for migrant workers would help legalize the situation of many migrants from the region (Department of Labour 2007).[3] Largely because of continuing legal restrictions, many skilled Africans who enter South Africa do not work in their professional fields, instead taking up positions that do not fully capitalize on their training and skills. Anecdotal evidence as well as research in progress suggest that substantial numbers of qualified Zimbabweans, for example, often work as waiters, newspaper sellers, and parking attendants. Many may not be registered with any government department or agency (Polzer, Kiwanuka, and Takabvirwa 2010).

Buthelezi's departure as minister of home affairs appears to have had the effect of allowing other parts of the government, notably Thabo Mbeki's powerful presidency, greater breadth of conception and maneuverability with respect to migration policy. The government has now become convinced of the significance of South Africa's serious shortage of skilled labor and is integrating it into a new phase of its economic strategy.

The leading edge of the government's enhanced economic strategy is the Accelerated and Shared Growth Initiative for South Africa (ASGISA), unveiled in 2006. The initiative is not a new policy but rather an attempt to better coordinate existing policies. ASGISA is officially described as "a limited set of interventions that are intended to serve as catalysts to accelerated and shared growth" (Mlambo-Ngcuka 2006). Its aim is to halve unemployment and poverty by 2014. To do so, the government estimates that the country must achieve economic growth of 6 percent a year from 2010 to 2014.

The shortage of skilled labor is a major impediment to the ASGISA vision of growth and distribution. Within the framework of its economic strategy, as amended by ASGISA, the government launched the JIPSA initiative, which aims to develop skilled workers. When it was initiated in 2006, JIPSA was headed by then deputy president Phumzile Mlambo-Ngcuka; it had the strong support of the national treasury and the presidency.

ASGISA and JIPSA seem to have vanished from government priorities. As a result, skilled migration has become the object of tensions between the Department of Home Affairs and the Department of Labor, which has increasingly insisted on playing a more prominent role in defining and implementing immigration policy, particularly through the Immigration Advisory Board (Department of Labour 2007). The Immigration Advisory Board, initiated in the early 2000s and set up in 2006, meets erratically and does not seem to play more than a symbolic role.

Other pressures make it difficult for the government to implement a skills acquisition policy single-mindedly. For example, many stakeholders seek to give priority to the employment of South Africans, especially black South Africans. The government asks foreign companies to advertise in the local press for positions that would otherwise be filled by expatriates.

A further complication arises from South Africa's African Renaissance foreign policy, under which South Africa aspires to lead the continent in a comprehensive regeneration. South Africa is faced with the challenges of simultaneously advancing its own national interests while also promoting the development of the continent (or more narrowly, the Southern African region). In some respects, South Africa's policy of recruiting skilled labor from abroad sits uneasily with a foreign policy that places high importance on stabilizing countries throughout Southern and Central Africa and encouraging their economic development. In attracting skilled labor from neighboring countries (box 2.1), South Africa may be making it less likely that those countries will be able to achieve the level of development to which they aspire.

Conclusion: Is "South Africa First" a Good Policy for Southern Africa?

The South African government recognizes that some of the most dynamic sectors of the economy are embedded in international labor markets in which skilled workers are encouraged to regard the entire globe as one vast

BOX 2.1

Successful Immigrants in South Africa

Notwithstanding formal obstacles to success, there are many examples of immigrants from Africa who have achieved success in South Africa. Among Zimbabweans, Trevor Ncube owns the *Mail & Guardian* newspaper, Strive Masiyiwa is chairman and chief executive officer of Econet Wireless, and Peter Moyo was executive director of both Alexander Forbes, a financial services company, and Old Mutual Life Assurance Company. Several prominent bankers are Zimbabwean, and many previously white-run corporations now have Zimbabwean executives in leading positions. The late Congolese entrepreneur of Rwandan origin, Miko Rwayitare, left Kinshasa in 1996. When he died, in 2007, his Johannesburg-based company, Telecel, operated in 14 African countries representing 40 percent of the Sub-Saharan African cellular market excluding South Africa. He also owned the first black-owned wine estate in South Africa. Kalaa Mpinga, the son of a former prime minister of Zaire (now the Democratic Republic of Congo), has worked as a senior executive for the Anglo-American company.

The recruitment of black senior managers from outside South Africa has several advantages for established South African businesses. It gives them access to knowledge and networks of influence in other parts of Africa, where they may be seeking to purchase assets or do business. At the same time, it enables them to demonstrate a commitment to black economic empowerment, which has become a political necessity, and even a legal obligation, in South Africa.

Foreign employment is not limited to the private sector; newcomers from other African countries are occasionally employed in public services. One example is Claude Mondzanga, a Congolese national who has served as the deputy director of the Baragwanath Hospital in Soweto since 1997. However, public services generally remain reluctant to recruit foreigners, preferring to hire South Africans.

Source: www.info.gov.za; www.whoswhosa.co.za; http://investing.businessweek.com/businessweek/.

marketplace for their talents. It understands that some governments aggressively encourage recruitment from abroad. At the same time, it counts organized labor as a key part of its constituency. Indeed, the ANC is formally part of a triple alliance consisting of itself, the South African Communist Party, and the Congress of South African Trade Unions. The ruling party is subject to significant political pressures based on both ideology and the demand to create or preserve jobs for South Africans.

In keeping with the neoliberal macroeconomic strategy it adopted in 1997, the government has thrown open the country's borders in many areas of trade. It is the leading architect and champion of the New Partnership for Africa's Development (NEPAD) and a leading force behind the abolition of the Organization of African Unity and its replacement by the far more dynamic African

Union. NEPAD in particular is a projection of many of the neoliberal economic views of the South African government. South Africa's policy toward its neighbors in Southern Africa has borne many of the hallmarks of a common market, with the progressive elimination of trade barriers between member states with a view to stimulating trade and wealth creation. The SADC trade protocol that came into effect in 2000 eliminated tariffs on some 80 percent of South African imports from the region. In 2008 all member countries except Angola and the Democratic Republic of Congo formed a free trade area.

The restrictions introduced by the 2011 Immigration Amendment Act, adopted amidst numerous protests from the business and human rights sectors, point in the direction of a more protectionist approach to the labor market. It remains unclear, however, how the new bill is supposed to address skills issues.

If the vision of a SADC common market is to be realized, South Africa will have to develop a regional economic and investment strategy. Under such a strategy, South African manufacturing firms would relocate their activities to countries in the region that offered cheaper labor, allowing South Africa to concentrate on high-knowledge industries. In the past, many officials in the Department of Trade and Industry advocated for such a regional industrial strategy, similar to policies followed by an earlier generation of industrializing countries in southeast Asia, such as Malaysia.[4] They broadly support the alignment of industrial strategy with a policy on migration that would facilitate the movement into South Africa of highly skilled personnel and create low-wage manufacturing jobs in neighboring countries. Such a strategy would also reduce the number of illegal immigrants into South Africa, by eliminating one of the main "pull" factors motivating them to travel south.

Government policy on these issues is increasingly influenced by the trade unions, which have strong influence over trade and industrial policy. The unions are, however, deeply divided, with a leadership that is open to regional perspectives on industrial and labor policies and an often strongly xenophobic rank and file. There are, consequently, tensions between South Africa's ambition to create a Southern African free-trade zone and perhaps even a common market and its desire to prioritize South Africans in job creation. Such tensions are visible in regard to migration. Thus, South Africa lowered tariff barriers within SADC but delayed agreement on the SADC protocol on the facilitation of movement of people for some 10 years.

Government migration policy is characterized by a number of contradictions. The government has expressed its concern at the scale of the African "brain drain." In the context of the UN High-Level Dialogue on Migration and Development, South Africa's former minister of home affairs Nosiviwe Mapisa-Nqakula spoke in favor of encouraging the African diaspora to participate in Africa's development. In conformity with such a view, stimulating skilled South Africans to return home is part of the JIPSA initiative. A delicate matter, however, is that a large proportion of these expatriate South Africans are white, and those who left in the 1990–94 period have often been regarded by South African government officials as people the country is well rid of. A policy of encouraging skilled people from the diaspora to return home might run into political problems in South Africa, as it would challenge some basic elements of the government's black empowerment policy.

The current administration seems divided on the approach to take. Its policies lack continuity with those of previous ANC governments, an aspect revealing the ANC's difficulty in defining a long-term strategy on the skills issue. Under Mbeki there was a sense that South Africa's serious shortage of skilled labor could be rectified in the short to medium term only by attracting skills from abroad and that a globalized economy implies a global market in labor for those with marketable skills. The Zuma administration does not appear to share these views. In addition, the management of migration within the Department of Home Affairs has not seen major progress or professionalization to date; the amended Immigration Act will only increase the bureaucratic burden, without effecting new administrative reform or providing a larger budget. If taken as indications of policy intent, such pendulum effects and administrative inertia indicate that, despite official rhetoric, government circles hold broadly negative views regarding the role of migration in skills development in South Africa.

Notes

1. Used in this context, the term *black* includes the categories referred to under apartheid as Coloured, Indian, and African.
2. Erasmus and Breier assessed the evaluations conducted by the Sector Education and Training Authority for the National Skills Authority as part of the national skills development strategy spearheaded by the Department of Labour. Based on these evaluations, they compiled a national scarce skills list, which served as the basis for the quotas published by the Department of Home Affairs.
3. Access to the South African labor market can be obtained through six types of permits: quota permits, general work permits, exceptional skills permits, intracompany transfer permits, business permits, and cross-border permits (such as the Lesotho six-month concession permits precluding waged work but allowing business activity).
4. Malaysia is widely admired both inside the ANC and among trade officials as a country that has overcome various postcolonial political impediments to become a highly successful economic power.

References

Business Day. 2007. "False Beliefs That Cloud the Skills Debate." January 3, 15.

Department of Health. 2010. Employment of Foreign Health Professionals in the South African Health Sector, approved by the National Health Council, February 5, Pretoria.

Department of Labour. 2007. *Labour Market Review 2007. Labor Migration and South Africa: Towards a Fairer Deal for Migrants in the South African Economy*. Republic of South Africa, Pretoria.

Erasmus, J., and M. Breier. 2009. *Skills Shortages in South Africa. Case Studies of Key Professions*. Human Sciences Research Council, Pretoria.

Financial Times. 2006. "Companies Hit at Immigration Law." April 19.

Mattes, R., and N. Mniki. 2005. *Restless Minds: South African Students and the Brain Drain*. Migration Policy Series 36, Southern African Migration Programme, Queen's University, Kingston, Canada, and IDASA (Institute for Democracy in South Africa), Cape Town, South Africa.

Mlambo-Ngcuka, P. 2006. "A Catalyst for Accelerated and Shared Growth (ASGISA)." Parliamentary media briefing by Deputy President Phumzile Mlambo-Ngcuka, February 6. http://www.info.gov.za/speeches/2006/06020615151001.htm.

OECD (Organisation for Economic Co-operation and Development). n.d. Database on immigrants and expatriates. http://www.oecd.org/dataoecd/18/23/34792376.xls.

Parliamentary Monitoring Group. 2006. "Deputy President Briefing on Accelerated and Shared Growth Initiative." February 6. http://www.pmg.org.za/briefings/briefings.php?id=246.

Polzer, T., M. Kiwanuka, and K. Takabvirwa. 2010. "Regional Responses to Zimbabwean Migration, 2000–2010." *Open Space: On the Move: Dynamics of Migration in Southern Africa* 3 (3): 30–34.

Southern African Migration Programme. 2000. *Losing Our Minds: Skills Migration and the South African Brain Drain*. Migration Policy Series 18, Southern African Migration Programme, Queen's University, Kingston, Canada, and IDASA (Institute for Democracy in South Africa), Cape Town, South Africa.

Statistics South Africa. 2003. *Documented Migration*. Report No. 03-51-03, Pretoria.

Chapter 3

Mobility and Municipalities: Local Authorities, Local Impacts, and the Challenges of Movement

Loren B. Landau, Aurelia Segatti, and Jean Pierre Misago

Global debates on migration and development typically focus on national policy frameworks and aggregate economic and social effects. South Africa illustrates the importance of subnational dynamics as the positive and negative consequences of migration are most acute at the level of the province and the municipality. In previous decades, the majority of South Africa's international migrants were concentrated in agricultural and mining areas. Since the early 1990s, both international and domestic migrants increasingly concentrate in the country's urban centers. Indeed, population movements—some predictable, some spontaneous, some voluntary, some forced—are now perennial features of South African cities and secondary towns (South African Cities Network 2004; Balbo and Marconi 2005).

Constitutionally empowered to be a leading force for development, local governments have been wary of addressing migration concerns. Their reluctance stems partly from the belief held by many local and national policy makers that immigration is exclusively a matter of national policy concern. Some local policy makers have yet to recognize the degree to which migration is transforming their cities. Others naively hope that heightened mobility is simply a temporary outgrowth of South Africa's democratic transition. Regardless of the reason, budgeting and planning exercises have largely excluded extended population projections and insights into the relationships between mobility, livelihoods, and community development—even as people continue to move into, out of, and between cities and the shortcomings of current planning exercises and interventions become evident. Without a substantial reconsideration of current approaches, concerns over access to services, physical and economic insecurity, and social conflict will only increase.

This chapter works from the growing recognition that migration, in all of its forms, is an important component of local governments' mandate within South Africa and across the region. Without the involvement of local governments, there is little chance of maximizing the development potential of mobility. Where local authorities ignore mobility or are poorly equipped to address it, their worst fears about migration are likely to be realized.

Most local officials have begun recognizing the benefits and risks of migration, but many municipalities are poorly equipped to address the issue. Whether a consequence of a limited understanding of population dynamics (that is, fertility, mortality, and mobility); conceptual, institutional, and political imperatives that prevent authorities from seeing or responding to migration; or the absence of a reasoned, empirically informed approach, municipalities are simply not keeping pace. By documenting these processes, highlighting shortcomings, and pointing to positive innovations, this chapter takes a small but significant step toward managing migration in ways that promote development and social cohesion.

This chapter draws on a broad range of data collected through surveys, participant observations, and interviews (109 conducted between 2002 and 2010). It relies most heavily on research conducted in 2010 in five municipalities: Johannesburg, the Merafong City Local Municipality, the Mossel Bay Local Municipality, the City of Tshwane Metropolitan Municipality, and the Nelson Mandela Bay Metropolitan Municipality.[1] At each site, the research team conducted individual and focus group interviews with municipal officials, law enforcement officials, community leaders, and representatives of political parties and labor unions as well as with representatives of the business sector, nongovernmental organizations, and community organizations.

Local Management of Migration: Policy Frameworks and Effects

At the municipal level, domestic and particularly international migration is positively correlated with economic growth and development. Although there are clear endogeneity issues in trying to determine the causal relationships between mobility and growth, it is likely that some of the observed economic development is caused by the arrival of new skills, investments, and trading connections. It is also undoubtedly the case that more prosperous and successful cities will continue to attract people from across the country and abroad. However anxious urban planners may be about an ever-expanding population, South African cities, like those across the world, have little option but to prepare for growing numbers of people.

The ties between mobility and human development (that is, education, income, and life expectancy) are less obvious (table 3.1). Although global evidence and research by the African Centre for Migration and Society suggests that movements to cities offer the fastest route to individual socioeconomic improvement and economic development, the aggregate effects are less clear. The ambiguous effect observed requires further research and analysis to explain.

Local authorities can play an important role in maximizing the economic and human development potential of migration. At the very least, they are critical in managing the social and political tensions often associated with the movements of people. As decentralization continues across Africa, as elsewhere in the world, and cities seek to establish themselves as relatively autonomous global players, the challenges of migration and responsibilities of local authorities will only increase.

The rest of this chapter explores the role of local government in responding to migration. It identifies both the challenges associated with developing such a response and the political hazards associated with maintaining current approaches. The discussion includes national trends, with particular attention to South Africa's two primary cities, Cape Town and Johannesburg. It highlights similarities and critical differences in the political calculus of migration management. Considerable attention is also paid to unofficial and semi-official responses to migration, in the forms of violence, discrimination, and economic

Table 3.1 Relationship between Urbanization and Human Development in South African Municipalities

	Percentage recent births	Percentage recent internal migrants	Percentage recent international migrants	Percentage recent migrants	Growth	Human development
Size	−0.154** (0.024)	0.099 (0.103)	0.177** (0.011)	0.124* (0.056)	0.167** (0.016)	0.403*** (0.000)
Percentage recent births		Correlated by definition	Correlated by definition	Correlated by definition	0.040 (0.305)	−0.069 (0.189)
Percentage recent internal migrants			Correlated by definition	Correlated by definition	0.137** (0.040)	−0.011 (0.444)
Percentage recent international migrants				Correlated by definition	0.233*** (0.001)	0.013 (0.434)
Percentage recent migrants					0.169** (0.015)	−0.007 (0.464)
Growth						0.022 (0.390)

Source: Authors, based on data from Statistics South Africa 2001; 2007 Community Survey.
Note: *** significant at the 1 percent level. ** significant at the 5 percent level. *significant at the 10 percent level.

exclusion. These actions contrast sharply with the steps South Africa has taken to institutionalize a human rights culture and the rule of law.

Local government is one of three spheres of government defined by the South African Constitution. Although the relationships between the governmental spheres are currently under review, the Constitution provides clear definitions of municipalities' roles and responsibilities, including legislative and executive authority over a number of matters. Section 153(a) of the Constitution explicitly demands that local government "structure and manage its administration and budgeting and planning processes to give priority to the basic needs of the community, and to promote the social and economic development of the community." Section 152(1) defines this "developmental duty" by noting that local government has various objects or purposes, including the promotion of social and economic development, a safe and healthy environment, and other responsibilities that clearly suggest some responsibility toward human mobility. The (nonbinding) White Paper on Local Government of 1998 argues that the challenge for local government is not how to run a set of services but how to transform and manage settlements—a challenge that can be met only if municipalities think of themselves as developmental local governments. Municipal authorities thus have a role to play, however ill defined, in addressing human mobility.

The impact and roles of local government are complicated by the division of labor across South Africa's governmental structures. Many of the social and economic concerns associated with movement are not explicitly within local government's mandate. The primary needs of migrants—shelter; access to health care, education, economic opportunities, and administrative justice; safety; security; and proper treatment—are formally the responsibility of national or provincial governments, although it is often municipalities that bear the responsibility and suffer the consequences when these delivery mechanisms do not function appropriately. If nothing else, there is an acute need for lateral and vertical collaboration and cooperation to ensure that various departments share information, coordinate responses, and appropriately allocate resources. The rest of this chapter considers the degree to which these conditions are being met.

Officials' Perspectives on Domestic and International Migration

Migration and mobility are hot-button issues in local politics and public administration in South Africa. Some local government officials see increasing migration and diversity as a positive sign of South African cities' emergence as trading and cultural centers. City planners in Cape Town and Johannesburg have begun outlining strategies for recruiting and incorporating highly skilled migrants and refugees into cities' socioeconomic networks.[2] At the same time, many municipal authorities feel overwhelmed, if not threatened, by domestic and international migration. In some locales, out-migration of the cities' skilled and affluent is raising the specter of economic decline and an ever-expanding underclass (South African Cities Network 2006).

Perspectives on what should be done about mobility vary. Attitudes include the belief that cities should do everything they can to limit migration and transience and promote permanent settlement; fears about the impact of migration on planning and meeting performance targets, the link between migration and crime (see chapter 4), the effect on trade competition, and the lack of reliable information and mechanisms to collect records of settlement within municipal boundaries; and a sense that however much migration might affect municipalities, it is fundamentally an issue for the Department of Home Affairs or other national departments. Each of these concerns is addressed below.

For many officials, migration is first and foremost conceived as permanent settlement—the move from one place to another. Understood this way, officials are quick to distinguish between the benefits likely to come from affluent pensioners and the highly skilled and the negative consequences of less affluent migrants. The issue is not only the need to expand services for the poor and vulnerable but the unpredictability and pace of such movements and associated demands. In the words of one Tshwane official, "Migration affects the quality of service delivery, because the municipality is always caught unaware by population movements. This creates permanent service delivery backlogs" (interview with Abel Mtshweni, deputy director, International Intergovernmental Relations, Operational Support Management, March 26, 2010). Another official in Tshwane noted, "We can't cope with the influx of people. How do we accommodate it?" (interview with A. Mosupyoe, Member of the Mayoral Committee for Health and Social Development, April 6, 2010).

If there is one common refrain among municipal officials with regard to migration it is the concern that it will impose a budgetary burden and undermine performance targets. There is also fear that providing for new arrivals will only beget further migration: "The more houses you build, the more the influx," noted the executive director of Corporate Services in Mossel Bay. More sophisticated perceptions of migration recognize the challenges of providing services and institutional frameworks for people with translocal livelihoods and families. There is often an explicit desire to plan in ways that promote permanent settlement and long-term socioeconomic investments in the current place of residence. To do otherwise is seen as both economically and morally dangerous.

Few officials had a clear idea of how they might incorporate migrants' livelihoods and service demands into their mandates. In many instances, management of migration is understood to mean "influx control"—the kind of policies that colonial and apartheid-era South Africa employed to keep "surplus people" out of cities. Given the unconstitutionality of such strategies, there was a sense that migration could not be managed. Without a proactive perspective on what can be done to address human mobility, the common refrain that "we can't cope with the influx of people" threatens to become a self-fulfilling prophecy.

Many municipal officials believe that migration management is not a local government mandate. Although some feel that local government should be considered more in migration policies, they are reluctant to tread on turf belonging to other spheres of government. An official from the Office of the Chief Whip in Tshwane noted that migration is considered a national issue and is not regularly discussed.

Tensions between national and local governments occasionally surface, but officials are generally reluctant to participate more actively in migration policy making. Some mayors (such as Amos Masondo, the former mayor of Johannesburg) and members of the South African Local Government Association recognize that a local government perspective is crucial to the development of future migration policy developments, but most municipal leaders do not share this view.

Around the world, migration is publicly and often politically associated with criminality and insecurity. A member of the Mayoral Committee on Community Safety in Tshwane, for example, noted that "Foreign migrants are a huge problem. Most come into the country without documents and are difficult to control. We do not know who, where; we cannot trace them. They are prone to crime as perpetrators or targets and victims." Others approach migration from a less Manichean position, arguing that migration contributes to competition for employment, business ownership, and housing.

Population Data: Collection and Use

The perceptions of most officials are founded on anecdotes and presuppositions; there have been almost no efforts to systematically document the effects of migration. Consequently, few municipalities can distinguish between domestic and foreign migration, permanent rural-urban migration and seasonal migration, or intra-city movements. Indeed, perhaps the most fundamental challenge to local governments charged with addressing migration and other development challenges is how little they know about the people living in their cities. Whereas national governments have the luxury of developing generalized policy frameworks, local governments and service providers are responsible for more focused and context-specific interventions.

This paucity of information extends generally to the urban poor. Efforts to map "poverty pockets" (Cross and others 2005) and review both national and local migration data represent some of the first attempts to understand South Africa's urban population dynamics (Dorrington 2005). However, many of these studies are based on incomplete census data, including inaccurate ward-level information and information on foreign-born populations, and are often purely descriptive. Although the Department of Cooperative Governance and Traditional Affairs (previously known as the Department of Cooperative Government and Traditional Authorities [CoGTA]) recognizes the need to improve cross-border and multinodal planning, including greater consideration of population mobility, planners have few tools for mapping the "functional economic geography of the city and its region [and] how the different components relate to each other" (South African Cities Network 2006).

The lack of data on migration affects South African municipalities in several ways. First, incomplete and inconsistent data migration are used as the basis for planning. Second, efforts to improve the capacity to collect, manage, and employ population data are hindered by political transitions and changes in policies. Third, in the absence of verifiable data and projections, local authorities continue to be influenced by stereotypes and incomplete readings of data.

Sources and Knowledge of Data

Across South African municipalities, population data are considered important for planning, budgeting, and other municipal functions, but, with rare exceptions, the collection and analysis of population data has rarely been a priority. Municipalities generally do not have units or even staff dedicated to collecting and managing population data or making existing data available for use in government departments. Outside the major metropolitan areas, authorities typically rely on scanty, incomplete, inaccurate, outdated, decontextualized information.

For the most part, municipalities draw population information and data from Statistics South Africa (StatsSA), often without a clear understanding of available indicators or how to process them at the ward level. In some instances, data from StatsSA are supplemented with commissioned surveys, studies by academic research institutions, data found on the Internet, or reviews of municipal service accounts. In most instances, directorates and departments use different sources of information—when they use data at all—for their programming and planning, all but ensuring that they are working from a different understanding of their constituencies' needs. There are also no guidelines or methodologies for research for planning exercises or support services within the central government.

Local and national planning and budgeting structures also provide mixed incentives for collecting and using data in municipal decision making. StatsSA is the most commonly used source of data, largely because it is the only source of data widely used and recognized by decision makers in other spheres of government (such as the Treasury, the Department of Cooperative Governance and Traditional Affairs, and various provinces). These spheres of government determine the financial support allocated to municipalities (through the local government equitable share system). Although they have little choice but to use them, municipalities recognize that StatsSA data are often outdated, inaccurate, and misleading.

The applicability of these data is particularly limited by issues of scale. Some of these concerns could be addressed through better engagement with StatsSA and other government departments, the development of local skills, and extrapolation of data from other sources. Municipalities need spatially localized trends that are neither well captured by national aggregates nor extractable by officials. The executive director of economic development in Nelson Mandela Bay expressed his frustration, noting that "StatsSA collects data at the ward level but presents at the provincial level, which makes its usage for planning difficult. We would need to spend a lot of money to get consultants to do additional analyses, to break it down to the metro level" (interview with Z. Siswana, April 16, 2010).

StatsSA does provide census data at the ward level, upon request. Processing these data requires specific statistical skills, however, which are generally not available at the municipal or even provincial level.

Municipalities could use local-level data generated by community development workers who are part of a government program created in 2004. The program is coordinated by the Department of Public Service and Administration, the Department of Cooperative Governance and Traditional Affairs, the provincial administrations, the South African Local Government Association, and municipalities. Where there is a good working relationship between ward leadership and community development workers, wards obtain population information from profiles regularly compiled by community development workers. Such data are not always available, however, because not every ward has a community development worker and because community development workers (who are deployed by and report to the provincial government) are not always willing to share their reports with ward leaders. This unwillingness stems mainly from an unclear relationship between provinces and municipalities over the management of these community development workers, who are seen by some as being sent out by the provinces to "spy" on local leaders and report corrupt behaviors (interview with community development workers in Merafong, June 2, 2010). This relationship seemed particularly tense in Merafong, where community development workers acknowledged that a redefinition of their mandate should be planned for after the next local elections. Ward profiles are therefore very heterogeneous, information is scarce, and methodologies are unclear.

Producing and Using Population Data: Multiplicity, Heterogeneity, and Illegitimacy

Many officials did not seem to be aware that they could use the data that are available or think these data could be useful in any way. An official from the Research Unit in the Tshwane City Planning Department claimed, "There are no mechanisms to know migration in the city. And this is worrying because the natural national population growth is decreasing. It is currently estimated at 1 percent in cities. So in cities without migration there is practically no population growth; but still cities do not have accurate information on population movements" (interview conducted April 7, 2010).

Even where new data exist, there appear to be institutional blocks to using them for planning purposes. For example, although the municipality of Nelson Mandela Bay conducted a demographic study in 2006 that included population projections to 2020, the director of the Integrated Development Plan stated that no information existed.[3] The chief financial officer of Nelson Mandela Bay noted that "people who provide stats do not provide projections, and that's unacceptable" (interview with Kevin Jacobs, chief financial officer, Nelson Mandela Bay, April 21, 2010). Population projections were thus not considered in planning or budgeting.

Issues of trust and institutional incentives underlie the reluctance to use locally collected data or data that do not come from StatsSA in planning processes. Part of this reluctance has to do with the range of often ad hoc methods used to update population statistics. For instance, the municipality of Mossel Bay updates its population figures using the average national annual population growth, whereas Merafong uses its own calculated average household size. Methodologies also vary widely (from satellite/aerial photographs to qualitative field studies). Although these approaches may satisfy the demands of particular municipal officials, the disparate approaches make comparison or aggregation difficult, making it hard to identify trends at the provincial, interprovincial, and intermunicipal levels. As discussed below, lack of comparability also makes it difficult to secure additional resources to support forward-looking planning.

Even within municipalities, there are often tensions over locally collected data and their implications. The executive director for special programs in Nelson Mandela Bay, for example, argued, "We need somebody to come up and work through these stats and tell us what we should believe. Otherwise each department uses whatever they think makes better sense to them. But StatsSA is one source not trusted by any department." Without a national body that provides reliable statistics and various departments that collect and use data as they see fit, there is little possibility of coordination or unified planning.

Decisions are at best based on the perceptions of officials who may have some empirical knowledge of the city and at worst by superficial and impressionistic ideas. The state of data collection at the national level and the lack of financial and human resources at the local and provincial levels call for a rethinking of planning that incorporates these uncertainties, improves data collection over the long term, and trains local staff to make informed projections and monitor trends. However, the institutional and organizational frameworks that would allow for these developments within local government structures seem to have been dismantled by political turnover and the concomitant losses of capacity and expertise.

Given this situation, it is not surprising that officials regularly lament the absence of a single department or person who could centralize, process, and make population data accessible to municipal departments. This kind of capacity once existed in large metropolitan areas. One Tshwane official revealed that "the decision was made to discontinue most of the research unit programs, which resulted in years of good work lost. It is difficult to make people on the top understand how critical research is. The rare reports we compile, such as city profiles, get submitted to and approved by the Council, but we have no idea how they are used for decision making and planning" (interview with Sharon Kaufman, Research Unit, Department of City Planning, Tshwane, April 7, 2010). The deputy director for metropolitan planning in the City Planning, Development, and Regional Services Department revealed that the research unit there had shrunk from 41 researchers to only 1 demographer and 1 researcher. She believes that the decline was caused by the fact that high-ranking municipal authorities do not understand the value of research.

Even in a municipality like Mossel Bay, where staff turnover and technical expertise did not seem to be a major problem, interdepartmental coordination and planning for data collection were poor, resulting in disagreements on the reliability of data and mandates over projections. Whereas Mossel Bay had a relatively stable and skilled technical and administrative staff that had served under both the opposition Democratic Alliance and ANC administrations, Merafong had many senior staff members holding acting positions for several years, with few opportunities to gain the skills required to reinforce their ability to be appointed in permanent positions.

Consultation, Planning, and Budgeting for Mobility

This section explains why planning processes have rarely included migration or other population dynamics. It emphasizes how the nature of planning and budgeting in South Africa, from popular consultation to the equitable distribution calculation, works against forward-looking planning that considers population dynamics. It shows how migration is viewed both as a default strategy to channel people into certain areas and as an obstacle to planning and budgeting, particularly for the poor. It concludes that forums and incentives for intergovernmental planning and budgeting are absent or stifled by institutional configurations and poor communication.

Consultation

Participatory planning (also known as community-based planning) emerged in the postapartheid dispensation as a way of realizing democratic transformation at the local level. This approach to planning was central to the ANC's transformation policy. Already highlighted as a principle in the 1994 Reconstruction and Development Programme, it was intended to ensure that the poor and marginalized had an effective mechanism for expressing their interests and needs (Bremner 1998). Participatory planning was subsequently incorporated into the new legislative and policy framework on local government through the White Paper on Local Government (1998), which recognized participatory governance and inclusiveness as central objectives of municipal institutions, and the Municipal Systems Act (2000), which provides for accommodating the needs of "marginalized groups." Participatory planning constitutes the basis for the preparation of Integrated Development Plans (documents intended to guide municipal investments and priorities for the following five years).

Paradoxically, given its democratic and developmental aspirations, the emphasis on participatory planning has created incentives for excluding the interests of migrants and discouraging officials from planning for migration dynamics (particularly population growth). This report is not the first to highlight shortcomings in the government's planning approach; it is the first to highlight the tendency toward a kind of "backward-looking programming" that is particularly damaging when trying to address migration. This tendency is rooted in a number of factors. For one, the need for public services that people express in consultation are filtered to select those that meet political imperatives and capacities. What is ultimately incorporated into municipal plans therefore reflects the needs of subsections of the poor population that accessed consultation forums at a particular moment in time, coupled with short-term political interests. In only a few cases do communities have the capacity or incentive to project demographic trends, and few residents are likely to ask their municipality to dedicate resources to future potential residents when their own needs are evident and acute. Given public attitudes toward migrants and the limited knowledge of migration dynamics, officials are unlikely to insist that resources be dedicated to unpopular, future residents.

A second limitation of participatory planning lies in the de facto exclusion of migrants (domestic and international) and migration issues from public consultations. The policy framework itself creates confusion. If the White Paper on Local Government and the Municipal Systems Act insist on "residents," the *Batho Pele* document (a statement of service principles) issued by the Department for Public Service and Administration refers to "citizens" in the section on local government participatory mechanisms. Noncitizens are not regularly invited to participate in community policing forums, stakeholder forums, residents' associations meetings, or meetings hosted by local ward councilors. There is often no formal prohibition on such participation, although such prohibitions have been reported anecdotally; almost all of the officials and community members in the country's secondary cities interviewed for this chapter reported the almost total absence of foreigners and recent migrants in such forums.

Some municipalities are working to overcome such exclusion. The city of Johannesburg, for example, has launched a number of initiatives to foster and encourage migrants' participation in dialogue platforms, including the Migrants' Help Desk, created in 2007, and the Johannesburg Migrants' Advisory Committee, established in 2010. Although laudable, it is not yet clear whether such well-intentioned efforts can overcome informal forms of exclusion. Nor is it obvious how the interests of migrants (especially foreigners) will be incorporated into planning processes if they go against powerful and more stable interests. There is also the danger that such consultation, like many forms of participatory planning, will be used simply to legitimate decisions made through other means (Cooke and Kothari 2001).

Planning

Municipalities' Integrated Development Plans reveal little mainstreaming of population dynamics into planning processes. In most cases, demographics are mentioned as a background element, not cited as the basis for development plans. The lack of reliable information is not the only reason for such blindered planning. Municipal officials have an ambivalent approach to population information: they consider it useful for the current management of development programs and for targeting "poverty pockets," but they are unable to use it to garner the financial support they need for future investment. In some instances, officials expressed concern that too much data might only highlight the shortcomings of what they knew were inadequate interventions given the scope of demand.

Migrants occupy an ambivalent space in officials' vision. Their arrival was viewed as a problem, as indicated by a town planner in Merafong who noted, "If we could, we would help everybody, but it is difficult because you cannot get information on these people because they do not have jobs and do not necessarily intend to stay here. You can't provide them with housing. Before they can see the house they are gone again" (interview with C. De-Jajer, town planner, Merafong, July 3, 2010). There was no hint that the municipalities' employment and housing characteristics may not be conducive to permanent settlement; that temporary migration may be systematic and predictable; or that apart from providing permanent houses or services, the municipality might develop other (not necessarily more costly) approaches to service delivery. Such oversights are reflected across South Africa. There is often a sense of despondency that nothing can be done. In one Merafong official's words, "With regard to rural-urban migration, there is actually not a lot we can do. . . . We do not see any other way of dealing with it [than to plan for permanent housing]" (interview with C. De-Jajer, town planner, Merafong, July 3, 2010). Officials continue to maintain the status quo, while recognizing that their interventions do little to address emerging needs. As the Merafong official noted, in the Spatial Development Framework "the idea is to throw money where economic development is feasible and where it is not possible to just supply or meet the basic human needs. We encourage these people to move into economically active areas." This means that smaller towns are unlikely to attract the resources needed to support current and future residents and that there are incentives to see the poor, regardless of origins, as temporary residents, for whom long-term planning is not needed.

The reasons outlined above, coupled with a normative bias toward stable populations and the need for bureaucratic accountability, mean that planning practice is often framed in ways that favor permanent residents and permanent settlement over transients and transience. In part, this emphasis reflects negative preconceptions of transient populations, but it is also probably a consequence of available instruments, bureaucratic rigidity, and comfort in planning for service allocation. This may be understandable, but it works against the interests of cities whose residents include significant numbers of people on the move. The Merafong town planner explains, "The reason is not to exclude those people, it is focusing on permanent residents first. It is difficult to cater to people who are highly mobile . . . it is almost impossible to cater to those people at the same time we are still dealing with our permanent residents, because they often do not require the same strategies" (interview with C. De-Jajer, July 3, 2010). Similar sentiments are expressed by planners across South Africa.

Whether explicitly anti-migrant or not, current urban development paradigms put poor migrants at a disadvantage. In opposition-held (ANC) Mossel Bay, for instance, the municipality has adopted a proactive line against informal settlements based on systematic dismantling and eviction in an effort to dissuade poor people from making the city their home. The strategy support executive explained the municipality's approach, a position that was much criticized by the (opposition) ANC in the municipality: "What we are trying to do is to discourage people from coming. As far as squatting is concerned, we have people who remove [their] structures. . . . You can only try to discourage people as much as possible" (focus group interview with ANC councilors, Mossel Bay, May 11, 2010).

Similar strategies have been adopted in the city of Tshwane. For its part, Cape Town has attempted to set a firm "urban edge" to prevent the footprint of the city from expanding (all while preventing densification). Within the city, Cape Town has managed its migrant population under the guise of environmental protection and public health. As in Johannesburg, efforts to maintain the urban edge or protect sensitive environmental resources often provide the justification for "decanting" or otherwise removing or restricting recently arrived and mobile populations.

Budgeting

Planners' mentalities and modalities of planning have at least three significant implications for the budgeting processes:

- Efforts to address the existing needs of permanent residents lead planners to overlook population and migration trends, even though future residents will demand resources and interventions.
- Even if planners engage in forward planning, their efforts are largely unsupported by the current system of resource allocation to local government (the local government equitable share).
- The planning and budgeting modalities generally reflect limited capacity to cater to the poor in general and the most indigent sections of the population in particular.

Strict reliance on 2001 census data (and subsequent national averages of population growth rates) and the lack of universally accepted interim data have undermined municipalities' ability to calculate demographic realities and trends. As the director of town planning in Mossel Bay notes, "We show we have the highest population in the district, bigger than George, bigger than Bhisho; but they are given more money than us. We use that information. Everyone is aware that Mossel Bay is the largest town in Eden District Municipality. Allocations for housing and [municipal infrastructure grant] money are not related to population figures."

Such a system provides a disincentive for forward-looking planning. Moreover, municipalities are generally unable to use studies they have commissioned or other data sources to influence their budget allocation to help bring it in line with changing demographics. As budget authority remains almost entirely national, gaps are created between needs and resources, and forward-looking planning and budgeting are discouraged. The chief financial officer in Nelson Mandela Bay thus explains:

> I was recently faced with a question of why we can't put in a proposal to the national treasury to increase our equitable share to support our poor because things have changed from when we used the baseline data of 2001. Now the issue is I can't put [in] a submission like that because the census at that particular time was used to calculate the equitable share. Remember the equitable share is so much. *So every municipality has been using the same information. So you can't go as an independent municipality and say I want my*

review. You must do all the municipalities at the same time. . . . Unless you have
information for the entire country, for all municipalities [emphasis added].

It is not only the absence of a universally accepted figure that is the challenge
but also the degree to which figures can highlight the needs of an "indigent" population. In Merafong the town planner considered the absence of agreed upon
data and projections as a serious problem because of the growing gap between
beneficiaries of grants and nonbeneficiaries, who could not be taken into account
by municipalities: "We have some of the worst socioeconomic conditions in the
province . . . and we have a large number of indigent people and we are actually
not getting enough funding for the indigents." If local authorities are expected to
respond to the needs of the poor, promote social cohesion, and invest, they need
strong, disaggregated data on the populations they are meant to serve.

Officials expressed frustration with the inadequacies in the local government
equitable share mode of calculation and their sense of powerlessness in redress-
ing inaccurate population estimates. By and large, they pointed to the need for
more frequent assessments of municipalities' populations, particularly in their
more mobile and indigent sections. The rigidity of the system and the absence
of efficient channels of dialogue for the reform of calculation modes seemed
to discourage local officials from taking the initiative. The principle of equity,
which lies at the heart of the local government equitable share system, was not
questioned, but its lack of flexibility and adaptation over time were criticized.
The domination of party structures over government ones in policy-making
processes was perceived as limiting the impact of popular participation, empirically based evidence, and officials' own assessments.

Intergovernmental Coordination on Planning and Service Delivery

Municipal authorities' frustrations with intergovernmental cooperation and
coordination are not limited to financial issues. At the heart of their discon-
tent are concerns over overlapping mandates and the monopolistic tendencies
of provincial and national authorities. Although communities interact directly
with municipalities, local authorities are often unable to address the demands
levied on them by other spheres of government with which they are ostensibly
equal. Field interviews confirm the following concerns raised by the Department of Cooperative Governance and Traditional Affairs (CoGTA 2009):

- Municipalities are often undermined by national and provincial government
  policies and processes (blamed for the failure of housing policy over which
  they have little authority, for example).

- The intergovernmental relation system does not effectively coordinate planning across the three spheres of government or strengthen accountability toward achieving critical and targeted development outcomes.
- National and provincial policy failures undermine local government effectiveness.

The CoGTA report emphasized two challenges: "intergovernmental conflict and competition over powers and functions between provinces and their local governments" and "national targets for service delivery that apply uniformly irrespective of the economic and institutional differences between municipalities [which] simply set municipalities up to fail" (CoGTA 2009: 11). Various frustrations and tensions are evident:

- Local government structures are not consulted in national migration policy making.
- The roles of the different levels of government (provincial and local, in particular) across various sectors are not clear.
- Local governments feel excluded from planning and budgeting processes, particularly by the national treasury.
- Priorities and goalposts for service provision to the poor are constantly shifting.
- Changes are made in policies regarding immigrants and asylum seekers (including relocating offices, changing work prohibitions, and formally enabling access to services) without consultation with or forewarning to local authorities.

Although municipal authorities were frustrated that they were not consulted on issues related to their population, they were rarely proactive advocates for their mobile populations. Many (quietly and anonymously) blame the hegemony of party structures for closing avenues for "upward" communication. Research conducted for this report failed to find strong leadership in lobbying for a rethink of the local government equitable share or other policy issues directly affecting municipalities' ability to address population dynamics. To some extent, larger cities like Cape Town and Johannesburg have developed parallel systems to address some of their concerns. Smaller and less well-resourced municipalities do not have this option.

In a number of municipalities, some degree of coordination with local big business was evident. Other municipalities consulted business with regard to population planning, particularly where the opening of specific businesses had resulted in substantial influxes of population (for example, in Merafong and Mossel Bay).

The Practice of Uncoordination: Security, Conflict, and Social Cohesion

Lack of coordination, planning, and consultation are evident in municipalities' efforts to address the ongoing threat of intergroup violence within South Africa's municipalities, particularly since the 2008 riots (see box 1 in the introduction). Since 2009 the president of South Africa has placed renewed emphasis on social cohesion, and the police and others have redoubled their efforts to fight criminality and violence. Although not explicitly about migration, these two initiatives nonetheless bring issues of mobility and security into sharp relief. Countering both crime and social fragmentation will mean overcoming a range of deeply ingrained and emerging forms of intolerance and bias. As people continue to move, the tensions associated with social and economic heterogeneity are becoming more acute (Cloete and Kotze 2009). Doing so successfully is expected to produce greater social equity and justice while limiting the opportunities for and exercise of criminality and socially destructive behaviors (including xenophobic violence). Although national institutional frameworks, policy priorities, and incentives are important in both shaping and preventing conflicts, the majority of tensions manifest themselves and must be addressed within municipalities.

Addressing issues of identity-based tensions and migration-related security in municipalities will require a shift in mindset, a change in attitudes toward migration among civic and community leaders that lends credence and practical political support to broader calls for cohesion and tolerance. Only by curbing explicit and implicit accusations against migrants will it be possible to create communities founded on principles of tolerance and inclusion.

Despite the evident need for action, officials have done little to explicitly manage tensions and insecurity associated with population mobility. Moreover, a range of practices by the police and others suggest a strong bias against new arrivals. In many municipalities, the South African Police Service arrest and detain foreigners. Under the guise of crime control, the police in Cape Town, Johannesburg, and other municipalities spend considerable amounts of their time tracking undocumented migrants—despite little evidence that doing so makes communities safer or more prosperous (Vigneswaran and Duponchel 2009; Vigneswaran and Hornberger 2009). Where the South African Police Service is not directly involved, other groups step in to fill their function. In Nelson Mandela Bay, for example, the Port of Entry police have taken on the role of immigration enforcement. In Mossel Bay, complaints about drug trading and other illegal activities resulted in a strategy of once-off raids rather than ongoing targeting of nonnationals and outsiders. The first ports of call for officers include foreign-owned shops, shacks, and homes. Such initiatives build credibility with some residents, but they reinforce the perception, largely unsubstantiated by fact, that foreigners are behind crime.[4]

It is important to understand the structural and political imperatives that motivate bias, harassment, and similar behaviors. Across municipalities, South African Police Service officials recognized that they were not satisfying residents' demands for justice and security. In almost all municipalities, citizens expressed frustration that there was little follow-up or investigation, just the occasional arbitrary raid. One officer noted that residents of Mossel Bay now take it on themselves to go to court when suspects are arrested. Once there, they warn the judge to keep the suspect in custody in order to avoid "justice" being done on the street (interview with Sergeant Jika, communications officer, KwaNonqaba Police Station, Mossel Bay, May 13, 2010). Elsewhere, the loss of faith in official systems has encouraged vigilante activity or mob justice. Given that many local residents see outsiders, South African and foreign, as responsible for everything from petty crime to drug trafficking and murder, these vigilante groups are wont to target outsiders. Limited resources and the desire to be seen as legitimate usually prevent the police from intervening to protect targeted and victimized subgroups (Hornberger 2009).

Some initiatives work to protect foreigners from xenophobic attacks. The Gqebera Trust in Nelson Mandela Bay initially emerged as a way of combating crime. Rather than organize to simply push out the Zimbabweans who were presumed to be behind problems in Walmer Township, the group organized to investigate criminal acts and to find out what had happened. Working with police and private security to collect and disseminate information, the trust has established itself as an important source of social capital. Although such initiatives cannot be replicated en masse, a credible organization and leader that can speak against prevailing xenophobic sentiments can be a powerful tool for promoting cohesion.

The lack of population planning creates a challenge for the police. Urban sprawl and increases in urban populations mean that urban police now have responsibility over both more people and greater territory than they used to. The growth of cities also means that security officials have to police a range of housing types, linguistic groups, and leadership structures. In places like Merafong, relatively unplanned expansion means that people are now living in areas without good transport infrastructure. The police in these areas lack maps that would facilitate navigation and patrols. Without additional financial support or planning, the police often find themselves thin on the ground and unable to establish a presence in the diverse communities in which they serve. According to a communications officer in KwaNonqaba in Mossel Bay, it takes years to update resources at police stations, meaning that "we will never match the need."

It is not only efforts to gain popular legitimacy that encourage the police to behave in arbitrary or overly assertive ways with regard to informal settlers or migrants. In Mossel Bay, for example, the police complain that pressure to "perform" comes from Parliament. In practice, this translated into policies about arrests and other benchmarks that allow individual stations or commands to demonstrate their effectiveness. The police admit that they arrest people just to fill their quotas (Vigneswaran and Hornberger 2009). In Johannesburg and elsewhere these arrests disproportionately target foreigners, who are less likely to have identity documents or business licenses. Such migrants are more likely than permanent residents to have cash (because they are traders or have trouble accessing bank accounts) and less likely to have strong allies within the community who could cause problems for overzealous police or resist extortion.

Community policing forums play an important role in structuring community relations, particularly about contentious issues of crime and security. However, the lack of state resources they receive means their operations rely entirely on support from community members. The consequence of this is that they become subject to those individuals and interests, however inclusive or exclusive, that are able and ready to offer resources.

Any effort to promote security and cohesion must incorporate private security companies. As a leader from Business Against Crime in Nelson Mandela Bay reports, "We've got 10,000 armed private security guards in the city . . . and they don't talk to each other . . . because they see [each other] as competition." They rarely engage with either the metropolitan police or the South African Police Service, often for the same reasons or because they do not wish to reveal their quasi-legal strategies to the police.

Obstacles to social cohesion are not limited to the police and security agents. In many instances, new arrivals are largely excluded from community leadership structures. Exclusion from such meetings helps reinforce a sense of difference and boundaries between groups. It also limits the information local officials would otherwise be able to collect from community members. The continued exclusion of new arrivals may foster a sense of transience that limits social and material investment in the areas in which they live. Providing a sense that new arrivals can influence the future of their residential municipalities can help create incentives for involvement and investment.

Conclusions

Social cohesion and tensions related to migration are likely to remain an important and dangerous trait of municipalities across South Africa. Recognition of the need to address these tensions is growing, but current conceptualizations and planning processes are likely to maintain or exacerbate current conditions.

Migration is generally not considered in municipal planning and implementation processes. The few initiatives that promote social cohesion have been short lived and superficial. The understanding of migration dynamics among municipal officials is limited by the absence of high-quality data, ignorance about the data that do exist, and a range of negative stereotypes associated with transience and international migration. This lack of understanding is not surprising given how widespread anti-immigrant sentiment is in South Africa.[5] If not addressed, the belief that migrants will undermine cohesion and efforts to reduce poverty may become a self-fulfilling prophecy. Policy must be based on an accurate and unbiased understanding of population dynamics, including poverty, mobility, and other dimensions. As long as popular sentiment remains firmly anti-immigrant and anti-migrant, there are strong incentives, however, for policy makers to avoid leaving the impression that they are "pro" migrant.

Consulting, planning, and budgeting processes entail challenges linked to the poor quality of population data. However, planning failures cannot be attributed to the lack of data alone—they also reflect shortcomings in broader governing frameworks. The way participatory planning is currently conducted within the municipalities studied is not conducive to outsiders' participation and does not encourage forward-looking planning in which populations' immediate needs are balanced with projections over time. Instead, authorities almost invariably perceive migration and mobility as a challenge to efficient planning, and preferences for permanent residents are expressed across municipalities, sometimes justifying anti-squatter policies. The equitable share system discourages the incorporation of the poor and transient, because municipalities receive no additional support from the national government for populations that are not captured in the national census. Officials are acutely aware of these inadequacies and express a sense of powerlessness in amending the existing system. Intergovernmental cooperation is lacking in many respects, particularly between CoGTA and the Department of Home Affairs with regard to decisions about foreign migrants and their access to certain rights and between municipalities and the provinces regarding mandates over service delivery, housing in particular. Lack of cooperation and clarity are often used to justify resorting to bylaws (municipal legislation governing trade and public space that can be used as justification to exclude). Although there are instances of cooperation with the corporate world on population and migration management, they remain anecdotal.

The prevalence of anti-immigrant sentiment calls for long-term structural changes in the distribution of resources and for bold education programs. But local government officials' perceptions are likely to preclude political innovation and legitimize local politicians' xenophobic/nativist actions. Visions expressed by local officials reflect apathy, powerlessness, and even at times the preference for executing top-down orders rather than taking the lead. Postapartheid transformation in the public service and the political hegemony of the ANC explain part of this sense of powerlessness. But if officials sense that the decentraliza-tion reform is nothing more than a new management model, they overlook the policy-making capacity that is expected of them. For the reasons outlined above, initiatives to improve migration planning must go beyond technical measures related to the collection and analysis of better data.

Although local governments in South Africa are slowly accepting their role in addressing the challenges of domestic and international migration, they face significant challenges in developing effective responses. In addition to the reluctance to see migration as a development concern, challenges include the following:

- *Involving migrants in civic affairs.* Cities are increasingly dedicated to foster-ing inclusion, but the objective of these efforts remains elusive because of the fragmentation and mobility of South Africa's urban populations. Because many people see cities as transit sites, they may not want to be included in their social or political structures.

- *Building trust.* The fluidity of migrant populations and their lack of incen-tive to engage in civic affairs make it difficult to gauge their interests and intentions through mechanisms that build mutual trust.

- *Informing policy with data.* Cities are unable to draw on data about citizens much less foreigners. In the absence of sound data, myths about migration and mobility continue to inform policy decisions.

- *Improving intergovernmental coordination.* In almost no instances have col-laborations between government departments been successful. This prob-lem is not unique to migration but is particularly evident given the need to develop multisite response mechanisms.

The consequences of the poor local response to migration are already evi-dent in a number of areas that are critical to South Africa's development:

- *Markets and financial services:* Migrants lack identity documents; they face discriminatory banking laws and lack access to credit.

- *Social services:* Discrimination, ignorance about migrants' rights, and poor record-keeping mean that many migrants, international and domestic, are unable to access social services where they live. The long-term economic and social consequences will be felt by both individuals and the communi-ties in which they live, particularly with regard to HIV/AIDS.

- *Vigilantism, violence, and ineffective policing:* Widespread xenophobia on the part of the police and citizens, coupled with ineffective policing, have led to vigilantism in many cities (see Misago and others 2010). As the police rarely investigate or prosecute these cases, such actions are slowly eroding South Africa's chances of establishing a rights-based system of law.

- *Accountability and planning:* South Africa's economic and political success hinges on developing accountable public institutions. The failure to protect populations and deliver services is undermining trust and civic engagement. Foreigners are frequently victims of political scapegoating, a process that distracts people from more fundamental structural and administrative problems.

Although citizenship and asylum laws must remain national, there is a heightened need for increased attention to subnational actors as they continue to assert their influence, through commission and omission, on the country's immigration and asylum regime. Cities and provinces need to recognize that they can, and indeed should be encouraged to, actively advocate for an immigration regime that helps foster inclusion and service delivery for all residents. Efforts must be made in collaboration with national, provincial, and neighboring local government officials, accompanied by broad discussions about the meaning of inclusion.

There is also a need for research at the local level conducted within a broad comparative framework. Although it is useful to develop aggregate trends, responses and attitudes may be shaped by the racial, economic, and political history of a particular neighborhood. Differences within cities may be as important as those between cities. There is a need to evaluate and critically analyze immigration and migration at the level of the city, as the effects will be vastly different for cities experiencing in-migration of foreigners and cities that are primarily destinations for South African citizens; cities that are net population losers will need to develop different metrics and projections to understand the challenges they face. Developing context-specific understandings will require heightened capacity for statistical, institutional, and social analyses. All spheres of government should be encouraged to collaborate in order to develop the capacity for data collection and analysis at all levels, and mechanisms should be created to ensure that these analyses are fed into decision-making processes. Doing otherwise will ensure policy failure and may help realize many planners' current fears about the effects of mobility on prosperity and security.

Notes

1. These municipalities were selected after a review of statistical data on the correlations between human development and various forms of mobility. For details on this selection and further background information, see Landau, Segatti, and Misago (2011). The research team included Kathryn Takabvirwa, Mpapa Kanyane, Nomusa Ngwenya, and Gugulethu Siziba; it was led by Jean Pierre Misago. The research for this chapter was supported by a variety of sources, including the Institute of Research for Development (France); the South African Local Government Association; the MacArthur Foundation; the Atlantic Philanthropies; and the Programme

to Support Pro-Poor Policy Development in South Africa, housed in the Office of the Presidency.

2. In 2005 Cape Town conducted a skills audit of its migrant population in order to better develop policies to capitalize on their presence in the city. Johannesburg has yet to follow suit, although it has officially recognized the potential contributions migrants make to the city.

3. Integrated Development Plans are five-year plans that flag the main directions for municipalities to attain the development goals they set for themselves.

4. In 2003 Detective Inspector Barney Dreyer said, "If we don't do something about the West African threat, we won't have a country left and (Nigerian President Olusegun) Obasanjo will be our president" http://www.iol.co.za/news/south-africa/west-african-drug-syndicates-rule-durban-1.116956. Although this statement reflects widespread perceptions, officials admit that foreigners make only a small contribution to South Africa's very high crime levels (Louw 2003; see also Harris 2001).

5. For more information on anti-immigrant sentiment in South Africa and its development over the past decade, see Crush (2008).

References

Balbo, M., and G. Marconi. 2005. "Governing International Migration in the City of the South." Global Migration Perspectives 38, Global Commission for International Migration, Geneva.

Bremner, L. 1998. "Participatory Planning: Models of Urban Governance: Porto Alegre and Greater Johannesburg." *Urban Forum* 9 (1): 111–19.

Cloete, P., and F. Kotze. 2009. *Concept Paper on Social Cohesion/Inclusion in Local Integrated Development Plans.* July 6, Government of South Africa, Pretoria.

CoGTA (Department of Cooperative Governance and Traditional Affairs). 2009. *State of Local Government in South Africa. Overview Report.* November. Pretoria.

Cooke, B., and U. Kothari. 2001. "The Case for Participation as Tyranny." In *Participation: The New Tyranny?* ed. B. Cooke and U. Kothari, 1–14. London: Zed Books.

Cross, C., P. Kok, M. Wentzel, K. Tlabela, G. Weir-Smith, and J. Mafukidze. 2005. *Poverty Pockets in Gauteng: How Migration Impacts Poverty.* Human Sciences Research Council, Pretoria.

Crush, J., ed. 2008. *The Perfect Storm: The Realities of Xenophobia in Contemporary South Africa.* Southern African Migration Programme, Queen's University, Kingston, Canada, and IDASA (Institute for Democracy in South Africa), Cape Town, South Africa.

Dorrington, R. 2005. *Projection of the Population of the City of Cape Town 2001–2021.* Centre for Actuarial Research, University of Cape Town.

Harris, B. 2001. "A Foreign Experience: Violence, Crime and Xenophobia during South Africa's Transition." Violence and Transition Series, Vol. 5, August, Centre for the Study of Violence and Reconciliation.

Hornberger, J. 2009. "Policing Xenophobia–Xenophobic Policing: A Clash of Legitimacy." In *Go Home or Die Here: Violence, Xenophobia and the Reinvention of Difference in South Africa,* ed. S. Hassim, T. Kupe, and E. Worby, 132–43. Johannesburg: the University of the Witwatersrand Press.

Landau, L. 2010 "Loving the Alien? Citizenship, Law, and the Future in South Africa's Demonic Society." *African Affairs* 109 (435): 213–30.

Landau, L., A. Segatti, and J. P. Misago. 2011. *Governing Migration and Urbanisation: Developing Approaches to Counter Poverty and Social Fragmentation.* African Centre for Migration and Society, University of the Witwatersrand, Johannesburg.

Louw, Danie. 2003. Interview conducted by Loren Landau, with Director, Hillbrow Police Station, Johannesburg, South Africa, July 18.

Misago, J. P., T. Monson, T. Polzer, and L. Landau. 2010. *2008 Violence against Foreign Nationals in South Africa: Understanding Causes and Evaluating Responses.* Forced Migration Studies Programme, University of the Witwatersrand, Johannesburg.

South African Cities Network. 2004. *State of the Cities Report 2004.* Johannesburg.

———. 2006. *State of the Cities Report 2006.* Johannesburg.

Vigneswaran, D., and M. Duponchel. 2009. "One Burden Too Many? A Cost-Benefit Analysis of Immigration Policing in Gauteng." Forced Migration Studies Programme, University of the Witwatersrand, Johannesburg.

Vigneswaran, D., and J. Hornberger, eds. 2009. *Beyond "Good Cop"/"Bad Cop": Understanding Informality and Police Corruption in South Africa.* Forced Migration Studies Programme, University of the Witwatersrand, Johannesburg.

Chapter 4

Migration Control, Documentation, and State Transformation

Darshan Vigneswaran

The government has been struggling to develop a coherent response to migration for more than a decade. Ever since the transition to democratic rule, illegal migration from neighboring countries has been viewed as a major challenge to the country's ambitious agendas of political transformation, economic development, and poverty alleviation. These challenges have been perceived in a variety of competing ways. The humanitarian lobby charges the government and South African citizens with neglect of legal obligations to foreign migrants. Nationalist critics complain that the government has not acted decisively enough against migrants who contravene the country's immigration laws.

Despite significant pressures on government to develop new initiatives and show results, the defining characteristics of immigration policy making over the past decade have been disorder, disunity, and despair. Leaders have struggled to translate policy into practice, having inherited a crumbling bureaucratic apparatus from the apartheid regime. Lacking clear direction from above, government agencies, offices, and officials have concocted immigration policy and practice "on the fly." These tendencies have been mirrored by the lack of significant regional initiatives by the Southern African Development Community (SADC). As evidenced by SADC's response to the ongoing Zimbabwean crisis, there is limited capacity for a coordinated regional response to migration and refugee flows.[1]

This chapter gauges the long-term impacts of this bureaucratic stasis on governance in South Africa. Its main goal is to explore how an ongoing state of crisis in this policy sphere is shaping the everyday practices of government bureaucracies, including both those charged with specific responsibility for immigration policy and those that have taken up this task. The main theme is the disjuncture between policy in principle and practice. Although the consensus across government is that current law and policy are inadequate and require substantial reworking, there is a de facto acceptance that government agencies and officials must continue to implement control-oriented policies and practices, including the arrest, detention, and deportation of "illegal foreigners." This disjuncture opens the way for opportunism and invention at the lower and local levels of state institutions. Government bureaucrats, principally in the Department of Home Affairs but also in the police, use the broad mandate for control-oriented immigration policy to craft spheres of personal influence and authority. These themes pose significant challenges for the government's development agenda, South Africa's security, and attempts to develop national and regional responses to migration.

This chapter draws on several sources of data, including parliamentary debates, newspaper reports, and unpublished material obtained from the government through requests made under the auspices of the Promotion of Access to Information Act, as well as interviews with about 20 past and present senior officials in Parliament, political parties, the Department of Home Affairs, and the police. Exploring the character of contemporary practice within government bureaucracies required 18 months of ethnographic research, conducted primarily at police stations in Gauteng but also at border posts, detention centers, and Department of Home Affairs' offices.

Postapartheid Reforms

In the late 1990s, there was a widespread political consensus that a new approach to immigration was needed—one that rid South Africa of the vestiges of the 1991 Aliens Control Act. Consequently, the Department of Home Affairs introduced a new legislative framework on immigration and refugees. The 1995 Draft Protocol on the Free Movement of Persons suggested a regional shift to a European Union type of migration governance. In the 1997 Green Paper on International Migration, a broadly representative team put forward the case that instead of focusing on controlling "illegals," the government should seek to "manage" migration flows in ways that served the national interest.

These moves were quickly countered by the Department of Home Affairs. The first White Paper on Immigration (1999) returned the focus to a control agenda and sought to renew commitments to various components of the 1991 legislation. Of particular note were a bundle of "community enforcement" measures that placed the onus on South African citizens to report the presence of foreigners in workplaces, schools, and hotels. The more significant issue revealed by the legislative process was the fact that no single government agency was in charge of migration (see chapter 1). In part, this was a legacy of the apartheid era, when responsibilities for enforcement were juggled by the various departments with responsibility for enforcing influx control. A confused mandate was ideally suited to a regime run by secret security agencies and networks, but it proved crippling in the postapartheid era. The ministries of justice, safety and security, and defense were each given new responsibilities to manage immigration under the draft legislation. None of these agencies was adequately consulted on these new tasks or willing to divert their resources accordingly. More important, with the possible exception of the army, none was prepared to relinquish its existing powers of immigration enforcement to a proposed new immigration agency.

Indeed, far from marshalling the nation behind the banner of immigration control, policy makers could rarely determine what their own officials should do. The Department of Home Affairs' capacity to control its own offices gradually deteriorated during the eight-year struggle to pass the new legislation. There was a breakdown in communication between the policy-making elite who drove the legislative process and the departmental officials in charge of enforcing immigration policy. The drafting team did not incorporate a thorough understanding of existing departmental strengths and weaknesses into their strategic framework or policy-making approach. For their part, senior officials never attempted to pilot new policies or make other organizational changes to facilitate implementation.[2] The result was that migration governance stagnated—and in some cases deteriorated. In the words of one official "in many of the places the function stagnated. It didn't die, it was just never done properly, because of this ongoing dispute of quite a few years" (interview with Willem Vorster, assistant director of investigations, Department of Home Affairs, July 7, 2006).

These problems were compounded by confusion between immigration duties and other forms of governance. Since the transition to democracy, the Department of Home Affairs has been responsible not only for the Chief Directorate for Migration (responsible for ports of entry, permits, refugees, enforcement, and deportations) but also for civic affairs (births, deaths, marriages, voter registration, and identification documents).[3] The main result has been that budgetary and human resources have been drawn away from immigration policing to other duties, including distributing identification documents to people in rural areas, conducting mass identification campaigns in the lead-up to elections, and dealing with peak migration flows through ports during special events (interviews with Claude Shravesande, chairman of the Standing Committee for Refugee Affairs, Department of Home Affairs, June 21, 2006, and Willem Vorster, assistant director of investigations, Department of Home Affairs, July 7, 2006).[4] Human resources have not simply been diverted from immigration enforcement. According to almost all senior officials, Department of Home Affairs' employees lack the competence to perform their tasks or fulfill their basic duties. A combination of old constraints from the apartheid era and poor management during the transition period has ensured that the Department of Home Affairs has never met its human resource needs. The department was historically the employer of last resort within the South African government, rarely attracting or maintaining the highest-quality civil service recruits (interview with Mario Ambrosini, former special advisor to the Minister of Home Affairs, September 22, 2006). Immigration officers have resisted incorporation into broader departmental decision making and strategy since the Aliens Control Bureau was transplanted into the Department of Home Affairs during the late 1970s. This infighting helped generate an institutional culture characterized by poor discipline and low morale (interview with Attie Tredoux, former chief legal officer, Department of Home Affairs, June 21, 2006, and Willem Vorster, assistant director of investigations, Department of Home Affairs, July 7, 2006).

As a result of the resistance of the Department of Public Administration, until recently the Department of Home Affairs was only allowed to demand that its entry-level officers pass standard 10 (two years of formal education before the end of secondary school) (interviews with Claude Shravesande, chairman of the Standing Committee for Refugee Affairs, Department of Home Affairs, June 21, 2006, and Willem Vorster, assistant director of investigations, Department of Home Affairs, July 7, 2006). The enormous sums spent by the department upgrading its surveillance technology have been largely wasted, as few immigration officials are able to use the technology to conduct routine status or identification checks.[5] These problems have been exacerbated by the mismanagement and politicization of departmental "transformation." The promotion of a new generation of directors and workers took place through forced redundancies of senior staff, with little consideration as to how the department could draw on the experience of senior employees (interviews with Claude Shravesande, chairman of the Standing Committee for Refugee Affairs, Department of Home Affairs, June 21, 2006, and Willem Vorster, assistant director of investigations, Department of Home Affairs, July 7, 2006).[6] The ANC has yet to address the problems of lack of esprit de corps, incompetence, and inexperience, which reached crisis proportions at the turn of the millennium.

Even if the department had the most competent civil servants in South Africa, it would still lack an adequate chain of command. The Department of Home Affairs does not possess the oversight mechanisms to regulate the performance of enforcement duties. In part, this problem stems from the transition to democracy. The Department of Home Affairs has been struggling to create a unified and centrally managed organization out of the disparate and spatially segmented apartheid bureaucracy.[7] As a result, its local branches appear to decide on their own how they will enforce immigration law. Officials have only a loose understanding of their mandate, which may diverge significantly from the principles espoused by departmental policy documents (interview with Willem Vorster, assistant director of investigations, Department of Home

Affairs, July 7, 2006). In some cases, this loose enforcement structure results in a peculiar state of affairs in which upper-level management relies on the judiciary to perform its oversight functions, checking and sanctioning the practices of junior staff (interview with Claude Shravesande, chairman of the Standing Committee for Refugee Affairs, Department of Home Affairs, June 21, 2006).

These problems do not stem solely from the limited competence of junior bureaucrats at the Department of Home Affairs: policy-making elites are not equipped to perform oversight functions or implement strategic change. They are particularly lacking in the realm of information management. The department appears to have lost large portions of its archives and to lack the means to readily access its own documents (interviews with Claude Shravesande, chairman of the Standing Committee for Refugee Affairs, Department of Home Affairs, June 21, 2006; Ivan Lambinon, former deputy director general for Migration, Printing Works, and Publication Control, Department of Home Affairs, July 14, 2006; and Ntlakana Gcinumzi, chief director of the Inspectorate, Department of Home Affairs, July 11, 2006). In the mid-1990s, the department could readily produce figures citing the number of workplaces visited and employers convicted of immigration offenses and clearly delineate between its own arrests of undocumented migrants and those made by other enforcement agencies.[8] In recent years, baseline figures on the total number of deportations appear to be the primary statistical measure of policy performance (interview with Attie Tredoux, July 21, 2006). Thus, officials have few means, apart from direct instruction, to ensure that their staffs learn from past successes and mistakes in the enforcement field.

Immigration Control in the 2000s: Giving Up Although Succeeding

As these and other problems with the Department of Home Affairs became more apparent to policy makers, senior officials expressed their disillusionment with the ideal of immigration control. In policy debates, this (often begrudging) conclusion originally stemmed from policy makers' reflection on speculative estimates of the number of undocumented migrants in the country. Although estimates based on sound demographic methods have been rare, guesses ranging from 1 million to 8 million continued to resurface in the press in the early years of the last decade. These figures led former director-general William Masetlha to report to Parliament in 2000 that "even in the unlikely event of all further illegal migration into the country being halted and their presence remaining constant at the 8 million ballpark figure, the removal of them at the current rate of 180,000 per year would take a total of 44 years" (Parliamentary Monitoring Group 2000).

In 2003 Mangosuthu Buthelezi, then minister of the Department of Home Affairs, came to the morose conclusion that "to think we will ever overcome the problem is a dream" (Peta 2003). Although couched in somewhat more measured tones, the ANC has made similar public acknowledgments since taking charge of the Home Affairs portfolio. Former Deputy Minister for Home Affairs Malusi Gigaba consistently reiterated that international migration was an "inevitable process" rather than a reversible trend (Gigaba 2010). Similar positions have been consistently voiced throughout the junior ranks of immigration officialdom— not surprising, given that undocumented migration is not a question of abstract figures for these officials but of the daily grind involved in regulating border crossings, processing permits, and investigating offenses. According to an official in the Immigration Inspectorate in Johannesburg responsible for detecting and deporting illegal foreigners in the country's most populous province, "It's really not humanly possible."

Despite this consensus about the limits of controls, there has been little clarity on what might be the main features of an alternative immigration policy. During his tenure, Gigaba consistently signaled the need to shift paradigms to a policy focused on migration "management." However, in the several years that he held the post, these themes were never strongly taken up. Instead, policy consisted of a series of tentative and ad hoc initiatives designed to address issues once they had already snowballed into crises.

The departmental response to the Zimbabwean crisis is a case in point. Since 2000, the political and economic crisis in Zimbabwe has forced large numbers of Zimbabweans to flee to South Africa and other neighboring countries in search of refuge, aid, and employment. As these problems worsened, it became clear that informal migration across the border between South Africa and Zimbabwe was increasing dramatically. In 2007 a flurry of media reporting documented Zimbabweans swimming the Limpopo River, ducking under fences, and evading border guards at the Beitbridge border post (Vigneswaran 2007). Despite these signs, the Department of Home Affairs did not pull back on its strict border regulations, deportation of illegal migrants, or lengthy case-by-case consideration of asylum applications. Not until the postelection violence of 2008 led to a further spike in refugee and migrant numbers did the department give serious consideration to new policy instruments that would address the crisis, including the establishment of camps on the border, visa-free entry into South Africa, and the creation of a special temporary permit for Zimbabwean nationals.

In the eight years before the Department of Home Affairs developed a Zimbabwe policy, officials were compelled to adopt their own approaches to the crisis. In the absence of clear signals or decisive policy changes at the top, government officials generally continued to implement control-oriented principles and practices. Police and army officials increased the resources devoted to patrolling the border with Zimbabwe, searching for new entrants and deporting them back across the border. Although recognizing the shortcomings of such approaches, officials expressed resolve to continue working in this fashion. In the glib assessment of the Musina police commissioner, detecting and arresting illegal foreigners could, at the very least, give you a "reason to get up in the morning" (interview with Commissioner Mathebula, South African Police Services, March 22, 2008).

In some respects, control-oriented solutions have hardened in the absence of competing policy options. In certain parts of Gauteng, the destination for large numbers of Zimbabwean nationals, police officials regularly encounter undocumented nationals in the course of their patrol duties. Lacking much direction from above, specific stations and officers have poured considerable time and energy into eradicating this "problem." On average, Gauteng police officers spend more than a quarter of their time at work searching for, arresting, and deporting foreign nationals (Vigneswaran and Duponchel 2009).

Another example of this trend can be found in the system for determining refugee status. Officials have been inundated with hundreds of thousands of requests for asylum by Zimbabwean nationals. In an apparent effort to cope with this administrative burden, officials have adopted a variety of short-cut techniques and procedures to expedite the process, almost all of which entail denying applicants' refugee claims (Amit 2010).

Similar stories can be told about a range of other policy initiatives, including efforts to address the backlog in asylum applications or to improve service delivery in the department and the decision by the South African Police Service to "deprioritize" immigration policing in the central province of Gauteng. Although policy makers have regularly and openly recognized the failures of control-oriented policies and flirted with alternatives, they have usually decisively implemented new policies only in conditions of crisis. In this context, lower-level officials have hardened their positions and approaches, resulting in an increasingly hard-line policy framework.

These dynamics do not play out only in particular offices or cliques within the administration—impacts also can be felt at the macro level. Over the past 15 years, while senior policy makers have slowly approached the conclusion that a control-oriented solution is ineffective, junior South African officials have collectively been developing a highly effective deportation system. Between 1995 and 2010, South Africa arrested and deported more than 150,000 people a year (Department of Home Affairs' Annual Reports; see appendix table C.6). In per capita terms, this makes South Africa one of the world's most prolific deporters of foreign nationals. Paradoxically, the more policy makers have realized that controls do not work, the more active policy implementers have been in enforcing controls. This trend abated somewhat in April 2010 with the temporary moratorium on deportations of Zimbabweans. The moratorium ended in January 2011, however, when deportations resumed.

Enforcement in Practice

Senior immigration officials have struggled to mobilize government agencies, principally the Department of Home Affairs, to implement immigration control policies. Despite—or perhaps because of—the lack of clarity from above, the bureaucratic corps have hardened their position on undocumented migration and poured increasing resources into their efforts.

This section sketches some of the implications these institutional developments have for governance of migration. It examines the enforcement of immigration controls at the border post with Zimbabwe, in permit-processing offices in the country's interior, and by street-level policing in Johannesburg. Although the largely ethnographic nature of these analyses precludes broad generalization, the snapshots suggest that regulatory structures in and practices of both the Department of Home Affairs and the South African Police Service have developed autonomous and extralegal mechanisms of controlling immigration. The main implication of these findings is that immigration policy in South Africa may be increasingly determined from below and resistant to direction from above.

The Border with Zimbabwe

A large proportion of informal entries to South Africa takes place east and west of the Beitbridge border post, which straddles the Limpopo River and separates the South African town of Musina and the Zimbabwean town of Beitbridge. Over the past few years, police in this area have considerably increased their capacity to control migration by establishing new reconnaissance and detention facilities and diverting general policing resources across the region into a range of other immigration enforcement activities (road blocks, patrols at bus stations, and so forth). This approach does not appear to be the result of national level policy or legislation but rather a product of the ad hoc initiative of local officials.

Although most of this activity lies within the legally and procedurally mandated authority of the South African Police Service, in their efforts to extend state capacity to regulate cross-border migration, police officials have often stretched the meaning of, or deliberately and directly flouted, the law. At the level of local strategy, the South African Police Service established a detention facility in Musina where suspected "illegal foreigners" (the term used in the Immigration Act of 2002) are housed and processed before deportation. Zimbabweans are often deported from this facility without oversight from the Department of Home Affairs or the opportunity to claim asylum.[9] South African officials have often acted outside their legal mandate to ensure that South African territory is defended against migration flows, illegally denying transit permits to about one in every five asylum seekers and entering into illegal quasi–pass law arrangements with farmers in the border area to prevent migrant workers from moving to the interior (Human Rights Watch 2006). Even officials who recognized the limitations of the border control ideal were resigned to their role in its regular reinforcement. As one police officer commented, "Sometimes we just let them in because we feel that even if we deport them they will come tomorrow ... they will never stop coming and we will never stop arresting them, it is like that here" (interview with police officer in Musina, March 22, 2008).

Immigration control is not always aimed at excluding migrants: in many cases immigration control serves as a front for corrupt practices. For at least a decade, smugglers have developed discrete and packaged services to assist migrants who can spare the cash to cross the border informally.[10] The loosely bound network of transport operators, negotiators, hawkers, guides, and (to a lesser extent) officials that run the human smuggling industry have created a parallel border management system. Although rarely impinging on the activities of smugglers themselves, members of the South African Police Services have on occasion become competitors for this smuggling trade. Indeed, a 2008 visit to Beitbridge revealed that the least expensive of the various smuggling services was wholly run by the South African Police Service. Officials at the Beitbridge border post charge R 50 (about $5.75) for undocumented entry to one side of the facility and R 50 for unauthorized exit on the other.

In summary, conditions on South Africa's borders suggest that immigration control functions are commonly implemented with little reference to centrally mandated law or policy. The Department of Home Affairs alleviated some of the pressure on its borders by signing visa-free movement agreements with Mozambique (2005) and Zimbabwe (2009). However, these moves have had only marginal impacts on the ongoing efforts of the South African Police Service to track and trace undocumented entrants, bolster border defense systems, and in some cases profit from informal movement of migrants across borders. Although various initiatives have sought to streamline border management over the past decade—including efforts to remove the army from involvement in border patrols and the designation of the Department of Home Affairs as the lead department for border management—they have not been effectively communicated to officials on the border, who appear to decide for themselves how the border should be managed.

Permit-Processing Offices

It is not simply the border that has proven resistant to central administration and policy. Similar dynamics are evident at permit-processing offices.

Once across the border, informal migrants have the limited "choice" between attempting to legalize their stay and attempting to ensure that their presence remains undetected. Migrants who prefer to legalize their stay find it difficult to obtain accurate information regarding the proper channels, except through the Zimbabwean Documentation Project, implemented in 2010 (see chapter 1). High demand for legalization services is reflected by the extraordinarily long and slow-moving lines outside all of the country's refugee reception offices (Forced Migration Studies Programme 2009).

Much like their colleagues on the border, officials at South Africa's permit-processing offices face what must appear to be a never-ending stream of migrants seeking to legitimize their stay. Many officials simply assume that it is their obligation to shore up South Africa's porous borders by deterring, undermining, and denying applications for asylum in South Africa. Often this deterrence does not take the "hard" form of citing a specific law that makes an individual ineligible to stay. Instead, officials erect "soft" barriers, including unnecessary delays, development of new "procedures," and failure to provide assistance during the labyrinthine application process.

Department of Home Affairs' officials commonly help transform bureaucratic procedures into major obstacles for migrants and, in some cases, their agents. Surveys conducted at these offices suggest that officials commonly make applicants wait longer to enter the office than the duration of their transit permits; interfere in applicants' efforts to fill out forms while not providing help to those who need it; and withhold crucial information from applicants, thereby increasing the likelihood that they will slip up in their interviews with status determination officers (Forced Migration Studies Programme 2007). Officials share a broad belief that migrants have an "easy ride," a belief that helps them rationalize and legitimize the persistence of informal administrative barriers. According to many clerks at the visa permits office, there is a need to make it more difficult for migrants to reside in South Africa, especially as migrants can enter South Africa on a particular permit and then change the purpose of their stay, something a number of higher- and lower-level officials termed "abusing the system."

The transformation process introduced by Mvuso Msimang from 2007 to 2009 focused on improving the ethic of service delivery at all Department of Home Affairs' offices. This project was performance oriented: it set targets for offices for the number of clients served, decisions finalized, and permits issued. Annual reports of the department indicate significant improvements across several indicators. However, in many cases these objectives were achieved through measures that closed off rather than opened up services to foreign migrants.

Street-Level Policing
For the majority of Zimbabwean migrants who fail to acquire or maintain a valid permit, life in South Africa can be an ongoing game of high-stakes hide-and-seek with the police and, to a lesser extent, officials from the Department

of Home Affairs.[11] In inner-city areas of Johannesburg such as Berea, Hillbrow, and Yeoville, large sections of the population are Zimbabwean, many of them undocumented.[12] The daily work of the South African Police Service and Metropolitan Police (patrolling city streets, raiding buildings, and conducting routine traffic inspections) often yields arrests of Zimbabwean migrants.[13]

During the period under review, the South African Police Service, while never formally adopting a policy on illegal migration, identified linkages between undocumented migrants and crime, referred to policing the illegal movement of persons as a major line function, and described the enforcement of immigration laws as a potentially useful method of dealing with certain categories of criminals (South African Police Service 1997). In pursuit of this independent agenda, they sought to beef up border-policing operations in conjunction with the South African National Defence Force (Hechter 1999). They also conducted large-scale operational policing in areas of high crime and dense migrant populations, which led to the arrests of large numbers of "illegal foreigners." Operation Crackdown was the most famous of these operations. In 2002 police, army, and metropolitan and Department of Home Affairs' agencies conducted coordinated sweeps of crime hot-spots, arresting more than 50,000 people for contravening the Immigration Act.

Citywide efforts have been bolstered by the actions of some individual stations. As part of the city's broader strategy to "retake control" of high crime areas that are believed to be beholden to armed criminal groups (City of Johannesburg 2004), the Johannesburg central police station initiated three policies targeted at informal migrants (suspected to constitute the accomplices and clients of criminal organizations). First, to "deter" illegals from coming to the precinct, the South African Police Service instituted a policy of charging suspected illegal foreigners with immigration offenses and asking the courts to impose maximum sentences (90 days in prison or a police cell).[14] Second, to combat migrant criminality, the police conducted raids on buildings and areas known to have high migrant concentrations, such as bars and squatter settlements. Third, the precinct deployed large numbers of "reservist" police officers to do most of the legwork for their regular "visible policing" sweeps. Reservists do not receive salaries and have a limited understanding of immigration laws, but they wear uniforms and carry firearms and account for significant numbers of arrests of suspected "illegal foreigners." Although senior officials realize that these policies create opportunities for corrupt behavior by junior officials, they regard such outcomes as unfortunate externalities of tactics that help reassert police authority over "crime-ridden" areas (interview with Superintendant Lategan, South African Police Services, April 8, 2008).

Junior officers also often autonomously make use of their powers under immigration laws. In the inner city, racial and ethnic profiling and interviews to determine an individual's immigration status appear to constitute the first step in most ad hoc police investigations. In the same way that police officers in other cities might use loitering laws, petty traffic infringements, and jaywalking to initiate investigations of suspects, in Johannesburg immigration law serves as the primary entry point into broader investigations (Herbert 1997). Indeed, policing in the inner city has come to resemble a vast immigration control exercise, albeit with a range of circumstantial and chance "spillover" effects on broader crime-fighting initiatives.

As with immigration enforcement on the border, policing in the city often involves high levels of corrupt activity. Police officers routinely engage in intimidation and extortion of, and simple theft from, Zimbabweans and migrants of other nationalities. Of 51 interactions between a police officer and a member of the public observed for this report, 35 percent involved the police officer soliciting a bribe. One in every four incidents involved the officer receiving or taking money or an object (often a cell phone) from the "suspect."

These practices at the level of local policing are unlikely to be significantly moderated by policy measures by either the police or the Department of Home Affairs. One of the central planks of the Zuma administration has been an increased focus on serious and violent crime. As part of this agenda, the former police commissioner of Gauteng Perumal Naidoo issued an instruction to all officers in his province to cease conducting immigration enforcement operations and adopt strategies that focused on the prevention of and response to priority crimes. Despite this order, officers in Gauteng have continued to arrest huge numbers of foreign nationals, vastly outperforming other provinces.

Resistance to policy instructions was also evident during the 2009–10 moratorium on deportations of Zimbabwean nationals. Despite the fact that Zimbabweans could not be deported from the Lindela detention facility, police officials from across Gauteng continued to arrive with carloads of suspected Zimbabwean "illegals" and leave them in Department of Home Affairs' custody. Thus, much like conditions at the border and in permit-processing offices, immigration control on the city streets has acquired a life of its own.

Conclusion

Despite its gloomy tale, this chapter gives some reasons for optimism. Over the past decade, the belief among senior policy makers that the government can solve its immigration problems through force alone waned. The xenophobic violence of 2008 served as a wake-up call about the dangers of institutional neglect. It is plausible to suggest that there are a series of openings for South African policy makers and their regional and international partners to offer new solutions and design new policy frameworks in the coming decade. This is a welcome departure from the strident nationalism of the apartheid era and the anti-foreigner tone of the Inkatha Freedom Party.

The overriding theme of this chapter is a cautionary one, however. Much work needs to be done for new ideas and principles to be realized in practice. The bureaucracy of immigration control in South Africa appears unresponsive to policy dictates. Decades of neglect have produced a range of deeply embedded control-oriented practices that lower-level officials adhere to regardless of the signals from above or the goals of their departments. Given these factors, immigration policy cannot be reformed merely by designing new legislation. Rather, reformers will need to engage with departments and provide new incentive structures to ensure that new policies are taken up and mainstreamed in everyday bureaucratic practice. Unless such efforts are made, key components of the South African state may become hollowed out by corruption and disorder, recalcitrant to policy prescriptions emanating from the center.

Notes

1. Over the past two decades, Zimbabwe has experienced a profound economic and political crisis, involving the collapse of economic production, hyperinflation, and mass unemployment, compounded by political conflict and repression. As a result of this crisis, hundreds of thousands of Zimbabweans have sought refuge and economic opportunity in neighboring countries and further abroad.
2. For a rare example of an official noting an intention to employ this approach, see the comments of a Western Cape immigration official in Wilhelm (1998).
3. To complicate issues, for a short period (1995–97), the Migration Directorate was also responsible for government printing and publication control (censorship and information management).
4. This statement contrasts with the official position stated by former director-general Billy Masetlha (apparently stemming from interdepartmental meetings on the issue) that problems lay in the total number of immigration officers (Parliamentary Monitoring Group 2000b).
5. "We've got one of the best systems in the world. And if you use it properly it is incredible what you can do with it. But they do not know that. Most of them don't have access to it. They have never bothered to get the access, because they have never been trained" (interview with Willem Vorster, assistant director of investigations, Department of Home Affairs, July 7, 2006).
6. The claim that these human resource issues stem from the department's small budget is countered by the fact that upper-level management positions in Pretoria and lower-level positions at the regional level have been routinely left unfilled.
7. The process of incorporating the former homelands agencies began in 1993–94.
8. See, for example, the figures cited in the appendix of Minaar and Hough (1996).
9. In May 2009 the Gauteng High Court ruled that the Musina facility was unlawful and unconstitutional and ordered it to be closed. Despite this rule, the Department of Home Affairs and the South African Police Service continued to use the facility (CoRMSA 2009).

10. One smuggler interviewed in April 2008 had been working in the area since 1995.
11. Even the possession of a valid permit may not provide immunity. In a survey of 404 detainees at Lindela, the center where migrants are held pending deportation, 68 percent claimed to have been in possession of a permit allowing them to be in South Africa when they were arrested. Almost half of those with such permits (47 percent) claim that their permits were valid at the time. For details of the study, see Sutton and Vigneswaran (2011).
12. A survey on livelihoods in inner-city areas found that at least one-third of residents were Zimbabwean (34 percent in Berea, 39 percent in Hillbrow, and 39 percent in Yeoville). About one-fifth of all residents living in these areas did not possess valid documentation permitting them to reside in South Africa.
13. In a separate survey, 60 percent of detainees at the Lindela detention center reported that they were originally arrested by the police or by a group of officials, including police officers. For a detailed explanation of these dynamics, see Vigneswaran (2008).
14. Custody of suspected "illegal foreigners" would customarily be transferred to the Department of Home Affairs.

References

Amit, R. 2010. *Protection and Pragmatism: Addressing Administrative Failures in South Africa's Refugee Status Determination System.* Forced Migration Studies Programme, University of the Witwatersrand, Johannesburg.

City of Johannesburg. 2004. *Johannesburg Inner City Regeneration Strategy.*

CoRMSA. 2009. *Protecting Refugees, Asylum Seekers and Migrants in South Africa.* Johannesburg: CoRMSA.

Forced Migration Studies Programme. 2007. *Barriers to Asylum: The Marabastad Refugee Reception Office.* University of the Witwatersrand, Johannesburg.

———. 2009. *National Survey of the Refugee Reception and Status Determination System in South Africa.* University of the Witwatersrand, Johannesburg. http://www.migration .org.za/report/national-survey-refugee-reception-and-status-determination-system-south-africa, retrieved on September 15.

Gigaba, M. 2010. Address at "Conference on Legal and Social Security Protection Perspectives on Migration in South Africa," University of Cape Town. http://www.info. gov.za/speech/DynamicAction?pageid=461andsid=7748andtid=11153.

Hechter, Z. 1999. "Ambush in a Thunder Storm." *Diverse Publikasies,* June 30.

Herbert, S. K. 1997. *Policing Space: Territoriality and the Los Angeles Police Department,* Minneapolis: University of Minnesota Press.

Human Rights Watch. 2006. *Unprotected Migrants: Zimbabweans in South Africa's Limpopo Province.* http://www.hrw.org/en/reports/2006/08/07/unprotected-migrants.

Minaar, A., and M. Hough. 1996. *Causes, Extent and Impact of Clandestine Migration in Selected Southern African Countries with Specific Reference to South Africa.* Human Sciences Research Council, Pretoria.

Parliamentary Monitoring Group. 2000. "Presentation to the Parliamentary Portfolio Committee on Home Affairs." By B.L. Masetlha, Director-General, March 7, http:// www.pmg.org.za/minutes/20000306-budget-briefing-director-general-and-minister. Accessed June 302011.

————. 2006a. "Deputy President Briefing on Accelerated and Shared Growth Initiative." February 6. http://www.pmg.org.za/briefings/briefings.php?id=246.

————. 2000b. "Minutes of the Portfolio Committee on Home Affairs." March 7.

Peta, B. 2003. "Illegal Immigrants Are a Perpetual Problem Compounded by Corruption, Says Buthelezi." *Cape Times,* October 14.

South African Police Service. 1997. *Annual Report* 1996/97. Pretoria.

Sutton, R., and D. Vigneswaran. 2011. "A Kafkaesque State: Deportation and Detention in South Africa." *Citizenship Studies.*

Vigneswaran, D. 2007. "Fact or Fiction: Examining Zimbabwean Cross-Border Migration into South Africa." *Migrant Rights Monitoring Project Occasional Report 2007/B,* Forced Migration Studies Programme, University of the Witwatersrand, Johannesburg.

————. 2008. "Enduring Territoriality: South African Immigration Control." *Political Geography* 27: 783–801.

Vigneswaran, D., and M. Duponchel. 2009. "One Burden Too Many? A Cost-Benefit Analysis of Immigration Policing in Gauteng." Forced Migration Studies Programme, University of the Witwatersrand, Johannesburg.

Wilhelm, P. 1998. "Fortress SA Bites Some of the Hands That Feed It." *Financial Mail,* April 10.

Chapter 5

Migration and Health in South Africa: Implications for Development

Joanna Vearey

Migration is a central determinant of health, requiring appropriate policy and program responses (MacPherson and Gushulak 2001; Anarfi 2005).[1] In the southern African region, migration represents a key livelihood-seeking strategy for poor households. In cases where migrants are able to provide a range of resources to their linked households (including money for school fees and healthcare), migration contributes to social and economic development at the household level. However, for these development-associated benefits of migration to be realized, migration itself must be managed in a healthy way; population mobility must be recognized as a central public health imperative.

The 2009 *Human Development Report* acknowledges that migration can contribute to social and economic development (UNDP 2009). Without the migration of skilled and semi-skilled labor, South Africa will not meet its long-term development targets (Landau and Wa Kabwe-Segatti 2009). This chapter argues that attaining development targets—including targets set by the South African government, as well as the internationally ratified Millennium Development Goals (MDGs)—requires (among other measures) a focus on the health of internal and cross-border migrant populations. Ensuring and sustaining the good health of populations is a critical development challenge within southern Africa, at both national and regional levels. Exploring migration through a public health lens highlights a range of tensions that need to be addressed in order to strengthen public health responses, including those of public healthcare systems, for all within the region. Such responses do not currently engage equitably with all population groups, and migrants, particularly cross-border migrants, experience challenges in accessing public healthcare systems in southern Africa.

Historically, migrants within the southern African region have been at increased risk of a range of negative health outcomes, largely because of their inability to access positive social determinants of health, defined as "the full set of social conditions in which people live and work" (Commission on the

Social Determinants of Health 2007: 44). It is not being a migrant per se that increases health risks but the context associated with being a poor migrant.[2] Positive social determinants of health include the health system, food and nutrition security, adequate housing and tenure, access to safe water and sanitation, secure livelihood activities, social networks, and family support. All of these determinants are affected by the socioeconomic and political context, including factors associated with governance and policy (WHO 2008). Migrants, both internal and cross-border, may be excluded from accessing preventative and curative care (through legislation or through challenges in accessing services), and they may reside in unhealthy spaces where health risks are high, such as hostels and other unhealthy spaces that disrupt social networks and family structures. Living in such conditions has been shown to be related to the spread of tuberculosis (caused by overcrowding) and sexually transmitted infections, including HIV/AIDS, exacerbated by the disruption of social and sexual networks within the region. Migration associated with labor can expose individuals to occupational health hazards, including silicosis among miners. Cross-border migrants are likely to face challenges in accessing the health system (a central determinant of health), resulting in delayed medical care and treatment. Migrants are also exposed to a range of communicable diseases (including HIV/AIDS, tuberculosis, and malaria) that require appropriate and often long-term treatment. Maternal and child health is affected when migrant populations are excluded from public healthcare systems. It is the social and political context, in this case related to migration, that results in differential exposures to health-damaging conditions, differential vulnerabilities to illness, and differential consequences of ill health.

Migrants are positively selected: they are healthy and of a productive age at the time they migrate. However, the conditions within which both internal and cross-border migrants reside in urban, and increasingly, informal urban, areas negatively affect their health, mostly through the inability to access positive social determinants of health (WHO 2008). Public health authorities are faced with the challenge of both maintaining the good health of migrants in urban and peri-urban spaces and responding to their needs once they return to (predominantly) rural areas once they become too sick to work (Clark and others 2007). To meet these challenges, health systems and public health programs must respond in a "spatially sensitive" fashion (Collinson and others 2010). A "spatially-sensitive" approach to healthcare provision requires that different levels of government engage across the urban-rural continuum in order to ensure that the system responds to the changing health needs of migrants who return home in times of sickness.

This chapter examines the unequal access to public healthcare experienced by migrant groups and the dangers it poses to public health. The health of migrant populations is about more than their access to public healthcare services. However, this chapter focuses on access to healthcare, itself a central determinant of health. It argues that denying migrant populations timely access to appropriate healthcare (including both preventative and curative services) puts the health of the entire population at risk. In a region where communicable diseases—including tuberculosis, HIV/AIDS, and malaria—are prevalent, it is essential that access to healthcare for all be ensured.

The chapter examines five key questions:

- Why is health critical in the relationship between migration and development?
- Does healthcare-seeking affect regional migration into South Africa?
- Does the presence of regional migrants negatively affect South Africa's public health system?
- How can the gap between health policies, which uphold the right to access emergency and basic healthcare, and the challenges experienced by regional migrants in trying to access public healthcare within South Africa be reconciled?
- How is the provision of healthcare to migrants affecting the health and livelihoods of regional migrants and other South Africans?

The chapter proposes a policy response to ensure that a process of "healthy migration" can be implemented within the region and outlines future research needs.

This chapter draws on a range of studies conducted in South Africa, including empirical studies by the African Centre for Migration and Society at the University of the Witwatersrand between 2007 and 2010. Initial research exploring migration and health focused on determining whether the rights of cross-border migrants to access public healthcare were being upheld and in collecting data to challenge prevailing, and unsubstantiated, claims from within policy spheres that migrants were coming to South Africa in order to access healthcare, including antiretroviral therapy for HIV/AIDS. This question led to the identification of additional research questions and ongoing research studies that focus on the complex linkages between migration, livelihoods, and health. These studies adopt a public health lens to explore how migration and health are interrelated. Employing a range of both quantitative and qualitative techniques, these studies allow the relationship between migration and health to be explored and implications for development to be discussed. (Details on the methodologies of these studies can be found in Vearey 2008 and Vearey and others 2010.)

Health, Migration, and Development: Protective Policy?

Progressive changes in legislation have been made since the end of apartheid that should help uphold the right to access healthcare for all in South Africa. Despite the changes, both internal and cross-border migrants continue to experience challenges in accessing public healthcare (ARASA 2008; Harper and Raman 2008; Amon and Todrys 2009; CoRMSA 2009; Human Rights Watch 2009a, 2009b).

According to the law, refugees and asylum seekers should be treated as South African citizens in terms of access to free public healthcare (Refugee Act of 1998, Act No. 130). Different categories of regional migrants are granted differential rights to access free public healthcare services. Noncitizens with work or study permits, for example, are supposed to be charged a fee at the point of use.

The multiple pieces of legislation and guidelines can be confusing. Section 27 of the South African Constitution guarantees "access to health care for all." The National Health Act (2003) and the Constitution ensure everyone in the country, regardless of immigration status, access to life-saving care. The Refugees Act (1998) provides particular rights to legally recognized refugees but is ambiguous regarding the rights of noncitizen groups to public health services, including antiretroviral therapy (UNHCR and the AIDS and Human Rights Research Unit 2006). The documents noncitizens hold (for example, refugee, asylum seeker, and the range of temporary residence permits) present challenges to service providers, who may not be familiar with different documentation. In addition, national guiding documents, such as the 2007–11 National Strategic Plan for HIV/AIDS and sexually transmitted infections, use the terms *asylum seeker, refugee,* and *foreign migrant* interchangeably, creating confusion for practitioners (National Department of Health 2007a).

South Africa began to roll out a free national antiretroviral therapy program in the public health sector in April 2004. Attempts have been made to clarify the rights of international migrants to such therapy. The 2007–11 National Strategic Plan specifically includes noncitizens (National Department of Health 2007a). A key guiding principle to the successful implementation of the plan is "ensuring equality and non discrimination against marginalized groups"; refugees, asylum seekers, and foreign migrants are specifically mentioned as having "a right to equal access to interventions for HIV/AIDS prevention, treatment and support" (National Department of Health 2007a). Priority Area 4 of the plan encompasses human rights and access to justice; goal 16 ensures "public knowledge of and adherence to the legal and policy provision" (National Department of Health 2007a).

In early 2006, the National Department of Health issued a statement clarifying that patients do not need to hold a South African identity booklet in order to access antiretroviral therapy. This statement has implications not only for international migrants but also for undocumented South Africans.[3] Additional guidelines on the provision of antiretroviral therapy for international migrants, asylum seekers, and refugees—developed through collaboration between the Southern African HIV Clinicians Society and the United Nations High Commissioner for Refugees (UNHCR)—supplement the National

Department of Health antiretroviral therapy guidelines (Southern African HIV Clinicians Society and UNHCR 2007). As a result of the lobbying of civil society groups and the UNHCR, in September 2007 a financial directive from the National Department of Health confirmed that refugees and asylum seekers—with or without an asylum seeker or refugee permit granted by the Department of Home Affairs—have the same right as South Africans to free basic healthcare and antiretroviral therapy in the public sector (National Department of Health 2007b).

Despite these policy guidelines and frameworks, international migrants continue to face challenges when they attempt to access public health services in South Africa (Pursell 2004; Landau 2006b; Vearey 2008; Amon and Todrys 2009; CoRMSA 2009; Human Rights Watch 2009a, 2009b). International migrants often struggle to communicate with healthcare providers (interpreters are not present), and some public health facilities generate their own guidelines and policies that run counter to national legislation, continuing, for example, to demand South African identity documents and denying access to international migrants (Vearey 2008; CoRMSA 2009). Although they rarely deny healthcare outright, frontline healthcare providers (including clerks and administrators) often act as "street-level bureaucrats," developing their own access systems for migrants (Moyo 2010). Regional migrants experience discrimination and negative attitudes from frontline healthcare workers, who often vent their own frustrations over working within an underresourced and overstretched public healthcare system on "the other" (Moyo 2010).

An additional problem is the inability of many lower-skilled international labor migrants to obtain the documentation they need to be in South Africa legally, caused by a restrictive immigration policy and poor implementation of this policy (Landau 2004; Vearey 2008). Access to documentation through the Department of Home Affairs is problematic for all international migrants, including refugees and asylum seekers (CoRMSA 2009; Landau 2006b) (see chapters 1 and 4).

South Africa is a member of the Southern African Development Community (SADC), a region with the highest HIV/AIDS prevalence in the world and historically high levels of internal and intraregional migration. In recognition of the important development-enhancing role that healthy migration can play within the region (Landau 2006a; CoRMSA 2009; UNDP 2009), SADC drafted a policy framework for population mobility and communicable diseases. The framework outlines the measures needed to address regional gaps in the control and management of communicable diseases (with a focus on tuberculosis, HIV/AIDS, and malaria) (SADC Directorate for Social and Human Development and Special Programs 2009). The framework makes reference to the principles endorsed in the founding charter of SADC, which emphasizes nondiscrimination; the African Charter on Human and Peoples'

Rights, which stresses the right to health; and the principles of equality and inalienability of rights.

Recently, migration and health have received renewed attention at the global level, through the 2008 World Health Assembly Resolution 61.17 on the Health of Migrants (Ghent 2008). The resolution calls on member states to ensure the health of migrant populations through a range of actions, including the following:

- Promotion of migrant-sensitive health policies.
- Promotion of equitable access to health promotion, disease prevention, and care for migrants.
- Establishment of health information systems, in order to facilitate the assessment and analysis of trends in migrants' health.
- The gathering, documenting, and sharing of information and best practices for meeting migrants' health needs in countries of origin or return, transit, and destination.
- Promotion of bilateral and multilateral cooperation on migrants' health among countries involved in the whole migratory process (World Health Assembly 2008).

Healthcare-Seeking and Migration: What Determines What?

Many people in South Africa believe that regional migrant populations are far larger than they are, that the movement of people is associated with poor health, and that regional migrants place an additional burden on the public health systems of destination countries (Southern African HIV Clinicians Society and UNHCR 2007). Globally, governments often blame "foreigners" for introducing and spreading disease (Amon and Todrys 2009; Harper and Raman 2008). The resultant marginalization of noncitizen groups has led to the conflation of health with the politics of citizenship, in many cases leading to the denial of healthcare to noncitizens (Grove and Zwi 2006).

International migrants continue to be portrayed as disease carriers who place burdens on the public health systems of destination countries (Grove and Zwi 2006; Harper and Raman 2008; Worth 2006). Concern over migrants has grown in the context of HIV/AIDS, with destination countries fearing that migrants bring the disease with them, potentially threatening the public health of host populations (Worth 2006; Amon and Todrys 2008). As a critical public health challenge in Southern Africa, the region most affected by HIV/AIDS globally, concerns relating to the disease need to be carefully considered within a context in which other communicable diseases (such as malaria and tuberculosis) are also prevalent; efforts to address the health of migrant populations must move beyond a focus on HIV/AIDS. In South Africa, increasingly violent xenophobic sentiments add a layer to the conflation of health and citizenship.

The African Centre for Migration and Society at the University of the Witswatersrand in Johannesburg conducted a range of surveys, reaching more than 6,000 respondents (Landau 2004, 2006b; CoRMSA 2009; Vearey and others 2010). The findings from these studies show that international migrants report moving to South Africa for economic reasons or to escape persecution, not to access healthcare services (CoRMSA 2009). Migrants are positively selected: the majority are healthy and young.

Findings from a cross-sectional household survey conducted in Johannesburg in 2008 show that rural households can benefit from migration through the receipt of remittances from urban migrants and that both internal and international migrants report that they plan to "return home" should they become too sick to work (Vearey, Nunez, and Palmary 2009); "home" is also the preferred place to die and be buried. This pattern appears to hold true for all categories of migrants, regardless of their employment status. Although both men and women report that they would return home to receive care, this movement is likely to be driven by the presence of women in the household "back home" who are able to provide that care.

These findings are supported by studies in rural South Africa that indicate that migrants tend to return home once they are too sick to work, usually because of tuberculosis or HIV/AIDS (Collinson and others 2006; Clark and others 2007; Collinson 2010). The sickness (and death) of urban migrants interrupts the flow of remittances and places a burden on the rural household that has to take care of the returning migrants.

Survey findings reveal that less than 5 percent of international migrants report ever bringing a sick relative to join them in the city; to care for ailing family members, migrants either send money or return home to provide care (Vearey, Nunez, and Palmary 2009). These findings challenge the assumptions that migrants move to urban areas in order to access healthcare services.

The National Public Service Access Survey conducted by the Migrant Rights Monitoring Project (coordinated by the African Centre for Migration and Society) polled more than 3,000 international migrants in five South African cities (Cape Town, Durban, Johannesburg, Port Elizabeth, and Pretoria) in 2007–08. These interviews were conducted with migrants seeking assistance at refugee reception offices and nongovernmental organizations (NGOs) that provide support to international migrants. Forty-five percent of respondents reported ever needing healthcare in South Africa. The longer migrants had been in South Africa, the greater the likelihood that they reported needing healthcare, indicating that migrants are not traveling into South Africa when sick in order to access healthcare. Thirty percent of respondents who reported ever needing healthcare experienced challenges when attempting to access public healthcare services. The most common challenges were being treated badly by a nurse, language problems, denial of treatment because of documentation problems, and denial of treatment for "being foreign." Undocumented migrants were the most likely to report problems, followed by asylum seekers and international migrants with other documentation (such as study and work permits). Refugees were least likely to encounter challenges when attempting to access public healthcare services in urban South Africa.

A 2007 cross-sectional survey of people receiving antiretroviral therapy at two government and two NGO sites in inner-city Johannesburg shows that international migrants encounter many more challenges than South African citizens do when attempting to access therapy in the public sector (Vearey 2008). The survey found that international migrants were frequently referred out of the public sector (often at the time of testing) and into the NGO sector. Many were unable to access antiretroviral therapy in the public sector because providers demanded South African identity booklets—in violation of national law. More than three-quarters of the international migrants interviewed accessed antiretroviral therapy in the NGO sector. The resultant dual healthcare system presents a range of logistical issues to healthcare providers and makes migrants reliant on a less sustainable form of access to care.

Do Regional Migrants Negatively Affect the Public Health System?

The public health rationale for providing healthcare to regional migrant groups is often overridden because of concerns about citizenship, legitimacy, entitlement, and a resource-constrained healthcare system (McNeill 2003; Grove and Zwi 2006; Amon and Todrys 2008; Harper and Raman 2008). South African policy makers and practitioners operating within the public healthcare system—including National Department of Health officials, facility managers, clinicians, nursing staff, and other frontline healthcare workers, including administrative staff—often voice concern about the financial impacts of providing healthcare (including antiretroviral therapy) to cross-border migrants. Some facilities generate their own guidelines that violate national law and deny (or make challenging) access to noncitizens. Some healthcare providers working within these institutions report that these guidelines prevent them from carrying out their job effectively. Some nongovernmental healthcare providers support the provision of healthcare to all within the country, regardless of nationality, and in many cases have set up services specifically for noncitizens.

Denying or delaying access to treatment and care leads to increased stress and sickness, reducing the ability of migrants to maintain (or regain) livelihood activities (Vearey 2008). It also raises serious public health concerns, as failing to treat people with communicable diseases may ultimately place the host population at risk, placing an even greater burden on the health system (Grove and Zwi 2006; Amon and Todrys 2008).

Unfounded assumptions prevail that international migrants are unable to adhere to antiretroviral therapy and that allowing them access to free therapy will result in a flood of HIV positive migrants into South Africa (Southern African HIV Clinicians Society and UNHCR 2007). A 2007 study on access to antiretroviral therapy (Vearey 2008) challenges these assumptions. It finds that half of the international migrants interviewed had been in South Africa for more than four years. The majority (76 percent) first tested for HIV in South Africa and 80 percent discovered their positive status while living in South Africa (Vearey 2008). Although the majority of international migrants included in the study tested for HIV and started on antiretroviral therapy within their first five years of being in South Africa, the longer an individual had been in the country, the more likely it was that he or she had tested positive for HIV and initiated treatment.

A clinical study conducted in Johannesburg (McCarthy and others 2009) indicates that, compared with citizens, international migrants receiving antiretroviral therapy had fewer hospital admissions, fewer missed appointments for antiretroviral therapy initiation, shorter median time to antiretroviral therapy initiation, better retention in care, and lower mortality. Overall, international migrants were less likely to fail antiretroviral therapy than citizens. This study provides strong evidence of good responses to antiretroviral therapy among international migrants and supports the recommendation of the UNHCR that antiretroviral therapy should not be withheld from migrant populations. These findings are supported by a study by the African Centre for Migration and Society that found no significant difference between the number of international migrant and citizen clients who reported they sometimes failed to show up for or did not adhere to treatment (Vearey 2008).

No costing studies have been undertaken within South Africa (or the region) to determine the financial implications of providing healthcare—including emergency care, basic care, and antiretroviral therapy—to regional migrants. Public healthcare facilities do not collect data on the nationality of or the documents held by their patients. As a result, facility-level data do not exist on the migration status of healthcare users.

Recent costing studies commissioned by the National Department of Health indicate that South Africa needs to invest in the provision of HIV/AIDS treatment for all who need it (Meyer-Rath 2010). Discussions regarding the introduction of national health insurance must acknowledge the presence of regional migrant groups. SADC is exploring healthcare financing mechanisms that might assist in addressing the cost implications of providing healthcare to migrant groups within member states. Despite the high levels of mobility and communicable diseases in Southern Africa, however, no costing studies have been conducted to assess the implications of regional financing mechanisms.

An additional factor to be considered is the role of NGO healthcare providers in the financing of healthcare. A range of NGOs provide free healthcare to both South African and noncitizen groups. It is important to acknowledge this contribution to the provision of healthcare, particularly within urban and border areas, where regional migrant populations tend to be concentrated. These urban and border areas have been identified as places where migrant populations experience the greatest challenges in accessing public healthcare services.

Particularly given the high prevalence of HIV/AIDS in the region, appropriate health responses are needed for South Africa's migrant population. Many changes in national policy and legislation have occurred in recent years; the data cited in this chapter may reflect a lag in the implementation of new directives. That said, legislation does not appear to be applied uniformly across public health facilities, raising concerns about the objectives outlined within the National Strategic Plan. The National Department of Health does not monitor the implementation of protective policy or hold to account facilities and healthcare providers that flaunt national directives. Upholding the right to access healthcare services for all within South Africa is likely to have a population-level benefit. South Africa needs to acknowledge health as a common public good and to ensure that funding strategies are developed to ensure that the health of all is upheld, including by monitoring the implementation of laws and policies.

Toward an Effective Policy Response

In order to ensure that the developmental benefits of migration are realized, a process of healthy migration needs to be facilitated (Vearey and Nunez 2010). All levels of government need to mainstream internal and cross-border movement in policies and programs. Public health responses need to be spatially sensitive in a way that considers the health of migrants (Collinson and others 2010). Policy makers need to recognize that most migrants move into urban areas in search of improved livelihood opportunities.

Including migration within policies and programs will help ensure that all migrant populations are able to access positive social determinants of health, including access to basic services (such as water and sanitation), adequate housing, food security, and public healthcare systems. The social determinants of health encompass "the full set of social conditions in which people live and work" (Commission on the Social Determinants of Health 2007). There is a need to understand the movements of both regional and internal migrants, particularly in relation to their healthcare-seeking and care-seeking migration decisions in times of sickness.

Migration is a global phenomenon. The 2009 *Human Development Report* identifies it as a key driver of human development (UNDP 2009). In Southern Africa, migration represents a key livelihood-seeking strategy for poor households. Where migrants are able to provide a range of resources to their linked households (including money for school fees and healthcare), migration contributes to social and economic development at the household level. For these development-associated benefits of migration to be realized, however, migration must be managed in a healthy way; population mobility must be recognized as a central public health imperative.

South Africa is structurally dependent on the migration of skilled and semi-skilled labor (Landau and Wa Kabwe-Segatti 2009). Attaining development targets—including targets set by the South African government, as well as the MDGs—requires (among other measures) a focus on the health of internal and regional migrant populations.

As a country of internal and cross-border migration, within a region of growing population mobility, South Africa must develop, implement, and monitor an evidence-based, coordinated, multilevel national and regional response to migration and health. Doing so requires spatially sensitive health and development responses that acknowledge the movement of people within South Africa and the region.

The 61st annual World Health Assembly adopted Resolution 61.17 on the Health of Migrants, which calls on member states (including South Africa) to promote equitable access to health promotion, disease prevention, and care for migrants (World Health Assembly 2008). Global, regional, and national meetings were subsequently held to discuss the resolution.[4] Recommendations from these meetings include the need to improve referrals between healthcare institutions (both within and across countries), develop "health passports" for internal and regional movement, ensure that support is provided to rural healthcare systems and households of origin, and provide ongoing training and support to healthcare providers.

In April 2010 South Africa's National Department of Health co-hosted a national consultation with the International Organization for Migration, UNAIDS, and the African Centre for Migration and Society. The consultation represented an important first step toward ensuring that migration and health are considered at the national level. It is essential that migration and health be considered within the linked agenda of migration and development and that the availability of data to inform intersectoral, evidence-based regional policies be strengthened (CoRMSA 2009).

Conclusion

Future research is needed to inform ongoing, sustainable, regional, spatially sensitive responses to migration and health in Southern Africa. There is an urgent need to conduct research in other countries in the region; data on health and migration focus on South Africa and Botswana. Research should attempt to determine the costs involved in providing (and not providing) healthcare, including antiretroviral therapy, to international migrant populations. Such analysis would help national governments ensure that appropriate responses to health and migration are budgeted and planned for in a spatially sensitive fashion.

Research on migration and health in South Africa highlights the "othering" of international migrants, particularly in the context of HIV/AIDS. An effective response to migration and health must find ways to address this issue. There is an urgent need to return to a public health approach to address the health of regional migrant populations. Such an approach calls on regional bodies, governments, civil society, public health professionals, and researchers to advocate for and ensure that the right of all migrant groups to access healthcare is upheld (McNeill 2003). Targeted trainings at the national, provincial, district, local, and facility levels of healthcare provision are required to ensure that access to healthcare is facilitated for all migrants within South Africa. Engagement should include the provision of appropriate and targeted information, particularly about client-provider interactions and how decisions by frontline healthcare providers affect health outcomes.

South Africa's public health system must be strengthened, particularly in terms of human resources, service provision, and an effective health information system. An initiative led by the Southern African office of the International Organization for Migration—in partnership with the African Centre for Migration and Society and in collaboration with the National Department of Health—involves finalizing and piloting a training program that aims to ensure equitable access to public healthcare for all migrant groups. The training, designed in response to a needs assessment, is targeted at different levels of the healthcare system, including frontline healthcare providers, facility managers, and National Department of Health decision makers. Healthcare, like other public sectors, is in need of more systematic mainstreaming of migration in its planning and implementation schemes. Policy cycles, however, move at their own pace, which has proved to be particularly slow in the case of migration in South Africa.

Notes

1. This chapter draws on Vearey (2011).
2. In this chapter, "poor migrants" are migrants who lack access to private healthcare in South Africa.
3. South African citizens may be "undocumented" because their births were not registered or because they have problems accessing identity documents; as a result of backlogs at the Department of Home Affairs, it can take many months to replace lost documents.
4. Meetings included the 2009 Migration Dialogue for Southern Africa, the March 2010 Global Consultation on Migrant Health in Madrid, and a two-day national consultation in April 2010 on migration and health in South Africa.

References

Amon, J. J., and K. W. Todrys. 2008. "Fear of Foreigners: HIV-Related Restrictions on Entry, Stay, and Residence." *Journal of the International AIDS Society* 11(8). doi:10.1186/1758-2652-11-8.

———. 2009. "Access to Antiretroviral Treatment for Migrant Populations in the Global South." *Sur– International Journal on Human Rights* 6 (10): 154–77.

Anarfi, J. 2005. "Reversing the Spread of HIV/AIDS: What Role Has Migration?" In *International Migration and the Millennium Development Goals: Selected Papers of the UNFPA Expert Group Meeting.* New York: United Nations Population Fund.

ARASA (AIDS and Rights Alliance for Southern Africa). 2008. *The Mining Sector, Tuberculosis and Migrant Labour in Southern Africa: Policy and Programmatic Interventions for the Cross-Border Control of Tuberculosis between Lesotho and South Africa, Focusing on Miners, Ex-Miners and Their Families.* Johannesburg.

Clark, S. J., M. A. Collinson, K. Kahn, K. Drullinger, and S. M. Tollman. 2007. "Returning Home to Die: Circular Labour Migration and Mortality in Rural South Africa." *Scandinavian Journal of Public Health* 35 (Suppl. 69): 35–44.

Collinson, M., J. Veary, P. Bocquier, S. Drimie, T. Quinlan, and W. Twine. 2010. "Reaching the Invisible: Hidden Links of Ill Health between South Africa's Cities and Rural Areas." Paper presented at the national conference on "Structural Poverty in South Africa," Johannesburg, September 20–22.

Collinson, M., A. B. Wolff, S. M. Tollman, and K. Kahn. 2006. "Trends in Internal Labor Migration from Rural Limpopo Province, Male Risk Behaviour, and Implications for the Spread of HIV/AIDS in Rural South Africa." *Journal of Ethnic and Migration Studies* 32 (4): 633–48.

Commission on the Social Determinants of Health. 2007. "A Conceptual Framework for Action on the Social Determinants of Health." Draft Discussion Paper, Geneva.

CoRMSA (Consortium for Refugees and Migrants in South Africa). 2009. *Protecting Refugees, Asylum Seekers and Immigrants in South Africa.* Johannesburg.

Forced Migration Studies Programme. 2009. *Zimbabwean Migration into Southern Africa: New Trends and Responses.* University of the Witwatersrand, Johannesburg.

Ghent, A. 2008. "Overcoming Migrants' Barriers to Health." *Bulletin of the World Health Organization* 86 (8): 583–84.

Grove, N. J., and A. B. Zwi. 2006. "Our Health and Theirs: Forced Migration, Othering and Public Health." *Social Science and Medicine* 62: 1931–42.

Harcourt, Wendy. 2007. "Editorial: Beyond Us and Them: Migration and Global Economic Development." *Development* 50 (4): 1– 5.

Harper, I., and P. Raman. 2008. "Less than Human? Diaspora, Disease and the Question of Citizenship." *International Migration* 46 (5): 3–26.

Human Rights Watch. 2009a. *Discrimination, Denial and Deportation: Human Rights Abuses Affecting Migrants Living with HIV.* New York.

———. 2009b. *No Healing Here: Violence, Discrimination and Barriers to Health for Migrants in South Africa.* New York.

Landau, L., ed. 2004. *Forced Migrants in the New Johannesburg: Towards a Local Government Response.* Forced Migration Studies Programme, Johannesburg.

———. 2006a. "Myth and Rationality in Southern African Responses to Migration, Displacement, and Humanitarianism." In *Views on Migration in Sub-Saharan Africa: Proceedings of an International African Migration Alliance Workshop,* ed. Catherine Cross, Derik Gelderblom, Niel Roux, and Jonathan Mafukidze, 220–44. Pretoria: Human Sciences Research Council Press.

———. 2006b. "Protection and Dignity in Johannesburg: Shortcomings of South Africa's Urban Refugee Policy." *Journal of Refugee Studies* 19 (3): 308–27.

Landau, L., and A. Wa Kabwe-Segatti. 2009. *Human Development Impacts of Migration: South Africa Case Study.* Human Development Research Paper 2009/5, United Nations Development Programme, New York.

MacPherson, D. W., and B. D. Gushulak. 2001. "Human Mobility and Population Health: New Approaches in a Globalizing World." *Perspectives in Biology and Medicine* 44 (3): 390–401.

McCarthy, K., M. F. Chersich, J. Vearey, G. Meyer-Rath, A. Jaffer, S. Simpwalo, and W. D. F. Venter. 2009. "Good Treatment Outcomes among Foreigners Receiving Antiretroviral Therapy in Johannesburg, South Africa." *International Journal of STD and AIDS* 20 (12): 858–62.

McNeill, P. M. 2003. "Public Health Ethics: Asylum Seekers and the Case for Political Action." *Bioethics* 17 (5–6): 487–502.

Meyer-Rath, G. 2010. "The Cost of the National Antiretroviral Treatment Programme: How Big Can We Go, and How Much Can We Save?" Presentation made at the Southern African HIV Clinicians Society Johannesburg Branch Meeting, Johannesburg, August 26.

Moyo, K. 2010. "Street Level Bureaucracy: The Interface between Health Personnel and Migrant Patients at Hillbrow Community Health Centre." Master's thesis, Forced Migration Studies Programme, University of the Witwatersrand, South Africa.

National Department of Health. 2006. *Memo: Access to Comprehensive HIV and AIDS Care Including Antiretroviral Treatment.* Pretoria.

———. 2007a. *HIV and AIDS and STI Strategic Plan for South Africa, 2007–2011.* Pretoria.

———. 2007b. *Revenue Directive: Refugees/Asylum Seekers with or without a Permit.* BI 4/29 REFUG/ASYL 8 2007. Pretoria.

Pursell, R. 2004. "Accessing Health Services at Johannesburg's Clinics and Hospitals." In *Forced Migrants in the New Johannesburg: Towards a Local Government Response*, ed. L. Landau, 93–98. Johannesburg: Foundation for Human Rights

SADC Directorate for Social and Human Development and Special Programs, 2009. *SADC Policy Framework for Population Mobility and Communicable Diseases in the SADC Region*. Final Draft, April. SADC Secretariat, Gaborone, Botswana.

Southern African HIV Clinicians Society, and UNHCR (United Nations High Commissioner for Refugees). 2007. *Clinical Guidelines on Antiretroviral Therapy Management for Displaced Populations*. Johannesburg.

UNDP (United Nations Development Programme). 2009. *Human Development Report 2009. Overcoming Barriers: Human Mobility and Development*. New York: United Nations Development Programme.

UNHCR (United Nations High Commissioner for Refugees), and the AIDS and Human Rights Research Unit, University of Pretoria. 2006. *Asylum Seekers in South Africa and Their Rights to ARVs*. Pretoria.

Vearey, J. 2008. "Migration, Access to ART and Survivalist Livelihood Strategies in Johannesburg." *African Journal of AIDS Research* 7 (3): 361–74.

———. 2011. "Learning from HIV: Exploring Migration and Health in South Africa." *Global Public Health* 6 (3): DOI: 10.1080/17441692.2010.549494.

Vearey, J., and L. Nunez. 2010. *Migration and Health in South Africa*. International Organization for Migration, Pretoria.

Vearey, J., L. Nunez, and I. Palmary. 2009. "HIV, Migration and Urban Food Security: Exploring the Linkages." In *RENEWAL (Regional Network on AIDS, Livelihoods and Food Security) South Africa Report*. RENEWAL and Forced Migration Studies Programme, University of the Witwatersrand, Johannesburg. http://www.ifpri.org/renewal/pdf/JohannesburgFinal.pdf.

Vearey, J., I. Palmary, L. Thomas, L. Nunez, and S. Drimie. 2010. "Urban Health in Johannesburg: The Importance of Place in Understanding Intra-Urban Inequalities in a Context of Migration and HIV." *Health and Place* 16 (4): 694–702.

WHO (World Health Organization). 2008. *Closing the Gap in a Generation: Health Equity through Action on the Social Determinants of Health*. Commission on Social Determinants of Health, Geneva.

World Health Assembly. 2008. Resolution 61.17, Health of Migrants. A61/VR/8. 61st World Health Assembly, Geneva.

Worth, H. 2006. "Unconditional Hospitality: HIV, Ethics and the Refugee 'Problem'." *Bioethics* 20 (5): 223–32.

Immigration Legislation and Policy in South Africa and the Southern African Development Community, 1986–2010

Immigration legislation and policy

Year	Major political events in South Africa	South Africa	South African development community	Rest of world
1986	Pass laws repealed. State of emergency declared. Labor agreement with Swaziland signed.	Term *European*, which made it compulsory for all immigrants to be able to "assimilate" with the European population of the Union, deleted from section 4(3)(b) of 1984 Immigration Act.		Immigration Reform and Control Act (United States) provides amnesty for 3 million undocumented immigrants, imposes harsher sentences on employers.
1987			Malawi ratifies Convention Relating to the Status of Refugees. Malawi ratifies Organization of African Unity (OAU) Convention Governing the Specific Aspects of Refugee Problems in Africa.	
1988	South Africa begins withdrawal from Angola and cooperates with Namibia's independence process.		Lesotho ratifies OAU Convention Governing the Specific Aspects of Refugee Problems in Africa. Malawi passes Refugee Act.	
1989	F. W. de Klerk becomes president, Eugene Louw becomes minister of interior, and P. J. Colyn becomes director-general of home affairs.		Mozambique ratifies OAU Convention Governing the Specific Aspects of Refugee Problems in Africa. Swaziland ratifies OAU Convention Governing the Specific Aspects of Refugee Problems in Africa.	
1990	Nelson Mandela freed from prison.		Angola passes Law on Refugee Status No. 8, promoting equality and nondiscrimination.	Immigration Act of 1990 increases annual number of immigrants allowed to enter United States to 700,000 a year. Dublin Agreements define common asylum policy for Europe.

Year				
1991	Interim Constitution negotiated.	Aliens Control Act, encompassing all previous legislation regarding admission and residence of immigrants, passed.	Mozambique passes its first Refugee Act No. 21.	Quebec authorized to manage immigrants' selection autonomously from rest of Canada.
1992	Interim Constitution negotiated. L. A. Pienaar appointed minister of home affairs, following death of E. Louw.			
1993	Interim Constitution adopted. D. P. A. Schutte replaces L. A. Pienaar as minister of home affairs.		Namibia passes its new Immigration Control Act.	Canada announces restrictions on immigration and ends family reunification program.
1994	First democratic multiracial elections held; Nelson Mandela elected president. Mangosuthu Buthelezi, leader of the Inkatha Freedom Party, appointed minister of home affairs, Penuell Maduna (ANC) appointed deputy-minister of home affairs.	Interdepartmental commission on internal migration appointed.	UN General Assembly passes resolution 45/158, International Convention on the Protection of the Rights of All Migrant Workers and Members of Their Families. Seychelles ratifies resolution.	
1995	Aliens Control Amendment Act passed. SADC nationals granted amnesty. OAU Convention Governing the Specific Aspects of Refugee Problems in Africa ratified.		Botswana ratifies OAU Convention Governing the Specific Aspects of Refugee Problems in Africa. Namibia ratifies Convention Relating to the Status of Refugees.	European Union members that ratified Maastricht Treaty implement Schengen Agreement, which abolishes internal borders, providing EU citizens with access to all labor markets within the European Union.
1996	Lindiwe Sisulu (ANC) replaces Penuell Maduna as deputy-minister of home affairs.	Government appoints task team to draft Green Paper on International Migration. Convention Relating to the Status of Refugees ratified.	Namibia passes Identification Act (on identity documents).	United States passes Illegal Immigration Reform and Immigrant Responsibility Act. Recession leads government to approve restrictions and facilitate repatriation of undocumented migrants.

(continued next page)

Immigration legislation and policy

Year	Major political events in South Africa	South Africa	South African development community	Rest of world
1997		May: Green Paper, which recommends separate legislation and policy for immigration and refugees, published. Public comments to be submitted until August. June: Southern African Migration Programme hosts conference on "After Amnesty: The Future of Foreign Migrants in South Africa." September: Southern African Migration Programme, Parliamentary Portfolio Committee on Home Affairs, and Department of Home Affairs host public conference on Green Paper. November: South Africa joins International Organization for Migration, which opens branch in Pretoria. December: Identification Act passed.		1997–2002: Successive U.S. Congresses adopt more liberal immigration policies, facilitating asylum and family reunification.
1998		March: Cabinet appoints Task Force composed of functionaries from the Department of Home Affairs and representatives of NGO to draft White Paper on Refugees. June: White Paper on Refugees open to public comments. Revised document submitted to Cabinet at same time as draft refugee bill, approved in November. August: Minister of Home Affairs appoints task team to draft White Paper on International Migration.	Mozambique, South Africa, and Swaziland agree on minutes of trilateral meeting of their ministers of home affairs.	United States and Canada sign Memorandum of Agreement on asylum application.

1999	General elections held; Thabo Mbeki elected president. Mangosuthu Buthelezi reappointed minister of home affairs, Lindiwe Sisulu reappointed deputy-minister. In December, Billy Masetlha replaces Khulu Mbatha as director-general of home affairs.	March: White Paper on International Migration, as modified by Cabinet, published; open to public comments until November. November: Beginning of public hearings on the White Paper organized by the Parliamentary Portfolio Committee. Minister of Home Affairs appoints task team in charge of drafting an immigration bill.	Mauritius passes Refugees (Recognition and Control) Act.	Tampere Summit defines need for common migration policy in Europe. 1999–2002: Increase in arrivals of Chinese refugees and undocumented migrants by boat in Australia. Australia signs agreements with China and the UNHCR.
2000	New bar code identification system (Home Affairs National Identification System [HANIS]) adopted. Local elections held. 1998 Refugees Act implemented.	February: ANC MP Aubrey Mokoena appointed chair of Parliamentary Portfolio Committee, replacing Desmond Lockey (ANC). Draft immigration bill open to public comments for six weeks. April: New application of Parliamentary Portfolio Committee to conduct public hearings on White Paper. Hearings take another four months. May–August: Public hearings on draft bill. July: Minister of Home Affairs organizes conference on comments on draft bill. August: B46 version of draft bill sent to Cabinet, which sends bill back to Department of Home Affairs with amendments. October: Parliamentary Portfolio Committee publishes report on the White Paper. Conflict between Department of Home Affairs and Parliamentary Portfolio Committee further delays adoption of immigration bill. November: Political parties' respond to report. Penultimate report of Parliamentary Portfolio Committee on White Paper on International Migration submitted.	Swaziland ratifies Convention Relating to the Status of Refugees.	European Funds for Refugees created.

(continued next page)

	Immigration legislation and policy			
Year	Major political events in South Africa	South Africa	South African development community	Rest of world
2001	Charles Nqakula replaces Lindiwe Sisulu as deputy-minister of home affairs.	B46 version of draft immigration bill amended. Revised bill approved by Cabinet. Programmed in Parliament for October 2001. October: B79 version of bill introduced in Parliament. Parliamentary Portfolio Committee starts working on it.	Mozambique and South Africa sign Second Joint Commission Policing Agreement for Joint Operations on Border Monitoring. Zimbabwe passes Immigration Act and Refugee Act.	Official launch of New Economic Partnership for Africa's Development, which adopts reversal of brain drain as one of its priorities. Hardening of U.S. laws on immigration and passage of numerous anti-terrorist laws and measures. Legal battles between NGOs and Bush government on foreigners' constitutional rights.
2002	Nosiviwe Mapisa-Nqakula replaces Charles Nqakula as deputy-minister of home affairs.	March: Crisis within Parliamentary Portfolio Committee over the immigration bill. Opposition parties ask for Aubrey Mokoena's dismissal. May 1: Mpho Scott (ANC) replaces Aubrey Mokoena as chair of Parliamentary Portfolio Committee; 23 amendments are adopted. May 9: Parliamentary Portfolio Committee adopts B version of bill. ANC announces intention to completely redraft bill. May 10–15: Inkatha Freedom Party and ANC negotiate over new bill, which is presented to Parliamentary Portfolio Committee and approved the same evening. May 31: Immigration bill becomes Immigration Act No. 13 of 2002. November: Immigration Act Regulations published; immediately challenged by advocacy groups in Constitutional Court.		Publication of European Green Paper on common policy framework for repatriation of undocumented migrants. Beginning of Australian extraterritorial policy for asylum seekers (clearance of asylum seekers before they reach Australian shores). United States releases report on human trafficking, ranking countries by standards for eliminating practice.

Year				
2003	Nosiviwe Mapisa-Nqakula elected chair of ANC Women's League. General elections held; Thabo Mbeki reelected president. Nosiviwe Mapisa-Nqakula replaces Mangosuthu Buthelezi as Minister of Home Affairs following departure of Inkatha from the government. Malusi Gigaba, ex-president of ANC Youth League, appointed deputy-minister of home affairs.	February: Regulations taken to Constitutional Court. April: Immigration Act and regulations implemented. May: Immigration Advisory Board established. June: Constitutional Court approves regulations. October: Immigration Amendment Act No. 19 of 2004 and its regulations published.		Ministers' Council of European Union adopts text on rights to family reunification, the first regulation on legal immigration since migration came under European competence. European Council in Thessalonic reasserts need for more convergence in asylum policies and immigration policies.
2004		July: Amended Immigration Act becomes law.		Green Paper on EU approach to managing economic migration published.
2005	President Mbeki removes deputy president Jacob Zuma from office following a corruption case.	Parliament passes additional amendment to Immigration Act.	Protocol on the Facilitation of Movements of Persons adopted by SADC.	EU policy plan on legal migration published.
2006	Corruption charges against former deputy president Zuma dismissed in court. South Africa becomes first African country to authorize same-sex unions. European Union and South Africa agree on Joint Country Strategy Paper 2007–2013.			African Union Strategic Plan on Migration and Development adopted in Khartoum. Millions of undocumented immigrants and their supporters take to the streets of large cities in the United States to protest against laws criminalizing undocumented immigrants. African Union adopts Migration Policy Framework on Africa.
2007		Prevention and Combating of Trafficking in Persons bill introduced.	Angola passes Act on the Legal Regime of Foreign Citizens No. 2, to address control and social integration of foreigners.	Canada proposes five-year plan to increase immigration (from 250,000 in 1992).

(continued next page)

		Immigration legislation and policy		
Year	Major political events in South Africa	South Africa	South African development community	Rest of world
2008	Home Affairs Minister Mapisa-Nqakula commissions migration policy review. Violence against foreigners breaks out in townships across South Africa, killing 62 people and displacing thousands. European Union-South Africa Summit held in Bordeaux, France. European Commission and South Africa issue Joint Statement of the EU and South Africa on the Occasion of the First SA–EU Migration Dialogue.		Tanzania and Zambia pass Anti-Trafficking in Persons Act.	European Union adopts Directive 2008/115/EC on common standards and procedures in member states for returning illegal third-country nationals.
2009	President Mbeki resigns after ruling party policy conference; ANC deputy leader Kgalema Motlanthe becomes president.		Zambia passes One-Stop Border Control Act.	
2010	Parliament elects Jacob Zuma president; Nkosazana Dlamini-Zuma appointed minister of home affairs.	March: Antitrafficking bill, intended to be fast-tracked by politicians for World Cup, tabled in Parliament. September: Government announces Zimbabwean Documentation Project, which regularizes undocumented Zimbabweans in South Africa. Project implemented amidst much controversy from October through December 31.		

Source: Authors.

How Many Are They? Migration Data Collection Issues

Policy makers responsible for the reform of migration policy in South Africa have struggled to ground their decisions in sound evidence. The difficulty they have found in doing so reflects the way in which migration data are collected and the tense and complex relationship policy makers have often had with researchers and experts. (For a detailed critical review of methods of measurement of undocumented migrants to South Africa, see Crush and Williams 2001.)

More than many other fields of public policy making, migration is subject to large discrepancies between knowledge and policy options. This gap is tied to two factors: (a) the difficulty of accurately measuring migration, given the large number of variables and contexts, and (b) the fact that migration touches on weighty and highly politicized issues including access to labor markets, nation building, citizenship, and belonging. These two dimensions are exacerbated by South Africa's geographic location, its weak capacity to control its borders and regulate immigration, debated definitions of nation-building, and paradoxically, historical legacy of absolute control over population movements (see Landau 2006). Since the end of apartheid, the protection of South African workers, particularly low-skilled workers, against competition from abroad has also attracted much attention from government and organized labor.

Two questions have dominated the South African migration debate: how many foreigners are in the country, and how many of them are illegal? A related question is how many South Africans actually leave the country to go live and work elsewhere. Behind each of these questions lie political and methodological challenges.

How Many Foreigners Live in South Africa?

Migration flows have increased over the past decade. According to the most recent census (2001), 345,161 foreigners lived in South Africa in 2001. This figure is clearly an underestimate; other sources have put the number of foreigners at 500,000–850,000 (Landau and Gindrey 2008).

Foreigners make up the majority in some Johannesburg neighborhoods, but most of South Africa—and even most of Johannesburg—has only small numbers of foreigners. Estimates for 2010 place the proportion of foreigners at about 7 percent of South Africa's 50.4 million residents (Landau and Gindrey 2008).

This number is higher than it was in 2000, but the percentage remains low compared with other "global" cities and regional powers. In Toronto, for example, more than 40 percent of the population was born outside Canada. About 6–7 percent of France's population was born abroad, but about 25 percent of the population is of foreign origin (Global Commission on International Migration 2005)

How Many Undocumented Immigrants Live in South Africa?

Before the repeal of influx control legislation in 1986, any African found outside a homeland without authorization to travel or live there was considered an illegal alien. Between 1986 and 1994, authorization to live in formerly white areas was relaxed somewhat for certain categories of black South Africans. However, tens of thousands of homeland citizens and African foreigners continued to be arrested and deported as "illegal aliens." Since the reincorporation of homelands into South Africa in 1993, and passage of the 1995 Citizenship Act, only international foreigners have been considered illegal aliens. Under current South African law, two categories of people can be considered illegal aliens: lawful entrants who overstay the duration of their permit and unlawful entrants (people who entered without documentation or with fraudulent documentation).

The number of undocumented migrants can be estimated using different methods: surveying migrants living in South Africa, calculating the number of people who overstay their visas, and examining the number of people arrested and repatriated by South African police and immigration services. All of these methods have serious limitations. Surveying migrants is almost impossible given their desire to stay invisible. Measuring "stay-overs," as they are called by immigration services, is unreliable, as they can leave the country clandestinely. In 1995, for instance, the Department of Home Affairs indicated that 708,927 "stay-overs" had been detected in the department's computer system. Arrest and repatriation figures provided by the police and immigration services measure police activity rather than migration flows. Official repatriation figures, which rose from 44,225 in 1988 to more than 300,000 in 2010, can at best provide indications of trends in policing and documentation activities. There is no reason to believe that these figures reflect the number of undocumented migrants in South Africa. A change in immigration regulations may suddenly modify the legal status of migrants and cause sudden increases or decreases in arrests and repatriations—as was the case with the moratorium on the deportation of Zimbabweans in 2010.

Official estimates are also problematic. In 1994 the South African police provided government departments with an estimate of the total number of undocumented migrants in the country, which they put at about 2 million people. In 1995 they came up with the figure of 8 million—20 percent of South Africa's population—an implausible figure that was immediately questioned by the press. Several reputable research institutes suggested unrealistic estimates of 3–8 million people. Such figures would mean that 2 people out of 10 in South Africa are undocumented migrants. These figures were immediately dismissed on the basis of observations and smaller-scale studies by demographers and migration specialists.

Many estimates seem to have come from a survey by the Centre for Socio-Political Analysis of the Human Sciences Research Council conducted between December 1994 and June 1995. Based on interviews with a sample representative of the South African population, this survey asked respondents how many foreigners they knew in their immediate surroundings. By extrapolating these figures, researchers calculated the total number of foreigners in South Africa. It then subtracted the number of legal immigrants to generate an estimate of the number of undocumented migrants, arriving at a figure of 8.2 million undocumented migrants in December 1994 and 9.5 million just six months later. Subsequent duplications of the survey inexplicably indicated the disappearance of hundreds of thousands of undocumented migrants. This methodology is considered extremely weak and unreliable by international standards, because of its obvious biases and inaccuracies. In 1995 the Human Sciences Research Council concluded that "there may be up to 9 million illegal immigrants here. The most accurate estimate may therefore be 5 to 6 million." (Minaar, Pretorius, and Wentzel 1995). Other researchers from the Human Sciences Research Council concluded that there could be as many as 12 million undocumented migrants in South Africa, later revising the figure downward to 5 million (Minaar and Hough 1996).

However fallacious, these figures confirmed popular suspicions and quickly filled a gap in official speeches. Over time, they became disconnected from the Human Sciences Research Council, which withdrew its estimates as methodologically flawed in the early 2000s (Crush and Williams 2001).

The effect of these figures on political rhetoric and policy formation cannot be overstated. In 1997, for example, the Inkatha Party minister of the Department of Home Affairs introduced his migration policy plans in Parliament by citing the following figures:

> With an illegal alien population estimated between 2.5 and 5 million, it is obvious that the socioeconomic resources of the country, which are under

severe strain as it is, are further being burdened by the presence of illegal aliens. The cost implication becomes even clearer when one makes a calculation suggesting that if every illegal costs our infrastructure, say R1,000 per annum, then multiplied with whatever number you wish, it becomes obvious that the cost becomes billions of rands per year.

In 2002 Billy Masetlha, the ANC director-general of the Department of Home Affairs, declared to the Parliamentary Commission on Home Affairs:

a study conducted by the Human Sciences Research Council in conjunction with the University of Pretoria (sic) estimated that in 1996, two years after the new dispensation and the opening up of the country to the world in 1994, there were between 2.4 and 4.1 million illegal aliens in the RSA at the time. Now, eight years later, one can safely say the minimum is at least above the estimate of 4.1 million, and probably substantially higher. This being the case it means that 10 percent or more of the population are illegal aliens. This equals most of the quoted unemployment figures.

Work by the Southern African Migration Programme and the African Centre for Migration and Society has generated far more modest estimates. Using internationally accepted demographic methods for such estimates, they place the total number of foreigners in South Africa, documented and undocumented, at about 3 million (these figures may now be higher as a result of the ongoing Zimbabwean crisis) (Crush and Williams 2001; Landau and Gindrey 2008). These more reasoned estimates have not, however, fed into the public or political discourse.

The 2010 Zimbabwean Documentation Project illustrates the South African government's use of grossly inflated figures. According to several official statements, 800,000 to 1 million Zimbabweans were projected to lack documentation. By the time the project was completed in December 2010, the Department of Home Affairs received fewer than 266,000 requests, mainly divided between asylum, work, and study permit regulations. This huge discrepancy between perception and fact raises numerous questions about the manipulation of such figures and the management of permit applications. Had Zimbabwean nationals been given access to adequate documentation upon their entry into the country between 2001 and 2008, they would not have become undocumented.

Estimating the number of South Africans moving to urban areas is also difficult. As discussed in chapter 3, researchers projected massive and unstoppable flows of people from former homeland areas into the cities. Malthusian pronouncements about the effects of urbanization appeared in provincial and municipal speeches and policies, especially in Gauteng and the Western Cape, the two provinces most affected by urbanization.

Demographers and economists such as Rob Dorrington (University of Cape Town) and Charles Simkins (University of the Witwatersrand) warn against policy makers' anxious and inflated claims. As Dorrington notes, there are demographic limits on the number of people who can move, and parts of the Eastern Cape—a major source area for Cape Town—are now almost depleted of the groups most likely to move. Simkins, who built a demographic model for the Centre for Development and Enterprise, argues that there is almost no way to know how many people have moved because of fundamental flaws in South Africa's official statistics, including the lack of an accurate population register during apartheid, poor sampling in the initial (1996) census, and different (and ineffective) techniques for measuring migration. According to him, "one of the reasons for lower projections is that black fertility has dropped more rapidly than was expected—an equivalent decline in fertility in a shorter period than it previously took whites. The notion that black people have some permanent 'cultural' predisposition towards large families is patently wrong" (Simkins, quoted in Bernstein 1995).

Measuring Emigration

The main difficulty for the government is in measuring the number and nature of departures. Studies reveal a large gap between recorded departures and legal settlements of South Africans in the top five countries of immigration. Meyer, Brown, and Kaplan (2000), for instance, note that figures provided by Statistics South Africa (based on data from the Department of Home Affairs) on people who left the country since 1994 represent less than half the number of South African immigrants legally recorded in host countries (mainly Australia, New Zealand, the United Kingdom, and the United States).

The absence of administrative measures to record departures in the Immigration Act of 2002 and its regulations is hampering efforts by of the Department of Home Affairs to measure emigration. Only fragmented figures on South African expatriates have been available since 2004.

References
Bernstein, A. 1995. "Planning for the Nation's Population Expansion." *Cape Times* (July 24). http://www.cde.org.za/article.php?a_id=309.

Buthelezi, M. 1997. "Keynote Address to the 1997 Southern African Migration Project Conference." Institute for a Democratic South Africa, Cape Town. http://www.queensu.ca/samp/document.html.

Crush, J. and V. Williams, eds. 2001. *Making Up the Numbers: Measuring "Illegal Immigration" to South Africa*. Migration Policy Brief 3, Southern African Migration Programme, Queen's University, Kingston, Canada, and IDASA (Institute for Democracy in South Africa), Cape Town.

Dorrington, R. 2005. *Projection of the Population of the City of Cape Town 2001–2021*. Report prepared for the City of Cape Town. Centre for Actuarial Research, University of Cape Town.

Global Commission on International Migration. 2005. *Migration in an Interconnected World: New Directions for Action.* Report of the Global Commission on International Migration. October, Geneva. www.gcim.org.

Landau, L. B. 2006. "Myth and Rationality in Southern African Responses to Migration, Displacement, and Humanitarianism." In *Views on Migration in Sub-Saharan Africa: Proceedings of an International African Migration Alliance Workshop,* ed. Catherine Cross, Derik Gelderblom, Niel Roux, and Jonathan Mafukidze, 220–44. Pretoria: Human Sciences Research Council Press.

Landau, L., and V. Gindrey. 2008. *Migration and Population Trends in Gauteng Province 1996–2055.* Migration Studies Working Paper 42, Forced Migration Studies Programme, Johannesburg. www.migration.org.za/sites/default/files/working_papers/2009/Gauteng_working_paper_ MSWPS42_0.pdf.

Masetlha, B. 2002. "Remarks to the Parliamentary Portfolio Committee on Home Affairs." Cape Town, 15/04/2002. http://www.queensu.ca/samp/ImmigrationBill Comments/DG150402.htm.

Meyer, J. B., M. Brown, and D. Kaplan. 2000. "Assessing the South African Brain Drain: A Statistical Comparison." DPRU Working Paper 00/40, Development Policy Research Unit, University of Cape Town. www.commerce.uct.ac.za/research_units/dpru/working papers/pdf_files/wp40.pdf.

Minaar A. and M. Hough. 1996. *Who Goes There? Perspectives on Clandestine and Illegal Aliens in Southern Africa.* Human Sciences Research Council Publishers, Pretoria.

Minaar, A., S. Pretorius, and M. Wentzel. 1995. "Who Goes There? Illegals in South Africa." *Indicator South Africa* 12 (3): 33–40.

Migration Statistics for Southern Africa

Table C.1 Foreign Nationals from Southern Africa and Indian Ocean States Legally Residing in Selected European Countries, 2008

Country	Angola	Botswana	Comoros	Congo, Dem. Rep.	Lesotho	Madagascar	Malawi	Mauritius	Mozambique	Seychelles	South Africa	Swaziland	Zambia	Zimbabwe	Total
Austria	40	5	0	110	0	30	30	45	20	10	390	0	20	50	750
Belgium	2,485	15	20	20,110	10	395	50	610	35	20	1,020	10	140	115	25,035
Bulgaria	0	0	0	0	0	0	0	0	0	0	20	0	0	5	25
Cyprus	5	0	0	100	0	0	0	10	80	10	260	0	5	110	580
Czech Republic	200	60	0	70	5	35	0	20	5	0	240	0	35	10	680
Estonia	0	0	0	0	0	0	0	0	0	0	5	0	0	0	5
Finland	360	5	0	0	0	0	15	20	25	0	160	0	110	20	715
France	7,725	20	23,190	37,460	10	18,275	25	14,045	125	210	1,240	25	60	100	102,485
Germany	4,940	60	30	6,130	25	520	90	760	1,820	170	3,375	25	225	470	18,640
Greece	5	0	0	45	0	35	5	20	20	15	275	0	25	30	475
Hungary	25	0	0	0	0	5	5	20	15	0	90	0	5	5	170
Ireland	590	215	0	1,680	30	5	125	4,070	10	0	5,080	20	130	1,350	13,305
Italy	1,555	15	5	2,570	20	1,215	45	7,950	350	600	725	10	255	205	15,520
Latvia	0	0	0	0	0	0	0	5	0	0	5	0	0	0	10
Malta	0	0	0	0	0	0	0	0	0	0	25	0	0	0	25
Netherlands	2,285	25	0	1,835	25	5	40	65	65	5	2,625	1,050	120	220	8,365
Norway	180	60	0	825	0	50	40	45	35	5	350	0	140	90	1,820
Poland	35	0	0	25	0	5	0	5	0	0	85	0	10	25	190
Portugal	27,305	5	0	210	0	15	5	5	3,345	0	595	10	10	40	31,545
Romania	20	0	0	25	0	10	0	225	0	0	80	0	5	15	380
Slovak Republic	25	0	0	0	0	0	5	0	0	5	45	0	5	5	90
Slovenia	0	0	0	0	0	0	0	0	5	0	5	0	0	5	15
Spain	1,580	5	5	1,505	5	85	30	115	250	20	830	5	25	65	4,525
Sweden	285	30	0	1,205	0	10	25	40	90	25	540	5	125	140	2,520
U.K.a	—	—	—	—	—	—	—	—	—	—	108,000	—	13,000	83,000	226,050
Total	49,645	520	23,250	73,905	130	20,695	535	28,075	6,295	1,095	126,065	1,135	14,450	86,075	453,920

Source: Eurostat 2010.

Note: Figures reflect residence permits valid as of December 31, 2008. — Not available.

a. Estimates, based on U.K. Government National Statistical Office, June 2009. (http://www.statistics.gov.uk/StatBase/Product.asp?vlnk=15147).

Table C.2 Foreign Nationals from Southern Africa and Indian Ocean States Refused Entry at the Border by Selected European Countries, 2008

Country	Angola	Botswana	Comoros	Democratic Republic of Congo	Lesotho	Madagascar	Malawi	Mauritius	Mozambique	Namibia	South Africa	Swaziland	Zambia	Zimbabwe	Total
Belgium	20	0	0	95	0	0	0	0	0	0	5	0	0	0	120
Cyprus	5	0	0	0	0	0	0	0	0	0	15	0	0	0	20
France	95	15	65	115	0	45	5	220	0	0	80	0	5	15	660
Germany	25	5	0	35	0	0	0	5	0	0	35	0	0	5	110
Ireland	15	30	0	45	5	0	70	5	0	0	350	15	10	75	620
Italy	5	0	0	0	0	0	0	5	0	0	20	0	0	0	30
Netherlands	0	0	0	0	0	0	10	0	0	0	30	0	5	10	55
Portugal	105	0	0	0	0	0	0	0	5	0	5	0	0	0	115
Romania	5	0	0	5	0	0	0	0	0	0	15	0	0	0	25
Spain	15	0	0	0	0	0	0	5	0	0	15	0	0	0	35
Switzerland	0	0	0	5	0	0	0	0	0	0	90	0	0	5	100
United Kingdom	55	30	5	70	5	10	20	320	5	75	890	15	25	90	1,615
Total	345	80	70	370	10	55	105	560	10	75	1,550	30	45	200	3,505

Source: Eurostat 2010.

Table C.3 Foreign Nationals from Southern Africa and Indian Ocean States Found to Be Illegally Present in Selected European Countries, 2008

Country	Angola	Botswana	Comoros	Democratic Republic of Congo	Lesotho	Madagascar	Malawi	Mauritius	Mozambique	Namibia	South Africa	Swaziland	Zambia	Zimbabwe	Total
Austria	15	0	0	20	0	0	0	0	0	0	5	0	0	5	45
Belgium	60	5	0	205	0	0	0	0	0	0	10	5	0	0	285
Finland	45	0	0	35	0	0	0	0	0	0	0	0	0	0	80
France	355	0	245	255	0	130	0	65	5	0	35	0	5	15	1,110
Germany	165	0	5	200	0	10	5	25	20	30	110	0	5	55	630
Ireland	0	0	0	10	0	0	0	20	0	0	10	0	0	0	40
Italy	5	0	0	10	0	0	0	30	5	0	10	0	5	5	70
Netherlands	115	0	0	45	0	0	0	0	0	0	5	0	0	5	170
Portugal	900	65	0	10	0	0	0	0	95	0	10	0	0	0	1,080
Spain	80	0	0	40	5	0	10	0	10	0	20	0	5	30	200
United Kingdom	150	35	0	330	15	0	485	555	10	90	880	25	180	4,055	6,810
Total	1,890	105	250	1,160	20	140	500	695	145	120	1,095	30	200	4,170	10,520

Source: Eurostat 2010.
Note: Includes countries reporting more than 10 illegal immigrants.

Table C.4 Foreign Nationals from Southern Africa and Indian Ocean States Returned Following Order to Leave by Selected European Countries, 2008

Country	Angola	Botswana	Comoros	Democratic Republic of Congo	Lesotho	Madagascar	Malawi	Mauritius	Mozambique	Namibia	South Africa	Swaziland	Zambia	Zimbabwe	Total
Belgium	15	0	0	80	0	0	0	0	0	0	0	0	0	0	95
France	50	0	45	130	0	90	0	30	0	0	20	0	0	5	370
Germany	30	0	0	55	0	0	0	0	0	0	5	0	0	10	100
Ireland	0	0	0	0	0	0	5	10	0	0	20	0	0	0	35
Netherlands	185	5	0	50	0	0	0	0	0	0	30	0	0	5	275
Norway	15	0	0	5	0	0	0	0	0	0	5	0	0	0	25
Portugal	50	0	0	0	0	0	0	0	5	0	0	0	0	0	55
Romania	5	0	0	0	0	0	0	0	0	0	15	0	0	0	20
Spain	55	0	0	5	5	5	0	0	0	0	20	0	0	10	95
Sweden	5	0	0	45	0	0	0	0	0	0	0	0	0	5	55
United Kingdom	125	55	0	120	25	5	365	715	10	170	1,580	40	135	500	3,845
Total	535	60	45	490	25	100	370	755	15	170	1,695	40	135	535	4,970

Source: Eurostat 2010.
Note: Includes countries reporting more than 10 returnees.

Table C.5 Legal and Undocumented Immigrants in and Emigrants from South Africa,
1980–2009

Year	Legal permanent immigrants	Legal emigrants	Official estimates of undocumented immigrants (millions)
1980	29,365	11,363	—
1981	41,542	8,791	—
1982	45,784	6,832	—
1983	30,483	8,247	—
1984	28,793	8,550	—
1985	17,284	11,401	—
1986	6,994	13,711	—
1987	7,953	11,174	—
1988	10,400	7,767	—
1989	11,270	4,911	1.2
1990	14,499	4,722	—
1991	12,379	4,256	2
1992	8,686	4,289	2.5
1993	9,824	8,070	0.245[a]/3
1994	6,398	10,235	2.4–5.1[b]/2[c]
1995	5,064	8,725	8.5[d]
1996	5,407	9,708	2–3[e]
1997	4,532	10,079	2–8[a]
1998	4,371	9,031	2–4.1[b]
1999	3,669	8,402	2–4.1[b]
2000	3,053	11,309	2.5–4.1[f]
2001	4,832	12,260	2.5–4.1
2002	6,545	10,890	2.5–4.1
2003	10,578	16,165	2.5–4.1
2004	10,714	—	2.5–4.1
2005	—	—	2.5–4.1
2006	9,235	—	3–6[d]
2007	3,817	—	3–6[d]
2008	2,393	—	3–6[d]
2009	4,083	—	3–6[d]

Source: Figures for legal immigrants and emigrants are from the Department of Home Affairs, 1980–2009.
Figures for undocumented immigrants are from the *South Africa Yearbook,* except where otherwise indicated.
Note: — Not available.
a. Department of Home Affairs.
b. Human Sciences Research Council.
c. Minister of the Department of Home Affairs, Mangosuthu Buthelezi.
d. South African Police Service Annual Report.
e. South African Institute of Race Relations.
f. Government Information and Communication Service.

Figure C.1 Annual Entries into South Africa Approved, 1984–2009

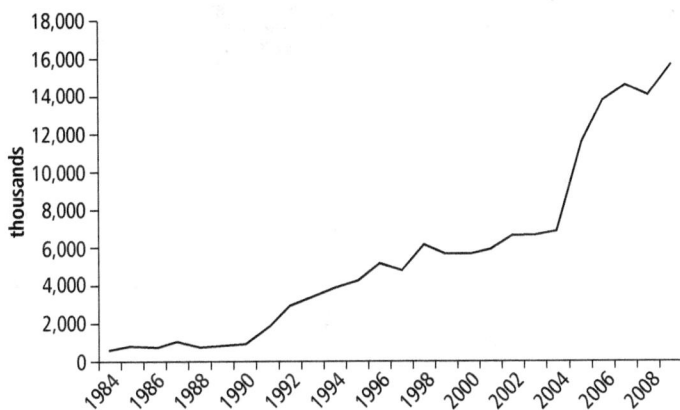

Source: Statistics South Africa, 1984–2004; Department of Home Affairs, 2005–10.
Note: Figures include entries for work, study, business, holiday, contracts, border traffic, transit, and unspecified purposes. Figure for 2008 is estimated.

Figure C.2 Annual Work and Study Permits Issued by South Africa, 1984–2007

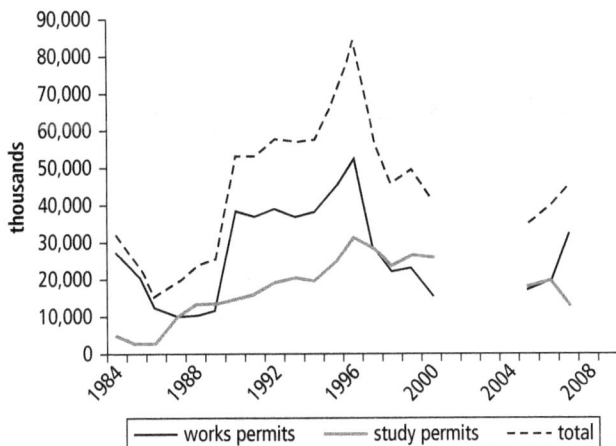

Source: Statistics South Africa, 1984–2004; Department of Home Affairs, 2005–07.
Note: Figure include new permits and renewals. Figures for 2000–03 are not available.

Table C.6 Number of Removals of Undocumented Migrants from South Africa, 1994–2008

| Year | Country of migrant | | | | |
	Mozambique	Zimbabwe	Lesotho	Other	Total
1994	71,279	12,931	4,073	2,409	90,692
1995	131,689	17,549	4,087	3,759	157,084
1996	157,425	14,651	3,344	5,293	180,713
1997	146,285	21,673	4,077	4,316	176,351
1998	141,506	28,548	4,900	6,932	181,286
1999	123,961	42,769	6,003	11,128	183,861
2000	84,738	45,922	5,871	9,044	145,575
2001	94,404	47,697	5,977	—	156,123
2002	83,695	38,118	5,278	—	151,653
2003	82,067	55,753	7,447	—	164,294
2004	—	—	—	—	167,137
2005	—	—	—	—	209,988
2006	—	—	—	—	266,067
2007	—	—	—	—	312,733
2008	—	—	—	—	280,837

Source: Department of Home Affairs, 1994–2010.
Note: The Department of Home Affairs has not released repatriation figures by nationality since 2004.
— = Not available.

Table C.7 Number of Refugees and Asylum Seekers in South Africa, 2001–09

Year	Refugees	Asylum seekers	Total
2001	18,605	4,860	23,465
2002	23,344	52,451	75,795
2003	26,558	84,085	110,643
2004	27,683	115,224	142,907
2005	29,714	140,095	169,809
2006	5,432	44,212	49,644
2007	9,727	58,584	68,311
2008	3,746	64,373	68,119
2009	9,000	364,638	373,638

Source: Department of Home Affairs, 2005–09.
Note: Figures for 2001–05 and 2009 are cumulative; figures for 2006–08 are for new permits only.

References

Department of Home Affairs. 1980–2010. *Annual Reports*. Pretoria.

Eurostat. 2010. Population database. European Commission, Brussels. http://epp.eurostat
.ec.europa.eu/portal/page/portal/population/data/main_tables.

South African Police Service. 1995. *Annual Report.* Pretoria.

South Africa Yearbook. 1989, 1991, 1992, 2001–05. Pretoria.

Statistics South Africa. 1984–2004. *Tourism and Migration Reports*. Pretoria.

Appendix D

Urbanization in Africa, 1950–2010

This appendix provides information on the actual and projected rural and urban populations for Africa as a whole and for each of its subregions. Figures for 1950–2010 are actual figures. Figures for 2015–50 are projections.

Table D.1 Actual and Projected Rural and Urban Population in Africa, 1950–2050

Year	Population (thousands)		Percent urban	Annual growth rate in preceding five years (percent)	
	Rural	Urban		Rural areas	Urban areas
1950	194,551	32,719	14.4		
1955	212,126	41,272	16.3	1.73	4.64
1960	231,926	53,123	18.6	1.78	5.05
1965	253,764	68,545	21.3	1.80	5.10
1970	280,269	86,523	23.6	1.99	4.66
1975	311,020	107,745	25.7	2.08	4.39
1980	347,631	134,605	27.9	2.23	4.45
1985	389,331	166,800	30.0	2.27	4.29
1990	433,504	205,225	32.1	2.15	4.15
1995	478,211	248,074	34.2	1.96	3.79
2000	524,861	294,602	36.0	1.86	3.44
2005	571,929	349,145	37.9	1.72	3.40
2010	620,053	412,990	40.0	1.62	3.36
2015	666,513	486,525	42.2	1.45	3.28
2020	707,253	569,117	44.6	1.19	3.14
2025	739,595	660,589	47.2	0.89	2.98
2030	762,895	761,293	49.9	0.62	2.84
2035	777,417	870,364	52.8	0.38	2.68
2040	783,375	986,240	55.7	0.15	2.50
2045	780,149	1,107,170	58.7	−0.08	2.31
2050	767,551	1,230,915	61.6	−0.33	2.12

Source: UN 2009, 2010.

Table D.2 Actual and Projected Rural and Urban Population in Southern Africa, 1950–2050

Year	Population (thousands)			Annual growth rate in preceding five years (percent)	
	Rural	Urban	Percent urban	Rural areas	Urban areas
1950	9,719	5,869	37.7		
1955	10,534	6,952	39.8	1.61	3.39
1960	11,447	8,277	42.0	1.66	3.49
1965	12,811	9,606	42.9	2.25	2.98
1970	14,335	11,118	43.7	2.25	2.92
1975	16,216	12,871	44.2	2.47	2.93
1980	18,221	14,752	44.7	2.33	2.73
1985	20,236	17,213	46.0	2.10	3.09
1990	21,479	20,502	48.8	1.19	3.50
1995	22,938	24,302	51.4	1.31	3.40
2000	23,730	27,657	53.8	0.68	2.59
2005	24,072	30,969	56.3	0.29	2.26
2010	23,947	34,021	58.7	−0.10	1.88
2015	23,218	36,439	61.1	−0.62	1.37
2020	22,325	38,809	63.5	−0.78	1.26
2025	21,368	41,307	65.9	−0.88	1.25
2030	20,295	43,741	68.3	−1.03	1.15
2035	19,130	46,015	70.6	−1.18	1.01
2040	17,915	48,119	72.9	−1.31	0.89
2045	16,684	50,068	75.0	−1.42	0.79
2050	15,471	51,917	77.0	−1.51	0.73

Source: UN 2009, 2010.

Table D.3 Actual and Projected Rural and Urban Population in Eastern Africa, 1950–2050

Year	Population (thousands)			Annual growth rate in preceding five years (percent)	
	Rural	Urban	Percent urban	Rural areas	Urban areas
1950	61,413	3,434	5.3		
1955	68,036	4,550	6.3	2.05	5.63
1960	75,952	6,047	7.4	2.20	5.69
1965	85,392	8,197	8.8	2.34	6.08
1970	96,395	11,211	10.4	2.42	6.26
1975	108,671	15,373	12.4	2.40	6.31
1980	122,355	21,138	14.7	2.37	6.37

(continued next page)

Table D.3 *(continued)*

Year	Population (thousands)		Percent urban	Annual growth rate in preceding five years (percent)	
	Rural	Urban	Percent urban	Rural areas	Urban areas
1985	138,919	27,043	16.3	2.54	4.93
1990	158,299	34,660	18.0	2.61	4.96
1995	176,891	42,983	19.5	2.22	4.30
2000	200,069	52,641	20.8	2.46	4.05
2005	223,636	63,778	22.2	2.23	3.84
2010	249,992	77,194	23.6	2.23	3.82
2015	277,792	94,663	25.4	2.11	4.08
2020	304,070	116,130	27.6	1.81	4.09
2025	326,793	141,973	30.3	1.44	4.02
2030	345,298	172,766	33.3	1.10	3.93
2035	359,518	208,143	36.7	0.81	3.73
2040	369,350	247,674	40.1	0.54	3.48
2045	374,276	290,999	43.7	0.26	3.22
2050	373,936	337,493	47.4	−0.02	2.96

Source: UN 2009, 2010.

Table D.4 Actual and Projected Rural and Urban Population in Middle (Central) Africa, 1950–2050

Year	Population (thousands)		Percent urban	Annual growth rate in preceding five years (percent)	
	Rural	Urban	Percent urban	Rural areas	Urban areas
1950	22,459	3,657	14.0		
1955	24,234	4,533	15.8	1.52	4.30
1960	26,401	5,687	17.7	1.71	4.53
1965	28,447	7,556	21.0	1.49	5.68
1970	30,783	10,161	24.8	1.58	5.93
1975	34,050	12,662	27.1	2.02	4.40
1980	38,214	15,578	29.0	2.31	4.15
1985	43,290	19,121	30.6	2.49	4.10
1990	49,072	23,741	32.6	2.51	4.33
1995	56,336	30,088	34.8	2.76	4.74
2000	61,574	36,486	37.2	1.78	3.86
2005	67,960	45,225	40.0	1.97	4.29
2010	73,318	55,592	43.1	1.52	4.13

(continued next page)

Table D.4 *(continued)*

	Population (thousands)			Annual growth rate in preceding five years (percent)	
Year	Rural	Urban	Percent urban	Rural areas	Urban areas
2015	78,367	67,781	46.4	1.33	3.96
2020	82,791	81,493	49.6	1.10	3.68
2025	86,369	96,522	52.8	0.85	3.39
2030	88,875	112,727	55.9	0.57	3.10
2035	90,157	130,005	59.0	0.29	2.85
2040	90,241	148,176	62.1	0.02	2.62
2045	89,170	166,963	65.2	−0.24	2.39
2050	86,992	185,977	68.1	−0.49	2.16

Source: UN 2009, 2010.

Table D.5 Actual and Projected Rural and Urban Population in Northern Africa, 1950–2050

	Population (thousands)			Annual growth rate in preceding five years (percent)	
Year	Rural	Urban	Percent urban	Rural areas	Urban areas
1950	39,852	13,130	24.8		
1955	43,206	16,359	27.5	1.62	4.40
1960	47,059	20,451	30.3	1.71	4.47
1965	50,588	25,748	33.7	1.45	4.61
1970	55,407	31,461	36.2	1.82	4.01
1975	60,827	37,798	38.3	1.87	3.67
1980	67,627	45,364	40.1	2.12	3.65
1985	75,239	55,227	42.3	2.13	3.94
1990	82,003	65,763	44.5	1.72	3.49
1995	88,059	75,884	46.3	1.42	2.86
2000	93,868	85,656	47.7	1.28	2.42
2005	99,107	96,338	49.3	1.09	2.35
2010	104,009	108,912	51.2	0.97	2.45
2015	107,877	122,718	53.2	0.73	2.39
2020	110,224	137,341	55.5	0.43	2.25
2025	110,736	152,385	57.9	0.09	2.08
2030	109,475	167,876	60.5	−0.23	1.94
2035	106,777	183,599	63.2	−0.50	1.79
2040	103,111	199,058	65.9	−0.70	1.62
2045	98,557	213,956	68.5	−0.90	1.44
2050	93,225	227,852	71.0	−1.11	1.26

Source: UN 2009, 2010.

Table D.6 Actual and Projected Rural and Urban Population in Western Africa, 1950–2050

Year	Population (thousands)		Percent urban	Annual growth rate in preceding five years (percent)	
	Rural	Urban		Rural areas	Urban areas
1950	61,107	6,629	9.8		
1955	66,116	8,878	11.8	1.58	5.84
1960	71,068	12,660	15.1	1.44	7.10
1965	76,525	17,439	18.6	1.48	6.40
1970	83,348	22,572	21.3	1.71	5.16
1975	91,257	29,042	24.1	1.81	5.04
1980	101,214	37,774	27.2	2.07	5.26
1985	111,645	48,196	30.2	1.96	4.87
1990	122,651	60,559	33.1	1.88	4.57
1995	133,988	74,817	35.8	1.77	4.23
2000	145,620	92,162	38.8	1.67	4.17
2005	157,154	112,835	41.8	1.52	4.05
2010	168,787	137,271	44.9	1.43	3.92
2015	179,258	164,924	47.9	1.20	3.67
2020	187,843	195,344	51.0	0.94	3.39
2025	194,330	228,403	54.0	0.68	3.13
2030	198,951	264,182	57.0	0.47	2.91
2035	201,834	302,603	60.0	0.29	2.72
2040	202,759	343,213	62.9	0.09	2.52
2045	201,462	385,184	65.7	−0.13	2.31
2050	197,926	427,675	68.4	−0.35	2.09

Source: UN 2009, 2010.

References

UN (United Nations). 2009. *World Population Prospects: The 2008 Revision.* Department of Economic and Social Affairs, Population Division, New York.

————. 2010. *World Urbanization Prospects: The 2009 Revision.* Department of Economic and Social Affairs, Population Division, New York. http://esa.un.org/wup2009/unup/.

Index

Boxes, figures, maps, notes, and tables are indicated by b, f, m, n, and t following page numbers.

apartheid (*continued*)
  migration data and, 44
  nationalism of, 117
apprenticeships, decline in, 71
ASGISA (Accelerated and Shared Growth
    Initiative), 31, 74–75
asylum. *See also* refugees and refugee
    policy
  healthcare and, 124–25
  municipalities and, 102
  numbers of, 158*t*
  Refugees Act and, 52
  refugees and, 36, 48
  Zimbabwean crisis and, 111, 112–13
Australia
  emigration to, 16, 71, 72, 73
  as "newfound land," 32

B
Bangladesh, migrants from, 9
banking laws, 101
Bantu education system, 71
Baragwanath Hospital, 76*b*
Batho Pele document, 91
Beitbridge border post, 112, 113
Belgians, independence of colonies
    causing emigration of, 36
bilateralism, 22–25
black consciousness movement, 53
black economic empowerment, 67, 76*b*
Botha, J. C. G., 37
Botha, P. W., 36
Botswana
  economic growth in, 11
  health data from, 132
  labor markets in, 24, 71
  migration system in, 71
  survey data from, 12
  xenophobic violence in, 11
brain drain
  African National Congress on, 50
  emigration and, 71
  government policy on, 73
  labor markets and, 24
  migration and, 39

significance of, 69, 77
Southern African Development
    Community position on, 68
brain gain phenomena, 39
British Chamber of Business in South
    Africa, 69
Brown, M., 149
Burundi, refugee movements in, 36
Business Against Crime, 99
Business Day (newspaper) on skills
    shortages, 69
Buthelezi, Mangosuthu, 42, 55, 58, 67,
    74, 110

C
Canada
  emigration to, 72, 73
  migration and, 16, 61*n*2
  as "newfound land," 32
capacity building, 5–6
Cape Town, local government
    responses to migration in,
    83, 84–85, 93–94, 96, 97,
    103*n*2
census data, 12, 88, 94, 100, 145, 149
Centre for Development and Enterprise,
    69, 149
Centre for Policy Studies, 40–41
Centre for Socio-Political Analysis, 147
Chief Directorate for Migration, 107
children, health risks for, 122
China, People's Republic of, migrants
    from, 9
Chinese Exclusion Act of 1882 (U.S.),
    61*n*2
citizens
  antiretroviral therapy and, 129
  citizenship, access to, 57
  "undocumented," 133*n*3
  violence against, 10*b*
Citizenship Act of 1995 (South Africa),
    146
City Planning, Development,
    and Regional Services
    Department, 90

High-Level Dialogue on Migration and
     Development (UN), 77
HIV/AIDS
   healthcare and, 123, 124
   migration and, 126–27, 129
   "othering" of international migrants
       and, 132
   social networks and, 122
   social services and, 101
Home Affairs Department
   bureaucratic procedures of, 114
   corruption in, 52, 58
   deportations and, 56
   discriminatory migration system
       and, 34
   emigration and, 149
   funding of, 58, 63n19
   immigration control and, 33, 106, 112
   institutionalized and reactionary
       interests in, 54
   leadership deficiencies of, 60
   migration data and, 44
   municipalities and, 100
   National Immigration Branch of, 54
   policing and administrative practices
       in post–1994 era, 54, 58–59
   postapartheid reforms and, 107–9
   refugee policy and, 48
   skilled labor and, 69, 70, 75, 78
   street-level policing and, 114–15, 116
   Zimbabwean crisis and, 110, 113
homosexual couples, rights of, 45b
Horn of Africa, political instability in, 12
housing, 92, 131
human capital
   skills shortages and, 69
   urbanization and, 83, 83t
Human Development Report 2009
     (UNDP), 121, 131
human resources, 107–8, 117n6, 132
human rights
   abuses, 32, 54, 56
   culture of, 84
   healthcare and, 124
   immigration policy, activism in, 43–46

migration policy and, 41, 54
refugee policy and, 48
undocumented migrants and,
   55–56
Human Sciences Research Council, 70,
   147, 148

I
IDASA (Institute for Democracy in South
     Africa), 41–42, 44
identity booklets, 128
illegal aliens
   deportation of, 146
   migration policy and, 44
   numbers of, 146, 147–48
   "racial" criterion of, 35, 37
imbizos (consultative meetings), 60
Immigrants Selection Board,
     37–38, 58
Immigration Act of 2002 (South Africa)
   ANC and, 51
   arrests related to violations of, 115
   consultative process and, 44, 45b, 46
   deportations and, 56
   emigration and, 149
   passage of, 45b
   Polokwane Conference and, 53
   reform of, 50, 52, 54
   skilled labor and, 73, 78
Immigration Advisory Board, 55, 75
Immigration Amendment Act of 2004
     (South Africa), 44
Immigration Amendment Act of 2011
     (South Africa), 33, 61n1, 77
Immigration Inspectorate
     (Johannesburg), 110
immigration policy, 1–2, 26, 31–66
   democratic reformist movement and,
       33, 42–49
   human rights activism and
       consultancy markets, 43–46
   reformists' breakthroughs, impact
       of, 46–49
   discriminatory migration system, 33,
       34–42

immigration policy (*continued*)
tools for transformation and, 37–42
two-gate policy in, 34–37
institutionalized and reactionary interests, 49–54
legislation and, 5, 26, 137–44
policing and administrative practices in post–1994 era, 33, 54–59
citizenship, access to, 57
entry and control, tightening of, 54, 55–57, 157*f*
Home Affairs and, 54, 58–59
xenophobic violence of 2008 and, 33, 60–61
Immigration Restriction Act of 1901 (Australia), 61*n*2
independence of colonies causing emigration of European settlers, 36
"influx control," 85–86
information systems, health, 126, 132
Inkatha Freedom Party, 42, 55, 117, 147
Institute for Democracy in South Africa (IDASA), 41–42, 44
Integrated Development Plans, 89, 91, 103*n*3
International Organization for Migration, 72, 131, 132
Internet, data from, 87

J
James, Wilmot, 42
Jews, 35, 36
JIPSA. *See* Joint Initiative on Priority Skills Acquisition
Johannesburg, local government responses to migration in, 83, 84–85, 92, 96, 97, 99
Johannesburg Migration Advisory Committee, 63*n*20, 92
Johnson-Reed Act of 1924 (U.S.), 61*n*2
Joint Initiative on Priority Skills Acquisition (JIPSA), 70, 72, 75, 77

K
Kenya, survey data from, 12

L
Labor Department, 75
Labor Market Commission, 58
labor markets
brain drain and, 24
regional migration and, 17–22, 20–21*f*
skilled labor and, 68, 77
language problems, 128
law enforcement. *See* police
legotlas (consultative meetings), 60
Lesotho, survey data from, 12
Limpopo River, 110, 112
local authorities. *See* municipalities

M
Maduna, Penuell, 51–52
Mail & Guardian (newspaper)
ownership of, 76*b*
on xenophobia, 41
malaria, 123
Malawi
migrants from, 71–72
refugees from, 24
survey data from, 12
Malaysia, industrialization in, 77, 78*n*4
Mandela, Nelson, 67
manufacturing sectors, 21, 25, 68, 77
Mapisa-Nqakula, Nosiviwe, 58, 77
marriages, fraudulent, 45*b*
Masetlha, William, 109, 117*n*4, 148
Masiyiwa, Strive, 76*b*
Mayoral Committee on Community Safety (Tshwane), 86
Mbeki, Thabo, 24, 45*b*, 51, 53, 74, 78
MDGs (Millennium Development Goals), 121, 131
men, "returning home" for, 127
Merafong City Local Municipality, 82, 88, 89–90, 92–93, 95, 98
Metropolitan Police (Johannesburg), 115

"spatially-sensitive" approach to
    healthcare provision,
    122, 130, 131, 132
"spillover" effects of policing, 116
spouses' rights, 45*b*
squatters, 100, 115
statistics on migration for Southern
    Africa, 5, 26, 151–59, 152–56*t*,
    157*f*, 158*t*
Statistics South Africa (StatsSA), 87–88,
    89, 149
*Statistics South Africa Labour Survey
    Quarterly* on international
    migrants, 21
"stay-overs," measurement of, 146
subsidies, 36, 62*n*7
surveillance technology, 108
Swaziland, survey data from, 12

T
tariffs, elimination of, 77
taxation, skilled labor emigration and, 73
Technology in Government in Africa
    Award, 58
Telecel, 76*b*
Toronto (Canada), foreigners living in, 146
"Toward Defining Service Delivery Impli-
    cations of Migration in Gauteng
    Province" Conference (2009),
    63*n*20
Trade and Industry Department, 77
trade unions, 68, 77
trust building and migrant populations,
    101
Tshwane municipality, 27*n*8, 82, 93
tuberculosis, 122, 123, 127
Turnaround Strategy, 58, 59
2008 tragedy. *See* xenophobic violence
    of 2008

U
UNAIDS, 131
undocumented migrants
    deportations of, 23, 56, 158*t*
    detention of, 55

healthcare and, 128
immigration control and, 109–10, 112.
    See also migration control and
    documentation
numbers of, 12, 109, 146–49
street-level policing and, 114–15
unemployment, 10, 75
unions, 68, 77
United Kingdom, emigration to, 16, 71, 73
United Nations
    High Commissioner for Refugees
        (UNHCR), 37, 38, 124–25, 129
    Office for the Coordination of
        Humanitarian Affairs, 12, 17
United States
    Latin American migration to, 11
    as "newfound land," 32
    quotas and restrictions on
        immigration to, 61*n*2
    regional power and, 22
    South Africans living in, 16, 72, 73
University of Pretoria, 148
University of the Witwatersrand, 123, 127
urban areas and urbanization
    effects of, 148
    health provision and, 122, 130
    human development and, 83, 83*t*
    migration and, 12–13, 25, 93
    poor in, 86
    remittances from, 127
    statistics on, 5, 26, 161–65, 161–65*t*
    "urban edge," 93–94

V
vigilante activities, 98, 101
violence against immigrants, 33, 51, 98,
        101. *See also* vigilante activities;
        xenophobic violence of 2008
visas
    free movement agreements and, 113
    thirty-day, 23

W
White Australia policy, 61*n*2
White Paper on Immigration (1999), 106

www.ingramcontent.com/pod-product-compliance
Lightning Source LLC
Chambersburg PA
CBHW062028270326

41929CB00014B/2358